'*On My Way to Jorvik* is the story of what happened behind the scenes when Jorvik first opened its doors to the public all those years ago. It was the way thousands of people discovered the world of archaeology and many of them, I'm glad to say, are still there. The huge appeal of Jorvik was personal: the displays spoke with individual Viking voices and they were so warm and human - just like this wonderful personal account by the man who designed it. I couldn't put it down.'

Professor Francis Pryor, MBE, FSA
Archaeologist, Prehistorian, Author and *Time Team* Presenter

'The opening of the Jorvik Viking Centre was a watershed moment in the history not only of archaeological heritage management but also of archaeology itself. The buzz among the global community of archaeologists was immediate. We were overjoyed that someone had managed to convey the excitement of our daily work to the rest of the world. I could not wait to see it myself, and I was not disappointed. The Centre was a tangible expression of the images that form in the minds of the archaeologists as they work hours, weeks, and months at excavations and in laboratories.'

Douglas C. Comer, Ph.D., RPA
Co-President, ICOMOS International Scientific Committee on
Archaeological Heritage Management (ICAHM)

'John Sunderland has written a witty, honest account of his journey from Wakefield to international designer. John's distinctive voice tells a hugely entertaining and informative story. At the heart of the book is his key role in designing and developing the Jorvik Viking Centre, an entirely new way of immersing people in the past. He gives a personal and hugely fascinating behind-the-scenes insight into the origins design and construction of this world-famous archaeological attraction in York.'

John Oxley, MBE FSA,
former City of York Archaeologist

On My Way to Jorvik takes the reader on an amazing, and amusing, journey back in time. It's a thoroughly readable and enjoyable insight into the birth pangs of a ground-breaking museum project, which was ultimately so hugely successful that it has been widely recognised as heralding the start of the heritage industry in the UK. I know that I am not alone in admitting that the Jorvik Viking Centre dramatically changed my life, and the lives of many of my industry colleagues, all because of the vision and creative genius of the author. It is a revealing story of the ride of his life, including the bumpy bits.'

Colin C. Pyrah OBE
Special Projects Director
Paragon Creative Limited

On my way to
JORVIK

A humorous memoir of how a boy with a vision became a radical
designer, created Dusty Bin, made films with Kenny Everett then
revolutionised visitor attraction design forever

A Memoir by

John Sunderland

ON MY WAY TO JORVIK
A humorous memoir of how a boy with a vision became a radical designer, created Dusty Bin,
made films with Kenny Everett then revolutionised visitor attraction design forever

Paperback ISBN: 979-8-9854400-0-3
Ebook ISBN: 979-8-9854400-1-0

www.johnsunderland.co.uk
Contact John Sunderland at: info@johnsunderland.co.uk

For Kathy

CONTENTS

INTRODUCTION

At 9:45AM ON April 14, 1984 the core group who developed, designed and built the original Jorvik Viking Centre sat apprehensively around a table in a conference room. The room was above the entrance doors and they were waiting for the Centre's first opening to the general public on its very first day, 15 minutes away.

Not one of them had any idea if anyone would turn up to see what they had done. In fact, no one dared look outside the windows to check.

As Project Designer I was one of those people, and perhaps the most nervous, as I had never designed an exhibition or museum in my life up till then. The amazing thing is, none of us had.

What was about to happen would change the lives of everyone in that room. And astonishingly, thirty years on the Jorvik Viking Centre is still going strong.

What was the special alchemy that happened amongst those people and the rest of the team? Just what was it that made Jorvik so engaging and so successful?

This is my memoir, a true story about a journey of a lifetime. It begins not in Viking times as you might expect. Instead my story starts in the realm of a young boy's imagination, back in 1961.

So please, if you will, indulge me and come along with me on my way to Jorvik.

John Sunderland
February 2014

1   KINGDOM OF TRUANT

THE SCHOOL YEAR HAD JUST begun, my first at Queen Elizabeth Grammar
School in Wakefield in the West Riding of Yorkshire in northern England. I
was eleven years old and as thick as a wooden toilet seat and shouldn't have been
there. It was a trick played on me by my mum.

Mum was keen on me going to Grammar School although I thought I didn't
really belong there, as I was so certifiably stupid, or so my dad repeatedly said.
I managed to gain a place via an unusual loophole – a Choral Scholarship with
Wakefield Cathedral. My mother arranged for me to sing my way in and once
there, I entered a parallel world of vocal indenture. A third of my waking week
as a kid was spent chained to the choir stalls. The good thing though was that
with a place in the local Cathedral choir came a paid-for scholarship at aged ten
in the junior division of the best school in the city, if not the county. But getting
into Senior School was the real prize, and for that I had to pass an exam. True
to form, I came in last. But I made it.

Mum said all I had to do was to wear the uniform and everything would be
fine. It wasn't. She didn't tell me about algebra or Mr Gatiss, the maths teacher,
the most feared master in the school.

In my head the holidays weren't over yet. It was still warm outside with long
balmy afternoons and the sun was shining. I could have been down at the beck
mending my dam. Yet here I was stuck in the classroom of terror, about to be
publicly ridiculed, tortured and hung in a basket from the school hall ceiling.

The pages of my open exercise book were as empty as the blackboard was
full of indecipherable marks. Not to the other boys though. They were scratching
around me like they knew what they were doing.

I sneaked another sideways glance outside as a twist of blue smoke floated
upwards from the grounds keeper's fire changing shape as it drifted like a lazy
ghost over the playing fields of pain. So this was growing up. They could keep it;
there was danger everywhere. My dad said I was a waste of space and stupid. Sat
there I did feel stupid and scared like a minnow in a tank dodging a piranha. My
saving grace was the vividly keen imagination I developed growing up. It helped

me deal with the effects of the heavy hand of my abusive father and to offset the challenges I faced at school learning facts and figures that seemed easy for the other kids. I learned to look at the world from a different angle and to live a lot in my head. I became really good at art but that didn't seem to count now like it had in junior school. Thankfully, we hadn't reached logarithms yet. David Smythe said they were murder even for boffins; I'd have to kill myself.

Mr Gatiss sat at the front behind a shortening pile of last week's exercise books; mine secretly marked on its spine with two extra staples. I could see it clearly; it was about three books down. I pushed my specs up my nose, flattened my quiff, took a deep breath to fill myself up with excess oxygen and stuck up my hand.

I had come up with a master plan to escape Mr Gatiss and his torture by algebra on Monday mornings and Wednesday afternoons. I had created a story and it was diabolically clever, wonderful *yet* dangerous, very dangerous in fact. Just the thought of it kept me in nightmares and diarrhoea for a week. Mum wondered where all the toilet paper was going. I even took a roll to school in my satchel *and* there were two insurance rolls in my desk.

My hand shook, but I kept it there waiting to be seen nerves or not; there was no turning back. This was it; do or die.

Mr Gatiss was well known for being able to see right through boys and know what they were really up to. Six formers, some as big as vans, were terrified of him, but I couldn't afford to be scared. I stared at him, my eyes as big as my national health lenses as my hand quivered overhead. Brian Sampson spotted me first, and then the other boys followed his gaze and turned to stare at me.

Trouble was the man I was to face, the Master who looked like a bullet, had seen it all before; he'd seen through them all, the boys who'd grown up to be surgeons and bank managers, accountants and chemists, vicars and scientists, the heroes, the villains *and* the dummies. They all remembered the legend that was Mr Gatiss, the knower of boys. Would he be a jump ahead of me? If he did, my life was worth less than an old school sausage.

'Yes, Sunderland?' he said, without lifting his helmet shaped head.

'Sir, please sir, I've something to ask you, *personally.*'

No one spoke up in his lessons unless they were about to pee themselves and most would have rather peed in their satchels first. It was rumoured he had nailed to his garage wall a large collection of first formers' scalps, small boys who had tried it on. Not one of those had asked to speak with him *personally.* Lucky for me, he was curious. He didn't say anything, just pointed to a spot next to his desk. I was about to go dancing on a mousetrap in miner's boots.

I got up and moved down the aisle between the desks with legs of lead that would have been speedy had I been going the other way. Faces of boys stayed turned towards me until I reached the end of the rows where I stepped into the deathly margin of no-boy's land.

As I made it to the side of his desk my upper body was entirely drained of blood and courage and my heart was thumping like the sound of Granddad bashing dust out of rugs. I was on the spot and in swiping range of his gorilla hands that it was widely said could squeeze the baked beans from an unopened tin.

'What is it, boy?' He spoke without looking at me from behind the shrinking pile of exercise books.

He was reputed to be the only master in the school to have a fountain pen filled with red ink that was really blood. He'd write 'Useless' and 'Hopeless' on my page of incorrect and non-existent answers or 'Useless, stupid dunce!' and 'Needs clinical help'. He put his hand out for the next book apparently not knowing it was mine.

'Excuse me, sir,' I said in a mouse-small voice. 'I have to go.'

'You know the rule, boy,' he said quietly but firmly with just a hint of razor steel being drawn from its scabbard. 'You should have gone before. You'll have to wait. Now go back to your desk, sit down, cross your legs and get on with your work.'

'No sir, I didn't *mean* the toilet, sir.' The class held its collective breath. They could hear me swallow, hear my heart whirring.

'Well, what *did* you mean?' he said leaning an ear low and close across the desk. You could have heard a moth burp as everyone by then had stopped breathing.

'I have to go to Hospital, sir,' I said with all the dry-throated sincerity I could muster, blinking wide-eyed behind my thick specs at a cheek of steel stubble dangerously close to mine.

'Hospital? Hospital? Why, what are you telling me, boy?' He returned to marking, eyes down on the last exercise book before mine.

'I'm going blind, sir,' I blurted out, 'and I have to be prepared for surgery with certain regular exercises and examinations at the Hospital Ophthalmic Department.' This was one he had not heard before. This was one 'the knower of boys' did not see coming.

He turned and leaned even closer, his face as unwelcome as a roused Rottweiler in a butcher's shop. I could see a forest of nostril hairs rising up into the darker caves of his skull beyond which I thought I could see glowing embers. He was so close I smelled the teacher smell of his ancient tweed jacket, the accrued aroma of years of wearing it in rooms full of malodorous boys.

He scanned me for lies with the penetration of a lie-detecting x-ray and removed his glasses. After a short pause, during which I was unable to breathe, he cocked an ear as he took out a folded plaid patterned hankie from his top pocket and began to slowly, pensively polish the lenses whilst pondering my entire wimpy knee-knocking being.

'I see,' he said.'And when do you have to go to Hospital, boy?'

'Well, now, sir. In fact I'm a little late,' I said, scrunching my eyes up behind my specs, covering up one lens and squinting at the clock and the second-hand which moved very slowly, unlike my heart muscles which were about to generate steam.

'And where is your note?'

'Note, sir? You should have been told by the office. They said I should come up in class.'

'Hmm, they did, did they? The ladies in the office, Mrs. Barley would that be?'

'Don't know her name, sir. I have to go each week, sir, from now on,' I said, knowing I was pushing my luck. But now with the adrenalin flowing, I had to get this in.

'And the sessions at the clinic unfortunately coincide with your double lessons, sir, on Mondays and Wednesdays.'

Now he stopped breathing in order to light the coals up his nose and looked at me with total fixed concentration like a dragon about to toast a peasant, primed for me to give myself away by any little twitch, looking for any whisker of self-doubt, any fault-line in my armour.

Inwardly, I focused, fighting my fear. I made my face inscrutable, truthful and sincere all at once, a thousand percent angelic choirboy, translucent with goodness and honesty, just like at the double-weddings sung for one-pound sterling, where we all had to pretend to be angels whilst scratching our bums. One good thing, at that moment, as there was no blood in my upper body, I couldn't blush.

My face was as white and as virginally innocent as the pages of my exercise book, incapable of sin. Yet, a deep dark voice inside my head (God I think on a direct line) was telling me this was such a huge lie for which I would burn in hell, the same hell I was already due for according to the Provost when he gave us the talk about self-abuse.

I'd be damned forever guaranteed, branded with each of the equations I couldn't do and prodded by devils with demonic red-hot fountain pens to do harder and harder calculations until the last decimal point of time. But even so, if I got away with it, it would be worth it.

I remember glancing outside again just then, beyond the windows to the bike sheds, and the backyards of terrace houses and salvation. I could be as free as that smoky ghost melting through the railings. That's where *I'd* be in a moment. I could do it, just mustn't waiver.

As I stood there, in the eternity of the pause between us, master and pupil, I envisioned all the wonderful hours I'd spend wandering round Woolworths, the milk-shakes I'd have incognito in the Shady Nook Coffee Bar, all the second-hand stalls I'd rummage through on the market, and best of all, the art materials department in Boots the Chemists and the *Eagle Press*.

Dad took over from God. 'You stupid little bugger! Can't you do anything right?' I heard as he shouted in my head so loud I thought the class could hear.

What was I doing committing suicide like this? I was probably going to be torn apart by the hairy gorilla hands of a mathematical monster. I'd be pinned against the blackboard and finished off with a thrust of his pen as he sucked the blood from my poor innocent heart. And all the boys would laugh and laugh till they were sick in their desks. Then I'd be carried out to the playing fields and hung by my shoelaces between the rugby posts, drying out, slowly dying, eyeballs pecked out by crows. I might last a week, perhaps longer, the object of loathing of the entire school.

Meanwhile Mr Gatiss, the knower of boys, held his unwavering gaze. I could feel him looking right through me. To this day I believe he knew what I was up to, but I like to think that in that scrawny weedy little kid in front of him with skew-whiff glasses and scabby knees, he recognised something that had been in him once. Maybe when he was in the war, as he ran for that German machine gun nest lobbing grenades and saving his mates with a bravery of tempered steel. Or maybe he was just too tired and worn down to care about some wimpy first former as he soft-pedalled his way to retirement.

'Well, Sunderland,' he said putting his spectacles back on, 'you'd better be off then. You shouldn't be late. Eyesight,' he said sliding them up his nose 'is a precious thing.'

My eyes opened so wide it's a wonder they didn't pop out and bounce across his desk. I'd done it. All my prayers murmured secretly in the choir stalls had worked. Thank you, God. Oh, thank you, Lord GOD Almighty and all the painted Saints and Mum for making me brave.

After that moment, he put his head down and never looked at me again, not once ever for the rest of my school days. For years, as I grew taller and broader and he grew older and greyer, as we crossed the playground from opposite sides, he remembered me, I know he did. It was as though we both shared a secret.

As I reached for my satchel below my desk I looked back and saw him take my exercise book without opening it and place it at the very bottom of the pile of those he'd already marked.

'Back to your books, boys,' he gently commanded. All heads went down as one. Only Denny, my new friend who sat across from me, looked sideways as I left the room with questioning eyes and eyebrows raised.

I reached the door, went through and looked back through the window. I hadn't shared my plan with him or anyone else. I'd kept it to myself. But he knew I was up to something. I saw him blow a little 'phew' from his cheeks.

'Back to your work, Dennison,' said Mr Gatiss without looking up. 'There's nothing to interest *you* out there.'

Seconds later I was out of the building, walking down the drive and trying not to break into a run. There was not another boy anywhere because they were all in classes. I saw the groundsman look at me from over his smouldering pile. As for Mr Gatiss, I could feel his eyes on my back as I walked, sure as I was that he could see me through the brick wall.

Just in case, I acted as though I was on my way to hospital. I walked sort of limply, trying not to bump into things, a poor almost blind child avoiding the goal posts. I kept this up all the way down to the gates. But then once round the corner, I jumped as high as I could and swung my satchel over my head, almost losing a toilet roll. FREE!

Little did I know I was taking my first steps on my way to meet the Vikings.

First question was, where to go for the next hour? I hadn't thought of that even as I was scheming hard in my private think tank during my Sunday night bath until the water turned body temperature. But one thing I realised, because I had scared myself silly with the hugeness of my crime against trigonometry, was that at least for the next couple of weeks I should lie low, very low, flat actually. But where could an eleven-year-old in a school raincoat carrying a new satchel hide out? The first place that came to mind wasn't far away.

I loved the City Art Gallery with its squeaky floor since visiting it during our first school trip and it was just five minutes away. That's where I went. I'd be safe there.

That first morning as a truant, the grand hallway of the gallery was illuminated by beams of dusty sunlight shining slanted from the large doors on the left-hand side of the hall. I looked through the windows in the doors to see if there was anyone about. God forbid there would be a party from my school. No, there was not a soul.

Inside to greet me was the familiar and pleasant aroma of beeswax and lino polish mixed with the scent of Brasso. The brass handles on the entrance door and bell and the plaques on the wall must have just been polished earlier that morning. Like the floor, the handles appeared to be untouched by human hand. I stared down at the brass that shone like gold, the golden handles to my Kingdom of Truant, alone in a world bordered only by my imagination, no masters telling me how or what to think now.

It was quiet. Hardly anyone ever went to the municipal Art Gallery, especially on Monday mornings. I was alone. It was perfect; there was even a toilet.

But first I had to pass down the entrance hall, past 'the Guardians' as I came to think of them, the gauntlet of high, dark paintings of local philanthropic City Fathers. I couldn't ignore them. They were all lit up for once and looking down at me, serious and unsmiling with their whiskered faces and thickly eye-browed eyes staring down from their frames: the Arkrights, the Hodgsons, and the Wainwrights. Then one spoke. I stood fast and looked up at a man with a cane and a top hat.

'I say, Hodgson, what's the boy doing in here. Shouldn't he be in school? Makes the place look untidy.' He checked the time on his gold fob watch. 'School time, look. I warrant, he must be a truant and therefore a liar to boot.'

'Yes,' said his neighbour through orange whiskers. 'He looks the sort that will come to no good, you mark my words.'

'Oh, leave him alone,' said the regal lady at the end of the corridor in a big green dress and hat, with a puppy and a parasol. 'He's here to improve himself. He's not one of your damn machine slaves. *This* boy is going to be an *Artist*, aren't you dear boy?' I looked round and saw she meant me. 'He won't be working in your pit, Cyril, or your mill, Donald, so you can both stop thinking of that. That boy is brave and fearless and a free spirit, a revolutionary. I can see by just looking at him that he has a surfeit of latent talent just dying to come out. Come on in, dear. Don't be bothered by these old walruses; you are *most* welcome.'

I hitched up my satchel, took off my cap and flattened my quiff. 'I am what she says,' I whispered to myself. 'Yes, I am. I am an Artist and I'm not bloody stupid.'

2   A BIG RESPECTER OF ART

From that morning on, I always remembered to smile at the nice lady and doff my cap. She always smiled back and her dog wagged its tail.

School trips to the Art Gallery were always special even though it had been hard to look at the pictures with all the giggling and pushing of the other boys jostling in front of a naked lady with a bowl of fruit and nuts. Being on my own was great; it had only been twenty minutes but already I was the Truant King in my own Palace of Culture. Then a door at the end of the hall opened with a swush.

A tall lady with glasses, grey cardigan, plaid skirt and big brooch squeaked down the hall holding a book. She walked right past me as if I was invisible, went through another door then immediately came out.

'You're not a school party are you?' she asked towering over me and craning to look in the galleries.

'No, Miss,' I said opening my satchel and taking out an exercise book and pencil, which I always carried.

'Parties are Thursdays, it is Monday,' she said. 'Such an interference, it really is. We always have to clean everything after you boys have been. Grubby fingers, dirty little boys. Don't touch anything, please, please. Look all you like,' she said smiling, 'but *touch* nothing. Is that understood?'

'I am not a party, Miss,' I said. 'And my hands are very clean. Personal hygiene is my hobby.' I presented my hand, the clean one, the one that I held up in class and that would send me to hell. 'And yes, Miss, I will not touch a thing. I am a big respecter of Art, Miss. In fact, I'm doing a project on it.' I was going to tell her what but she cut me off thankfully.

'Good, that's the ticket.' She straightened up and stared at me curiously like I was some kind of strange insect. 'Good!' And with that she disappeared through the door again. That was the last time I saw her.

In the galleries downstairs, there were other much nicer paintings than the gloomies in the entrance hall. In the large and airy rooms the painted pictures shone as if from their own light. Old fashioned, they seemed as huge as the scenes portrayed. I felt like I could step right into them.

There were battles and castles and strange landscapes with tiny cows and sheep and people playing flutes standing about in fields like they had nothing better to do, and ruins, and ladies in floaty dresses playing little harps.

Others had big rearing horses with soldiers on top waving swords. In another sailors were on ships firing cannons. If I looked at the paintings long enough, they came to life. When they did I found I could enter the scenes.

'Keep your head down, boy. Aaaagh!' shouted a soldier who I saw shot in the leg (the blood was vermilion – Grandpa had a tube, he was an artist my Grandpa). 'Those damn Frenchies have got me, boy!' he exclaimed manfully and painfully.

The blood looked very real and the battle looked exciting but as I didn't want to get blown to bits I stepped back out of the frame.

'I'm going to get help!' I shouted back to the soldier and then moved on.

'That's me fine lad!' yelled the wounded hero after me. That was a lie though, the second big one I'd told that morning.

In the next, the landscape with the ladies with the big bosoms was nice, and nobody was getting shot. I stepped in and onto a grassy hill. A breeze was moving the trees and swans came down out of the sky and landed on the lake, below a little temple. There was music; I went up to the shepherd with the flute.

'What's it like standing still in a painting all day,' I asked. He took his flute away from his lips.

'Oh, it's not bad really, young sir. It's a living, better than getting shot by old Boney,' he nodded to the painting next door. 'Worst part is that I have to keep playing this same bloody tune.'

'The sheep don't seem to mind,' I said.

'Course not,' he said. 'They're sheep.'

In the upstairs galleries there were also paintings called abstracts. They reminded me of ones I'd seen in books in the art room at school. I liked them too even though there were no people in them, but if you looked hard enough you could see things. I imagined it was like looking into the artist's head. But I didn't step into them; I thought I'd get lost.

And fantastically, in one room, standing on plinths like Saints at the Cathedral were sculptures by Henry Moore and Barbara Hepworth. Both of them, so Percy Beak our art teacher had told us, were famous and connected to the North of England, and even better, to our city. After all, back then, Wakefield was hardly a centre of culture. I knew their names though and that they were famous sculptors. I'd read about them; they made things with holes to go in front of banks and town halls.

So when I read on the little plaques that the sculptures had been given 'By the Artist to the City' I felt really proud like I owned them. And in a way I did.

I thought it would be amazing to make something like that – something no one had ever thought of, something that looked like nothing in particular, but at the same time felt like something *very* familiar. A thing that people would want to keep, show off, something that would make people *think* when they saw it. Not everyone thought that way. When we came on the trip from school, the other boys thought the sculptures were daft. The pubescently more advanced ones were only interested in stuff with tits and bums and the younger boys followed them.

'It's got a hole in it, sir,' said dummy Mellor, picking at a spot on his pimply cheek as he spoke.

'What's it supposed to be, sir?' said Prancett.

'I think they're great,' I spoke up, despite the put down expected, which was swift, silent and painful to both ankles.

'You're as stupid as that thing with the hole in it Blunderland,' whispered smelly Fishgill.

'Yeah, like the inside of your head, Blunders,' said Martin Cane.

'You probably want to bonk it,' another sniggered, 'cause it's got a hole. Too big for you Blunders, you little stupid nit.'

I didn't want to bonk it whatever that was. I wanted to shrink in size and explore it and put it in my satchel and take it home.

Now I had it all to myself. Smelly Fishgill was doing physics, ha! And I was here. The sculptures reminded me of caves and the rounded shapes of rocks on the beach and the white cliffs at Flamborough Head where Grandpa took us in his Ford Pop every summer.

As there was no one else about, I ran my clean hand over the surface of the Henry Moore and felt the cold shine and smooth curves and I looked through the holes.

It was all right. There was no one else upstairs; I would have heard them. So I took out my hanky, found a clean bit on it, and polished off the sculptures where I'd touched. I thought it best, being after all a Great Respecter of Art.

In the Art Gallery and everywhere else for that matter, I never took my gabardine raincoat off or my school cap, even though it was warm in there in winter. The coat and cap with the school badge was, I realised, my disguise. It turned me into an anonymous schoolboy. I was incognito (I'd heard that word in a film). I was just a kid doing a school project, not a junior conman hiding from the algebra police.

But even with a disguise, I had to be on my guard all the time, listening for footsteps on the lino. Once a lady in a blazer approached me; she had on a badge that said 'Volunteer.' I didn't hear her coming, as I was chatting with a Venetian Gondolier; she pounced on me.

'And why, young man, aren't you at school?'

Inwardly I knew that facing off with Mr Gatiss and telling the biggest lie in the universe meant I could bluff my way through anything. So I looked her in the face, took off my cap, smoothed my quiff, pushed up my specs and very politely said I was doing an Art Project. I showed her the notes and sketches I'd done for real in my book and copies I made of the paintings and sculptures, and then turned the tables by asking her a question.

'I have a question, Miss.'

'Oh?' She looked taken aback. She hadn't volunteered to be asked questions.

'Yes, do you happen to know the origin of oil paints and what were the main colours used in the fourteenth century in the Renaissance Religious palette? Was there a convention on the use of colour or was it defined by available materials?' (I'd read that in my dad's Home Encyclopedia, the one about the Artists of the Renaissance.)

That stumped her; she had no idea. I hadn't either, but it worked.

'Well, er, young man,' she said, 'that's a *very* intelligent and interesting question. I think I'll let you discover the answer for yourself. Self-education is the best in my book. Carry on, dear.'

Although I saw her patrolling the place occasionally, she, like the curator lady, never spoke to me again.

Sometimes a travelling exhibition would stay for a few weeks. Whilst the other boys were juggling equations, I was experiencing colour and wonder instead. So as time went on, I swapped Mathematics for Matisse.

Then I met Cezanne. I loved his paintings. Percy Beak had reproductions in his file. I was there alone in the Art Gallery in our crap city all soot black buildings, smoke and fog, boring shops and a river that smelled like black bleach. But into my Kingdom of Truant came these wonderful pictures of landscapes full of sunshine and olive trees, another world somewhere far off, but so real.

I imagined what it must have been like to stand in front of an easel under the sunshine of Southern France, looking day after day at one haystack. (I read the leaflet that came with the exhibition so I knew where he lived and painted and what he did.) I just had to visit and have a chat. I stepped into one of the paintings he did of his favourite mountain, Mont Saint Victoire.

'Bonjour, Monsieur Cezanne, what are you painting today?' (We'd started doing French in school.) He was standing in a stubbly field with a big hat on and seemed pleased to see me.

'Bonjour, Jean, nice to see you again. Look mon ami; look at the mountain.'

'But you did the mountain last week,' I said.

'Yes, but look closely. Here is the one I did on my last visit and see now how differently she looks today.'

'It's the same mountain,' I said. I knew because the painting he showed me was next to this one on the gallery wall.

'Yes, mon Dieu! Of course it is the same mountain. The mountain has not changed, the rock has not moved, but the light shining upon it has, look.'

'So the colours and shadows are different,' I said. They were, and they changed almost as I watched.

'Oui, c'est ca. I am painting light, not rocks and trees. Fascinating, do you not think?'

I liked talking to Monsieur Cezanne, but worried that if I spent too much time in the hot sunshine (something we seldom got in the West Riding) I'd get a tan under the rim of my cap. Try explaining that at home in November.

'Mum, it's *not* a tan, it's *hormones*.' I knew I had hormones; I just had no idea what they were or what they did, but it seemed to cover a lot.

Spending time with the artists had an effect on me. I started to look at the countryside around where we lived differently and tried to copy Cezanne's style next time I got a chance to paint. I didn't tell anyone where I got the idea.

'Now where did that come from?' Percy Beak asked one lunchtime when I was up in the art room painting. I loved Percy Beak.

'It's the fields and the copse near where I live, sir,' I said.

'You're a regular little Cezanne, Sunderland,' he said, and he couldn't have said anything better.

Even though it was heaven in the Art Gallery, I couldn't hang about there all the time. I needed more places to lie low in.

The City Museum was the same as the Gallery; it was free, and nobody ever seemed to go there. But getting there was dangerous because I had to pass Mum's office, right in front of where she sat at a desk by the window.

The Museum was across the street beyond a wide lawn with little bushes. To get to it there was only one thing to do; I ran quickly jumping from one bush to another, making short little runs when I thought she wasn't looking. I managed halfway across the lawn when I discovered I wasn't alone.

'Eyupp,' said a young woman with a bouffant hairdo and red lipstick. There was a bloke with her in the bushes. He had shiny Brylcreemed hair and a quiff about a foot long. 'What are you doing running about in the bushes?' she said.

'I'm doing a survey for school on shrubbery; it's a project.'

'Pull the other one, kid,' said the bloke pushing my shoulder. 'You've nicked off from school haven't you?'

By now I discovered that deflection was the best defense.

'Well, so what are *you* doing behind this bush?' I said.

'None of your business, little boy. Cheeky, isn't he Candice?' said the man. 'Go on, bugger off. This is our bush,' he said slipping his arm round her waist.

'Do you like girls?' asked Candice. She smelled of perfume, the sort Mum wouldn't wear because it made you cheap.

'Not much,' I said and dashed off, unseen from the windows.

'You will,' said the greasy quiff, giving Candice's bum a squeeze. She giggled.

I thought I was in the clear, but just when I made my next dash and safety was in sight, a big dog started chasing me. It barked a lot, so I stopped and threw it a stick. Whilst it was gone I made it to the other side of the lawn and got behind another bush by the roadside.

I didn't know a policeman standing at the kerb with his bike was watching me. He beckoned me over.

'Now then, sonny, how come you're running about in the shrubbery at this time of the morning? See that sign, what does it say?' I looked at the sign.

'"*Keep off the grass*", that's what it says, "*by order*". That's an offence and that is what you were doing. And why aren't you at your lessons?' He looked at the badge on my cap. 'From Queen Elizabeth I see. Good school, you shouldn't be missing any of it. I never had a chance.'

'It actually says, "No *walking* on the grass", that's why I was *running*, sir,' I said politely, looking up and smiling. He was about nine feet tall with a big black hat on and a truncheon. Funny, like the nuns at the Cathedral he seemed strange close up; I'd never been so near to a policeman.

'Are you trying to be funny, lad?' he said ominously pulling out his notebook and a pencil.

'No, sir, sorry sir; I was running because I'm late.'

'Late? Late to where?'

'The Museum, sir.' I thought I should say why. 'Fossils, sir. It's a project.'

'Well now then,' he said putting away his notebook. 'Now you're talking. Be sure to look in cabinet number five, bottom left '*Harpoceras Falciferum*'. That's mine, I found it on a trip to Whitby when I was a lad and gave it to the Museum. They were very pleased.' I took out my notebook and he spelled it out for me. 'Well, you better be off, cabinet five at the bottom, don't forget.' And with that he patted me on my cap and walked into the street to stop the traffic for me.

I reckoned as I crossed that someone who worked for God was licking his pencil ready to score down another huge point for hell. Telling a giant fib to Mr Gatiss was one thing, fibbing to a wounded soldier another; but a barefaced lie to a policeman could get me a custodial sentence or a year in solitary. That's why I decided to opt henceforth for the truth, better yet a real good story.

There were lots of scary stuffed dead things at the Museum lurking in the shadows in cases on the ground floor, things that I thought would like to pull you in with them. And there were lots of other interesting-looking things with labels, which I couldn't understand but wished I could. But most of all when I got in there I thought it spooky and I wished Denny had been there with me; but of course he was still doing equations, poor sod. But it wasn't all scary at the Museum.

There was another gallery upstairs, up the wooden squeaky staircase. In the middle was a large room-sized 'box' that went up to the ceiling. The outside didn't give too much away, apart from some words of description on a panel that I didn't bother to read.

On one side there was an opening about the size of a small window. It was for people to look through and into whatever was inside. It was too high up for me, so I stood on my satchel to peer in.

Inside was a perfect complete little room all made of wood with dark carved panelling. There were thin candles and a grate with sticks in it. The furniture was unelaborate, dark and wooden, the chairs straight backed and uncomfort-able looking, whilst in the middle was a table with grey metal plates, goblets and knives. Underfoot, the floor was made of wooden planks with what I took to be rushes scattered about.

It was a reconstructed room within a room. I'd never seen anything like it before and it became my favourite place in the whole Museum. I stood on my toes and stared in every visit, taking it in for minutes on end. I reached up and hung on until my calves ached.

In a way it was no less scary than the glass coffins downstairs with all the dead things in and I reckoned was most likely inhabited by a family of ghosts. When I was older I learnt it wasn't a modern 'reconstruction' (a word I didn't even know then). Rather it was a complete Jacobean room carefully removed with all its bits and pieces from an old house and rebuilt so you could have a view of how people lived back in the early 17th century.

Others might have thought it was still and unmoving, but to me it was almost alive. There was this *potential* for something to happen, as though someone had left a moment ago to go perhaps to the kitchen to make a venison and pickle sandwich and would be back any moment. That's what it felt like to me; it was riveting. I felt as though I was looking back in time.

If there was anywhere I was going to disappear, it would be there into that room, adopted by lonely ghosts, never to be seen again, living forever in the Kingdom of Truant in another century. I could almost see them: a man came in dusting snow off his shoulders:

Jacob: 'The privy is frozen again, my dear.'

Elizabeth: 'It's of no concern. I shall not require its services until the spring.'

I stood there flattening my satchel and uneaten banana, staring in, willing it to be real, willing the people to be real, imagining Jacob and Elizabeth sat there warming themselves by the fire, chatting about Jacobean things, this and that. At the same time I scared myself, thinking that maybe I could *make* them appear through the power of imagination.

Perhaps the room *was* as real to the ghosts who once lived in it, even if it was now in a museum. Maybe they didn't know. Haunted perhaps only in my mind, yet there *was* something about the room, something that made it less dead and empty than the cases of stuffed birds. It wasn't still as they were; it was animated, alive, and it took me some time to see what made it that way though it was in plain sight.

It was the clock, made, if I remember right, of brass and wood. It looked simple and primitive and had a long pendulum. I was mesmerised, watching as it swung slowly to and fro. I could see cogs going round inside, like the inner workings of a prehistoric robot. The clock ticked loud and regular like a mechanical heartbeat yet so much slower than the tick . . . tick . . . tick of my watch or the movement of the second hand of the electric clock that metered out anxiety in the classroom.

As I looked in and watched and waited for something to happen, willing it over the pain in my legs, I didn't realise what seeds were being sown in the sub-soil of my eleven-year-old mind, what things would eventually flower from them in my life because of that room. I never forgot my wish to see that room from the past come alive.

Besides the Art Gallery and the City Museum, the third part of my new extra-curricular life was going to the Playhouse Cinema.

Though grungy to say the least, it was the better of the three cinemas in the city. The auditorium smelled of damp old air and even older people. Every time I went, the same shadowy huddled figures were there. Like me, they were the cheap-rate matinee people, the pensioners and the homeless.

In those days you could stay in the cinema all day if you wanted, starting early in the afternoon with the first show. Best thing was that the cheap matinee tickets meant truanting kids like me could get in on pocket money, but I was the only one.

I would look up the films in advance from the adverts in the Wakefield Express, the local paper, but wasn't choosy. I saw everything that was going; musicals, war films, comedies, cowboy films and science fiction. Trouble was, I was skipping double maths on Wednesday afternoons, the last two lessons of the day. But even though I ran down from the school to the cinema I always missed the beginning of the feature. Once I thought I might get a reduced price for my ticket, but then thought better of asking about it. When you are incognito you don't want to cause a stir.

I saw some great films and some absolute stinkers. I saw films that made me laugh like a drain and some that scared me half to death. All of them transported me to another world on a magic carpet of an old cinema seat, sat there alone with eyes as big as the flying saucers that hovered over Washington D.C. And I got to meet the stars. Rick was my favourite in his white jacket.

'How's it going, kid?'

'Fine, thank you.' I was sat at the bar with him.

'What's a kid like you doing in a crummy place like this?'

'I am incognito, Mr Bogart,' I said pulling down my cap.

'You know not to ever use my real name. I'm in role; I get paid for it. Call me Rick like everybody else in this flick.'

'Okay, Mr Rick.'

'You should know this stuff kid, if you're incognito. Smoke?'

'No sir, I don't.'

'Good going, these things will kill you. Like a shot of bourbon? Sam, a shot on the house for the kid.'

' Er, Mr Rick, have you got any fizzy orange instead?'

'Tough guy, huh?'

I knew all the stars and they all knew me.

Getting in was never a problem. The woman behind the window at the ticket booth never looked up (or down in my case), she just spoke to my cap. Once inside, if ever someone came round with a flashlight I just slid down in the seat.

'A half, please Miss,' I said at the window and never a question was asked. Maybe the lady in the kiosk mistook me for a midget. There was usually a double bill with cartoons and the sort of adverts for local restaurants and plumbers that were slides rather than film.

'After the film why not try the Golden Moon Restaurant, New Delhi, just nine thousand miles from the cinema' and 'Bert Smith, Plumber, round the bend but reliable.' I loved these ads and laughed out loud. No one else did.

The only time you could see who you were sharing the place with was when the lights came up. Then the illusionary world disappeared to be replaced by the reality of the crumbling old theatre and the prospect outside of a cold and rainy winter afternoon. With the lights up, I nervously looked round at the gaunt faces of single old people, mainly old men, and the few huddled couples and occasionally the gigglers and gropers on the back seats of the balcony above. Those I could only hear and not see.

Occasionally there were some people, who spoilt it for the other patrons, someone with a terrible cough for instance, or a drunk, or worse a gibbering nut case who wouldn't stop talking. Once there was a bunch of Teddy boys taking the mickey and singing along to the songs in the Sound of Music.

The manager usually sorted them out with a wave of his flashlight, telling them to shut up or get out. I thought he was really brave. But one good thing, there weren't many perverts; at least I don't think so. I was spoken to only once.

She was an old woman in a fur coat who smelled strongly of pee and lavender. She touched me on the shoulder from the seats behind. I froze and sat still as a frightened mouse, moving only my eyes from under the peak of my cap. I didn't do anything, but as I didn't respond she leaned closer. Then I smelled the tobacco and mints on her breath.

'Here dear, would you like a sweetie?'

Never accept sweets from a stranger, Mum had said. She offered me a Mint Imperial from a crumpled paper bag.

'You on your own, dear?'

I didn't move. She stuffed the bag close to my face over the seat. I had no option. Mum would have been so mad. I took one hard white, slightly warm mint that looked like a little bird's egg. At the same time I caught a glimpse of her thick red lipstick and heavy black mascara. She looked like a monster.

'Yes, er no, I'm doing a project for school.'

'How nice. Bet you're a clever boy. Would you like to come and sit with me, or shall I come and sit with you for company?'

I had to think quickly.

'No thanks,' I said, 'I'm saving seats for my teacher who will be here very shortly to check on me.'

Then I heard a familiar cinema voice.

'That old dame bothering you, kid?'

'Oh, no,' I said to Mr Rick.

'I could send the boys round.'

'No, really, I'm fine. Thanks Mr Rick.'

I wasn't. She scared me, but telling her about my teacher must have worked. That was the last Mint Imperial I got from her, if she really was a 'her.' She had a deep voice.

The main problem going to the cinema was that it took most of my pocket money to get in. Otherwise I'd be tempted to spend more on a choc-ice or one of those frozen triangular blocks of orange that almost gave you frost-bite in your fingers. Those were dangerous because after you sucked on one for an hour it dyed your tongue bright orange for a week, and of course you didn't know you were doing it. An orange tongue would be difficult to explain at home without major fibbing that I had caught a mysterious disease.

So during the intermission, I tried my best not to look at the usherette with her illuminated tray of lollies, choc-ices and cones and stared instead motionless for ten long minutes at the moth-eaten curtains, thankful that temptation disappeared when the lights went down.

But, oh, how I loved the films. Thank you Mr Gatiss. Thank you trigonometry.

Now what started to happen to me was that the paintings, the museum, and the films all started to sort of gel together in my head, and though at first I didn't realise it, I had a big idea brewing.

After a few weeks I started thinking about what I saw. The films fascinated me. How was it that from the reality of the auditorium with its snuffly inhabitants and peeling paint you could become completely transported, within seconds, to another world and across time? As though the theatre itself had completely dematerialised. And thoughts along those lines somehow connected up with my Jacobean room experience. Wasn't it all very much the same?

I wondered hard and long about how was it that you could lose yourself in a story, set in the wild west or deep below the Atlantic in a submarine and still be sitting on a threadbare seat with its springs coming up your bum in boring Wakefield. What was it in a story that took you away and absorbed the audience so completely? And why, when I looked hard and long enough at a painting would a story appear in my head about what was happening?

Then, one glum afternoon after mooching around the museum for the umpteenth time, looking into glass cases with faded labels and the constable's fossils, I had a thought that changed the subsequent direction of my life and I think it's fair to say, the lives of many others.

Why couldn't museums be more like films? What if things in the museum could tell their own story? What if you could be *inside* the story instead of outside it? People would love it; *I'd love it.* Everything in the museum must have a story to tell rather than just a label to wear. As I walked through town on my way to choir practice, the world changed around me. Everything and everyone *is* a story, one that is either known, anticipated, to be discovered or about to unwind.

To this day I don't know why this idea got to me the way it did. It was so powerful and wonderful it wouldn't let me go. But I was eleven. How did I know what the future had in store?

Never to go away, I put the thought on a shelf at the back of my mind whilst for a few more months until the end of my first senior school year, my truanting life carried on.

Every now and then I could afford a choc-ice because occasionally I was surprisingly flush with cash. Either, because the choir had sung at a wedding at the weekend for which we got paid a guinea, or more profitably, I sold one of my oil paintings.

My career as a professional artist began incongruously in a fish shop in our village of Calder Grove.

Frank's Fish and Chip Shop (by heck, it was a bloody good fish and chip shop) stood by the road at the bottom of the hill. It's fair to say it was more important to the residents than the Post Office.

In the early sixties fish and chips was *the* dietary staple for working people like us. Exotics like curry and chips and so on were to come on the scene later. Back then your choice was simple: cod and chips (the cheaper fish) or haddock and chips, luxury. Or more basic: a bag of chips or chips with scraps on (scraps being the bits of fried batter that floated on the liquid lard in the pan) and a Technicolor treat *mushy peas*, which as a kid, I was convinced were shipped in from another planet.

I remember how the warm parcel of fish and chips felt in my arms on a winter night, and how the smell came through the paper. (Some people said that blindfolded they could taste what particular newspaper their chips had been wrapped in.) I hurried back up the hill to our bungalow with an order of haddock and chips four times, while Mum got out the plates and spread marge on slices of white bread. Wonderful.

Frank himself was not just a fryer of fish; he was an entrepreneur with a vision. He saw a world full of his chip shops with global franchises and was always on the lookout for gimmicks to get him free publicity. He dreamed of battering the world.

As I said, thick I was at the normal academic things, and sports a waste of time, but I could draw and paint since birth, and I couldn't stop. Grandpa had been an amateur artist and I think I got it from him. Next to the smell of fish and chips, the smell of oil paints would make me dizzy with joyful anticipation.

I don't know how Frank heard about my painting habit but one day, when I went in after school for the usual with scraps on, he asked to see some of my paintings.

So I took a small selection of pictures (my Cezanne period) down the hill in a plastic bag and showed him a few over the counter while he dropped a flaccid battered fish into the bubbling fat.

'Not bad, lad,' he said. 'I'll give you an exhibition, if you like,' as he slapped another large piece of cod around in the batter tray. 'You can show them and sell them in the café. Put them on the walls in there,' nodding through to the room that served as a sit-down dining room.

So I did. About ten of them went up on the walls above the ketchup, brown sauce, and malt vinegar bottles. My paintings of trees and fields, mainly executed on bits of hardboard I nicked from my dad's shed, hung decorously between wall lights with red tassel shades on either side of a giant double size photomural of a Norwegian fjord with tall conifers which met symmetrically in the middle.

Frank's wasn't exactly the Guggenheim, but at least you could always get 'twice and four penneth' and a carton of mushy peas while you were picking up on The Culture.

Frank wasn't really a patron of the village art scene; he wanted my exhibition for another reason. He was nothing if not inventive and he saw it as a novel way to promote his shop and his brand to the country. Frank knew how to promote things.

One morning before setting off for school, the phone rang. Mum looked surprised and shocked in the same expressive moment as she held the receiver out to me and whispered, 'Graham, it's the BBC. They want to speak to you.' (At home I was called by my middle name.)

'Hello?' I said cautiously.

A lady with a plummy southern accent replied. She said she was calling from *Today*. This was a national daily news and current affairs radio programme broadcast Mondays to Fridays between seven and nine which everyone in Britain and the universe listened to. In fact, we had it on in the kitchen when she called.

Frank had somehow got the show interested in doing a tongue-in-cheek piece about 'Art and fish and chips; do they mix?'

She talked to me like I was a real artist and not a kid. In the next few minutes they had me do a live interview over the phone, talking about exhibiting in a fish and chip shop. Mum had to turn off our kitchen radio because of what they said was feedback. Besides my little piece they had customers interviewed at the café (a local radio reporter had done it the day before) expressing their views about the paintings. It wasn't what you might call a highbrow discussion.

Reporter: 'So sir, I see you are enjoying the fish and chips. But I wonder, are you also enjoying the art on the walls?'

Local: 'That's not what I'd call art, pal. My dog could have done that. Now pass t' brown sauce and bugger off.'

No doubt Southern England's view of northern cultural life or lack of it was well reinforced. Southerners at the time (the people who lived somewhere 'down South') had a fascination with the eating habits of Northerners, and especially Northern delicacies like mushy peas and black pudding. However Frank got his national publicity and I got on radio and ended up selling a painting or two for the price of 'four times with scraps on'.

But daft as it may sound, getting on the BBC taught me a lesson; that I *could* do something with the only thing I did well. I could produce something original and catch people's imaginations. It strengthened my feeling that I wasn't so dumb and useless as I felt at school. By the end of my year of truancy and now pushing twelve, I began to really blossom as an artist. Just as well because at the end of the summer term in July, my academic ability remained steadfastly un-blossomed. However, things on the art side improved immensely on return to school in September when I made a breakthrough from fish and chip shop sales and began to sell paintings to school masters.

A few mates and I already lived in the art room. I'd rather be up there at break than kicking some stupid ball around the playground or worse being kicked around myself. So I had lots of time to do paintings.

My dad was often violent and nasty tempered and I think hugely frustrated with his life and humble job after fighting in the jungles of Burma during the Second World War. He came home with malaria still in his veins. It was shocking to see him when it raised its ugly head. I don't know what it was that made him take his anger out on me though. Being smacked around and verbally abused was one thing, but worse than that he never once acted like a loving father. That's why other men that I respected became the father figures who I wanted to please. Percy Beak our art master was one such man; gentle and kind and much too nice to be a master of spotty teenage boys. Percy had the most beautiful artistic handwriting and a black shiny fountain pen with a gold nib. He also pulled from his pocket a terrific black bone-handled penknife with a little silver shield on its side that I positively lusted after.

Percy chose a painting or drawing each week for *Picture of the Week*. I was lucky to have a few of mine chosen. One caught the eye of two schoolmasters; Mr Grimshaw, the music master, whose own talents were also wasted on pimply thirteen-year-olds and Mr Kent, our form master. Both of them commissioned me to do a painting.

That was fine, the painting bit. But then actually asking your masters to pay for something you did was not the easiest thing in the world.

Mr Grimshaw was pleased with the piece I did for him and his wife. It was a large cityscape rendered in Indian ink on glossy white paper. Without asking the price when I produced it he handed over ten pounds, a huge sum then. I think Dad was only making five quid a week at the time. But Mr Kent, embarrassed by the transaction, worked out a price for my painting whilst walking across the playground with me self-consciously in tow. I was in no position to bargain and he didn't give me much of a chance. Instead of asking me how much I wanted he said:

'Right, Sunderland, how much was the hardboard that you did the painting on?' He carried it wrapped up in brown paper under his arm to which I replied, 'I got it out of my dad's shed sir. It cost nothing.' Having said that, I already knew I was on a loser.

'How much was the paint?' he asked mid-playground.

'About two shillings, sir,' I replied, head down as we dodged between the footballers.

'So how much time did you put into doing it?'

'I did it in a day, sir.'

'Right, shall we say a shilling an hour, yes?' He should have been a captain of industry or a banker instead of a chemistry teacher.

'Yes, sir,' I said.

So the miserable miser gave me ten shillings and said, 'That'll about cover it then,' and walked off with my painting. Ten bob, effectively one-twentieth of what the music master paid. I'd been robbed. No wonder I hated chemistry as well as maths.

The following day he came up to me again, a little sheepishly this time. We were in the corridor outside the form room. He told me (in so many words) that his wife had been angry with him for being so tight-fisted and for not recognising the artistic value of the original Junior Cezanne he'd bought her.

He told me she loved it at first sight and immediately had him hang it above the fireplace in their lounge. So in the corridor with shaking fingers he poked into his well-zipped wallet and coughed up a fiver. Five pounds, yes, rich. This art business was going well, who needed logarithms?

Fifteen pounds between the two paintings, I could buy myself a Mini for that. I just had to be good at what I loved doing and did best. There was a future in this art stuff.

Still, Mr Kent got his own back. The swine recommended that I stay down in the same class at the same level for a repeat year because I did so badly at everything except art.

But during that year there was one positive change; I had a different kind of maths master, one who was more sensitive. He spent a great deal of time without fear or threat trying to get me to understand how algebra actually worked. He sat there patiently at my desk many times, one on one, taking me through equations, waiting for that magic moment when something in my brain would click. When it didn't, same with trigonometry and logarithms, there was the realisation that I had some kind of dyslexia when it came to numbers and symbols, that it was real, I wasn't just being thick and lazy. After that I was sort of let off the hook. I was left to meander in the mathematical world alone doodling in the margins the pressure taken off me whilst my talents in other directions blossomed.

Interestingly, decades later, I would be calculating costs for multi-million pound museum projects in my head and planning complex spaces in the same way. Eventually I was able to estimate the costs of major projects surprisingly accurately without ever writing down a number. I would *feel* the answer, more gut than brain. I realised that I could do maths and geometry all along, intuitively.

3 BLUE BOTTLE IN
THE BARREL

IF THE STIGMA OF MY situation wasn't bad enough at school, an unhappy home life had taken a miserable turn for the worse.

Mum and Dad were arguing all the time and there was always the threat of violence. The only time we could relax was when he was down at The British Oak with his boozing pals. No surprise then when one day after choir practice Mum introduced me to 'a new friend', Trevor. I was no fool. Trevor was her fancy man and he became a surrogate secret father to my sis and I, and curiously enough a man who helped me tremendously on my way to the Vikings of York.

Whilst the tension in our bungalow was rising daily, I became infamous at school for being so obviously one lobe-sided, something that was now becoming apparent to Mum too. Mr Gatiss, a year before, had finally blown my cover when he wrote in my end-of-year school report the immortal words: '*Mathematics Report* – John has made no progress whatsoever on account of his non-attendance of lessons. I hope the eye surgery will correct his vision problem.'

I had to explain. When I told Mum about my truanting she almost fainted. But I decided it best not to share the story of the 'funny lady' who wanted me to share her Mint Imperials.

'I'm only any good at art, Mum. It's not my fault,' I said in tears standing guilty before her. After that Dad couldn't care less about what I did at school and Mum backed me for what I was.

Though I never did improve much academically over the next six years of grammar school, I made up for it in creative ways. I loved writing, English and stories in history as well as acting and singing in the school musicals. I virtually lived in the art room.

Miraculously, I somehow scraped through my 17, achieving just enough to get into the sixth form, which was bliss. Four-fifths of my periods were spent in the art room, the other few in a small class of English scholars.

One day to my absolute surprise I was called to the Headmaster's office. I thought after six years that someone had snitched on me about my truanting days. Instead he made me a Prefect; I, who'd never worked out an equation in my life, was now a badge-wearing teachers' helper and junior disciplinarian.

At home in the early summer of my last school year, I finally stood up to my dad. I was helping him in the garden when he began to swear and shout at me as usual, calling me belittling names loud enough for the neighbours to hear. By then I'd not only grown physically bigger than him, I'd also gained physical confidence in spite of his battering. I wouldn't take it anymore and had an all-out fight with him then and there. When I threw him into the rose bushes he knew he was bested and the abuse of my mother and me stopped. But the atmosphere at home was deadly. He hardly spoke and never to me during the summer months as he and I waited for my departure to college.

During those weeks I had a pretty serious diversion. I met a trainee nurse at a party. Sue was lovely and different, her own person, not some dopey high school girl with a paddock and a pony. I fell for her pretty quickly.

She was training to be a mental health nurse at the hospital, Stanley Royd in Wakefield, where coincidentally my granddad had worked as a male nurse most of his life. I managed to land a summer job there.

It wasn't hard to get a job there. Not many teenagers chose to spend their summer holiday before college wiping old men's bums, and other similar unpleasant personal services all of which required serious scrubbing of the hands afterwards. Sue was eighteen and making nursing her career. I was just nineteen before leaving school (a year older than most for having been kept down that year). We met up after shifts, still with the stink of the wards on us, and soon fell in love. To be honest I really fell for her *and* her lovely hard-working family too who soon adopted this oddball arty grammar school kid she took home. I spent as much time there as I could, away from Dad.

Stanley Royd stood behind high spiked railings. A Victorian institution in every sense, it was daunting, black and grim like a prison for the incarceration of unfortunates of a barmy disposition. The place was steeped in local stigma. It was where for a hundred years mentally ill relatives who'd 'gone funny' or had trouble with their 'nerves' were dumped out of sight and forgotten.

'Sh** shovelling', as it was technically described, was basically the main and only skill required for my holiday job. There was one advantage to the job if you were a nail biter; it was a sure-fire cure.

Grandpa had worked as a charge nurse on a lock-up ward long before the drug Largactil (known as the 'liquid cosh' in the trade) had been introduced. His ward was full of the violently insane. I have often thought what a hellhole it must have been in the decades he worked there, but never once did I hear him complain.

I was always very sensitive to smells and the only connection I recalled as a child with him and hospital was him coming home after his shift with a dour, sour smell on his clothes and skin, like a whiff of putrefied rat, like dead air and sadness.

College and escape beckoned, but it was eight weeks away when I spent my first day of my summer job on the geriatric ward where, with Grandpa's help, I landed my Nursing Assistant job. It turned out to be the best further education a young man could have had, a bit like doing Voluntary Service in hell, but, boy, did I get a different view on life.

The ward was basically an old shed, painted an institutional cream, with the limp balloons from last Christmas hanging from the metal beams above the beds, as unnoticed as some of the patients.

Sharing days with those poor old souls, trying to communicate, taking them to the toilet, changing their dressings and stinking sheets came as an extra education that I never expected, a kind of finishing school for life.

It took some getting used to; it was a smack in the face of reality, a far cry from the art room and the Cathedral choir. I didn't realise how lucky I was. It was a shock to learn that caring for the elderly mentally ill was what many people did every day for a living. Working there gave me a precious insight into the working life of my grandfather too. For thirty-five years, day after day he was locked away with lost ghosts and shrieking ghouls, the really crazy ones. My old gentlemen were just faded shirts hanging in the wardrobe of time compared to those poor demented sods behind the locked gates.

During that summer, my respect for the staff, some of who were real saints, grew with every depressing faeces-soiled day. But I also saw the other side; I saw physical and mental cruelty doled out by a few sadistic so-called nurses, those who saw defenseless old men as inhuman and treated them as such.

I grew up quickly in those few weeks, witnessing as I did all sides of human nature. I saw both true selfless human goodness at work and real wickedness side by side, whilst in the patients I saw the complete collapse of the human condition, and several of the patients living in an institutionalised limbo, an off-world colony right next door.

One of the old men had a real impact on me. He must have been in his seventies; it was difficult to tell. He had a genteel face and soft hands with long white fingers like piano keys and china and the soft palms (which I held sometimes when I had to help him to the toilet) of a country vicar.

As he sat on the toilet in that comfortless door-less cubicle in the cold morning I could picture him in the pulpit and see him at the door of his church, handsome and holy in his dog collar. It was interesting how it was possible to have a sense of who the men had been before dementia immersed them in their chartless fog.

Now this genteel old gentleman had become completely lost for all his service to his flock and God, who appeared to have given him up. He couldn't do a thing for himself, but unlike most of the others on the ward, he wasn't completely alone for his equally elderly and refined wife came and sat with him every afternoon without fail.

She was on the ball and obviously the bond between them was as complete as the wedding ring on her elderly finger. Sadly he didn't recognise her. I felt tears well up often when I saw them together; there was so much love there at least from her. It takes a while to get hardened they say in the nursing trade.

She sat at his bedside throughout the long afternoons of visiting hours when time seemed to stand still in the ward, stroking his thin scratched hands whilst with milky eyes he looked at her with a furious curiosity.

Every day she brought him oranges and bottles of stout and bags of wrapped sweets and put them in his drawer to have later. His wife thought he was enjoying the things she brought him, but I was told what really happened and where they went, that some of the staff took them. I wanted to say something. Then I thought that at least it was something for her – the thought that he enjoyed the stout and the mint humbugs she brought. She didn't need to know.

His was a rare case, having his wife visit. Most of the inmates didn't have visitors. They were long since abandoned or they unknowingly survived friends and siblings who passed before them.

Some of the old men had had lives that were simply tragic, victims of awful accidents of history, fate and place. It was as though their stories had been locked away with them, too awful for society to bear.

Several had started out in life being born at the time of the First World War with congenital illnesses like syphilis, which their fathers contracted in French brothels passing it on to their innocent wives, lovers and babies back in Blighty after the war was over.

So these poor souls who wandered the ward or were tied to their chairs had been born with syphilis and condemned to a life of derangement, apart from the rest of humanity. Worst of it was they didn't die; the institutions in which they had lived all their lives kept them going, if you could call it living.

Later at home after the shift, I had to get it out of my system, so I had a bath to get the smell off. And then if I wasn't seeing Susan I turned to drawing what I experienced in my sketchbook. Drawing during times like these was a bridge for my spirit; the lines on the paper were like cables anchoring me whilst I was trying to make sense of it all.

It wasn't difficult to see how some of the less good-natured nurses left kindness behind and became hardened and in some cases cruel. The constant noise on the ward alone was enough to do it. In those days not all the staff, as far as I, an untrained assistant could see, were committed nurses. They weren't. The thankless daily tasks they had to perform in such an environment put them at the bottom of the nursing prestige scale.

Amidst the decay, stench and dementia there was surprisingly a sense of community, a sense of identity of the ward and its incumbents. This came from the nurses who cared. To them the ward was a large family with its characters like any family. They treated their charges with ongoing respect and with as much comfort as could be mustered, remembering birthdays with cards and small gifts for the patients without relatives. What amazed me was how they developed a way of communicating across the awful void of insanity. But I wondered as I looked at the card on the bed stand, if anything got through to the patient.

Occasionally, there was a funny side to daily life on the ward, the kind of thing that kept us all from going nuts.

One hot August afternoon I came on for my shift. For once it was bright and sunny inside. The regular staff was having their shift-change meeting in the office. I stepped out into the ward to do a check round to see who needed changing or cleaning up.

I was surprised to see six men all facing the same way standing in the middle of the open space that ran the length of the ward. They were in two lines with three patients in their ward gowns on either side and all were swaying side to side, slowly and in unison. I had never seen them do anything in a collective way, even hold a conversation, yet strangely here they were, all looking off to the front silently, their eyes fixed on some other place, time or horizon beyond the confines of the ward.

I approached one elderly gent at the front.

'What are you doing, Bill?' I asked as he gently swayed to and fro.

Eyes unblinking fixed forward he heard me, and without looking at me said, 'Don't you fret lad; you're safe now. We'll soon be home. We're just coming to port, not long now. I'll buy you a pint after we've docked.'

I choked up. It seemed they all believed they were docking onboard a troop ship after the war, soon to be de-mobbed and on their way home. It was as though Bill and his friends occupied a parallel universe made up of a collective experience and shared memories. They were all happy; I could see it in their eyes. They survived the war and would soon be home.

The summer of 1969 passed by in a cloud of romance and disinfectant. I hung up my white coat for the last time on the ward at the beginning of September and took the train south. I was accepted for my Foundation year at Bath Academy of Art, the oldest art college in England, famous for being located in a rural idyll, located ten miles outside Bath in Wiltshire, in the picturesque village of Corsham.

Truth about my five years of art and Design College is that I very nearly blew it in my first year at Corsham. In fact I was really close to packing up the idea of being an artist and designer. That is until I met someone truly inspiring.

During my first year at Corsham all that way *down south*, I felt very lost and lonely, a northern fish out of water. I had hardly ever been to the southern counties, the accents and the attitudes of students and locals seemed very different to people up North. And back then there really was a north-south divide, and the prejudices worked both ways.

My Yorkshire accent set me apart, so I felt. I developed a really fat Frank's Fish and Chip Shop chip on my shoulder that served to alienate me more. The other students were mainly from the southern counties or from abroad, so with my 'eeh by gum' accent I felt like an outsider. And worse I took all the friendly jibes about the dark satanic north to heart and was soon wondering why I had come so far south for my Foundation year. The reason was of course, to get away from my father.

So whilst all the other new students were pairing off I found myself alone in the freezing cheerless room at my digs with a Penguin chocolate biscuit stolen from the pantry below for company and a letter a night to write to Sue, my new fiancée back home in Wakefield, for conversation.

Weekends were the worst. Whilst the others were off somewhere I hung out in the student common room, with nowhere else to go. As I got more and more depressed my course work suffered and the Art Room Star status from school days in me faded. So this was college then, the art college I dreamt of going to. It should have felt great to be there. That's when I met her; another outsider if ever there was one.

Julie was about 4'6" tall, weighed about six and a half stone if that, had long jet black hair down to her waist which shone like polished anthracite, warm brown eyes that sparkled in a deeply tanned face and a smile that could melt Antarctica if she ever got down that way.

She had polio as a child and wore calipers on her skinny chicken bone legs, and her tiny hands and chipolata fingers were likewise crippled. But it was only her body that had borne the brunt of her illness. She was the most luminous person I had met to date; she literally shone with light and life.

Her loveliness of spirit was undimmed by her physical affliction. She couldn't hold a pencil properly or a paintbrush or work with scissors or set type, all the things everyone else did so easily. Notwithstanding, I never did find out why with such disabilities she had been desperate to enrol at an art college of all places. For her, everything at college was physically difficult, yet she attempted each new project with great smiles and courage. I met her for the first time one autumn term weekend, early on, because like me she was alone most weekends.

She came to the common room in the gatehouse to do some drawing, that's when we really connected. I watched her try to hold a piece of charcoal and to make it do what she wanted it to do on the paper. She would have hated my pity or sympathy, the last thing she wanted, but inside my heart went out to her. Not because of her disabilities, but because of her indomitable courage. I came to learn that what drove her was her innate creativity, which had to find expression.

Julie was an ex-colonial. Her parents were farmers in Kenya and her under-standing of England was naïve yet utterly charming. Like the way many Americans think England and the English are all Big Ben, muffins, high tea, Mary Poppins, fog and the Queen, Julie believed it too. And in the gorgeous surroundings of Corsham with its chocolate box Flemish weavers' cottages, beautiful lush landscape in which milk and honey virtually flowed, it was easy to think that *jolly old England* was indeed just that.

I fitted into her diorama of England too. My accent amused her, and she assumed things about my character and personality because I was from the North. That also fitted into her storybook vision (I was Heathcliff in glasses). To her I had definitely sprung from the darker end of the country and lived on nothing but bitter beer, fish, chips and black pudding (not far wrong actually, but I didn't admit it).

That Sunday, alone in the gatehouse, we talked a lot about where we came from, our families, our dreams and ambitions. She didn't seem to worry that she came to England with very little money, most having been spent on fees for the college. And she hadn't any clothes other than the red plaid skirt and the same blouse and jumper, as though for an eternal summer. She had no warm clothes, having only experienced the heat of Africa.

Later as winter arrived in Wiltshire her deep tan disappeared. She sometimes appeared blue with cold, but never complained. It was as though in robbing her of a full range of movement and stature, nature had compensated in making her more alive, naturally joyful and more optimistic than other people. Julie was elemental and yet frustrated and confounded by all activities that were part of our course. Still she knew inside that she was an artist and a designer, and at the point that I doubted my own creative drive and choice of future, she made me feel the same and put me back on track.

I realised because of her how very fortunate I was to have creative talent; that I'd been blessed with it, not cursed. And she made me feel fortunate for things I took for granted, like being able to hold a pencil and make it do what I wanted it to do. While she was imprisoned by her physical disabilities and restricted in the expression of her creative ideas, my student colleagues and I were able to move freely in the world wherever our creative paths led.

At Christmas Julie stayed a long cold fortnight in Corsham alone whilst I went back home to my fiancée. On my return Julie was glad to see me and me her.

'Eee lad,' she said, pulling my leg, when I first saw her after getting back. 'What were it like down t'pit on Christmas day, weren't turkey all black?'

We were never to become more than good friends. I had a life elsewhere with someone else to which I knew I would return in a few months. We drifted apart over the rest of the academic year. I've often wondered whatever happened to the unique and lovely Julie. She was an inspiration.

4 BIRTH OF THE BIN

I OBVIOUSLY NEEDED MORE STRUCTURE and discipline than was offered at Corsham. After one year in that blissed-out picture-postcard pot-smoking rural hippie heaven and after having been all but kicked out for doing hardly any work, I scraped into a place on the graphic design course at Birmingham Polytechnic. I hated the idea of Birmingham and its Poly, but four years later I felt very differently.

Birmingham Poly was as opposite to a rural idyll as one could imagine. Over the next three years studying graphic design and a post-grad year studying film production, I gained good qualifications and found my professional self. By the end of my college days I was determined to become a freelance graphic designer, illustrator, animator and independent filmmaker. I emerged with a Diploma in Art and Design with Honours, Dip. A.D. Hons. (The Hons. bit I was especially proud of.) After getting my Diploma I spent another exhilarating year on a post-graduate course learning how to make films. Vikings, museums and exhibition design were not even on the rim of my consciousness. But that 'museums like films' idea slept on in me. What I didn't realise then was all these media were tools that could be used in various combinations in interpretation and in the telling of stories.

As I discovered my aptitudes and abilities in graphic design, illustration and film, both live and animated, film seemed to be the most attractive.

What I really loved though was animation in all its forms. Early on in the year a young producer from the BBC visited college and looked at our work. There were only three of us on the post-grad film course. He liked my stuff and commissioned me to make several short animation films to be shown on the programme he represented, a religious series aimed at young people in what was then nicknamed 'the God slot', between 6pm and 7pm on Sunday evenings.

These short shorts provided a vehicle for my humour, and it was the first time I saw my work on television. At the time I along with other young emerging animators were influenced by the wonderful Terry Gilliam animations on *Monty Python* which was still new, so I guess my first efforts were somewhat derivative, all screaming nuns and paper cutouts.

On a more serious level where in fact there were no laughs at all but plenty of screams, I spent most of the year writing, directing and producing a 30-minute live action documentary about Mental Health Services. The film followed the story of a young woman who suffered a nervous breakdown. It was a big subject for a young guy to tackle. At the time there was much talk about the de-institutionalisation of Mental Hospitals and dumping, sorry, placing more ex-patients out in the community. I had seen institutionalisation first-hand in the geriatric ward of Stanley Royd, but none of my old boys there would have made it back in the community.

In order to research the subject, I got a holiday job the summer before my post-grad in the hospital where Susan was continuing her nursing training at Erdington in Birmingham. The experience of working on a ward occupied with people who had suffered breakdowns of one sort or another gave me the direct experience on which to base my film.

I finished it in time for the post-graduate year's assessment and the film earned me my higher degree. As I sat there with the external assessor viewing it, when it came to the titles I noticed for the first time that I spelled 'Polytechnic' wrongly as 'Politechnic'. It didn't make any difference; I passed. That done and after a total of five years at college it was out into the real world and the future, whatever it may bring, wherever it may lead.

College over and now aged twenty-four I married Susan who had come to Birmingham to complete her training and to set up home with me. It was time to decide which direction my freelance career should take. I had one major aspiration; I wanted to be a movie mogul, well perhaps not a mogul, but to make films anyway.

As this was likely to be nothing more than a dream, hard reality dictated that we should return to the security of the North. There the part-time holiday work I did for my father-in-law in his scrap metal business would, God forbid, turn into solid full-time. So while most of my college peers headed to London to find themselves careers in design, we headed back North to 'eee by gum' land in grotty Wakefield. It was as though I couldn't escape the place; but at least now with both of us having graduated we could lead our own lives.

We rented a red brick 'semi' on a grim and featureless housing estate made up of identical red brick houses and identical people. Sue got her position back at her old hospital but returned as a fully qualified nurse.

When we set up home on that dreary estate we began our new life with the princely sum of one hundred and thirty pounds in our joint piggy bank. And that was down to Sue; she was the breadwinner while I looked for work. We were desperately hard up, yet she agreed that given my passion for filmmaking, I should give freelancing a go, but she put a time limit on it. I had three weeks in which to land a job or if not go and work full-time for her dad.

I think she thought if she gave me enough rope I'd hang myself and come down to earth where she and the other real people were. My dream though was to produce, write and direct independent films, no less. Industrial to start with, then I'd work my way up to mega-movies. This you might imagine and you'd be dead right, was quite a sizeable ambition in a place like Wakefield. Not exactly the movie capital of the West Riding.

So sure was I that it was my intended profession that one night driving home late in our old rusted Hillman Imp, after being stopped by a policeman for speeding (which in the Imp was something of a feat), I gave my profession, straight faced, as 'film director'. This made the officer laugh so hard he tore up the charge sheet and told us to get off home with a caution delivered through sniggers and giggles. He said I was the best laugh he had all week.

Undeterred by the laughing policeman (what did he know after all?) and powered by enthusiasm, panic and desperation as our piggy bank had all but lost its rattle I thought the best way to get my first film job would be to start cold-calling companies in the city.

So I spent the days of what were going to be the last weeks of freedom before reality came knocking, sitting at the kitchen table with a copy of the local telephone directory going down the list of companies and making calls to complete strangers.

I had the innocent hope that someone on the other end would say, 'Oh, we've been waiting for someone like you to call; we're urgently needing a promotional film made by a budding genius like you about our bakery/dye-works/rhubarb farm. Can you start tomorrow, or better, today, and where do we send the cheque?'

It wasn't quite like that. The replies usually were more along the lines of, 'You what?' Click. Freelance work wasn't going to come that easy it seemed, especially for an aspiring junior movie mogul. Just then, as the piggy bank rattled its very last we discovered we were going to have a baby. Timing is everything.

Sue came home from a hard day of nursing where she pulled incontinent old ladies up and out of beds and lugged them onto toilets and into baths whilst suffering the onset of morning sickness to find the Film Director long in the face, as devoid of good news as our little piggy bank was now of funds.

All I had to report to her was that I got through the D's; then the M's, then the T's and no takers. But dauntless, she encouraged me to carry on all the way to the Z's; might as well get it out of my system. In the background, as those first hopeless days ticked by, was the prospect of working full-time for my new father-in-law Jack. As a scrap metal dealer Jack made a ton of money, and he had a job for me if I wanted it.

Except for Mum who was very supportive of whatever I wanted to do as long as my heart was in it, everybody else in the joint family said it would be the thing to do whilst we got on our feet. A career in 'Art and Design' was seen in those days as an unpromising job prospect in the working-class circles I came from. They thought it was my 'arty phase' and soon I'd come to my senses, like getting over a nosebleed or the flu.

Jack had no sons. He had three daughters, my wife being the eldest. So the prospect of a son-in-law coming in to the business was promising to him, even an arty wimp like me. To Sue it made a lot of sense. A job with a reasonably fat wad of mucky cash to bring home at the end of the week seemed like a good idea especially with the baby on the way. And if I went to work for her dad there'd definitely be a future in muck and guaranteed income for our new family, no doubt about that.

So with thoughts about working for Jack in the macho world of the scrap metal trade as an alternative career to being a film maker, I decided to redouble my efforts to land my first film commission. The alternative was too horrible to think about.

Trouble was I was getting worryingly close to the end of the telephone book and still with not a prospect in sight. My three weeks to find my first commission were almost up and Sue was beginning to grow out of her uniform. Having got almost to the end without any openings whatsoever, I eventually reached the W's. *The Wakefield Express*, the local newspaper, was near the top of the W list. So holding out little hope, I gave them a call. Little did I know that in dialling that number I was taking a giant step on my way to Jorvik. Funny how life works.

Getting through to Colin Pyrah, the Production Director who was also responsible for marketing and promotions, I introduced myself. To my jaw-dropping surprise he told me my calling was timely, they were *indeed* considering having a new promotional film made. Then I couldn't further believe my ears as he invited me to come in the day after and show them my reel. When Sue came home that evening I had at last something positive to report.

I turned up the next day at the newspaper offices and ran them my college film reel on an old film projector. My show featured a BBC commission cartoon or two; a weird little film I made based on the poem *The Dong with the Luminous Nose* by Edward Lear, and of all things, my no-laughs-allowed documentary on Mental Health Services in Birmingham, which I spent my post-grad year making. A documentary about a patient in a mental hospital hardly seemed appropriate in the circumstances but they seemed to like it.

The projector whirred as the actress playing the woman who was recently admitted into hospital clenched her teeth as the electric shock therapy passed through her skull. And I wondered what on earth were they going to make of this? But no matter how incongruous it seemed to me, they saw something in it, because right after watching it Colin hired me to make their film. I could have jumped over the river.

As it was, the budget they offered me was paltry, two and a half thousand pounds. Not a lot even then, just enough to buy the crew a few beers and packets of crisps. Undeterred though, realising this may be a loss-leader but could be my passport into industrial film making, I gathered a small professional crew together and asked Phil Swerdlow, a mate from school who I'd always regarded as a great talent, to join me to write and produce the film.

We needed to get smart and street-wise straight off. This was a real commission for a real company, not some student thing. Contracts would have to be drawn up and signed. Real money was being invested, not much, but a lot more than I'd seen in a while; I even had to get a business bank account just like a real movie mogul.

We did have one pretty big advantage though that made up for our greenness and lack of experience. While I was at college Trevor, Mum's fancy man, had landed a job at the new Yorkshire Television studios in Leeds. His position in the Sound Department put him in the production heart of the company and most importantly to me, meant he was able to help us. The first thing he did was fix up a meeting with me and a young editor at the studios, Chris Page; he was about our age and we struck it off straight away.

Chris had a great sense of humour, liked pubs and most importantly knew what he was doing. Trevor then put us in contact with a cameraman who did regular freelance work for the station. Once we worked out a deal with him, we had the production team.

We were a young and enthusiastic bunch; I estimate the average age of our team was 26 and full of energy. This was real. It was scary and exciting in equal measure. But I had started on the freelance path, my own boss for the time being at least. The prospect of working on the tip receded and although we were still broke, I at least, felt ten feet tall.

Four months after starting the production process we delivered the first print. The finished film was just short of thirty minutes in length and we made and delivered it within the budget of two and a half grand, and no major screw-ups.

Colin was delighted with the finished product and only having to pay a fraction of what they'd have had to pay if they'd gone to an established company. As for Phil and I, we survived and were now officially in the business with a completed project under our belts. Sue was not so sure.

Neither my client Colin nor I realised that making the film was the start of our working relationship, and that we were both now on our way to Jorvik.

At the television studios, Trevor was always on the lookout for jobs for me. When I told him I was interested in a full-time job at the studios in the Graphics Department if I couldn't get any more independent film work, he put out feelers. Not long after he landed me an interview with the head of that department.

I went along to the interview full of confidence with my Birmingham portfolio under my arm crammed with good stuff, and had my interview in the department amongst people my age who worked there. They sat at drawing desks and produced all manner of graphics, for light entertainment shows, children's shows, regional daily news broadcasts, dramas, documentaries and the nightly weather forecasts, to name but a few.

It was a very busy place and hummed with activity, a set-up where Dave's (the head of the studio) proclivity for the booze didn't seem to worry anyone, they all just got on with it.

It's worth pointing out that in those days there were no computers to assist in production, no Illustrator, no Photoshop; what appeared on screen was mostly produced by hand and the rub down letters of Letraset; so I thought my skills might just fit in. But I was wrong.

Disappointed that I wasn't offered a position on the studio staff, I was instead offered something much better. Dave read me right; I would have been bored out of my crust. There's a limit to how much Letrasetting *rain, sleet, snow, fog* a weather forecast artist can take. Much better, he said, he'd give me regular freelance work and was true to his word.

I set up a small studio at home in a spare bedroom. First they had me produce illustrations promoting movies they were to show later in the week. While it doesn't sound like much, it was really challenging and they paid me ten pounds for each one.

From movie captions for grown-ups I graduated to story illustrator on pre-school kids' programmes where I could earn more money per job. While the kids' programmes were more challenging at first, they were also a lot more satisfying to do. I had to take a story and produce a series of colour paintings on 16" by 20" white sheets of board. When broadcast the story would be narrated by an actor sat at a piano, while the illustrations brought the story to life for the little kids watching.

When I delivered a pack of these drawings to the studios, I showed them to the director and discussed the camera moves. She would then write down a list of instructions on moves, pans, zooms, fades, mixes and cuts, which would go with the story. Once again, little did I know that this work was taking me closer to the Jorvik Viking Centre and teaching me a thing or two about creating spatial illusions and the importance of the interaction of words and images even if who was watching was only three years old and sat on a potty in front of the telly.

I carried on producing illustrations for the same programme for a couple of years. Over that time my little studio room in our semi became filled with small plastic bottles of colours; this for the doll's dress in the series, these for Scallywag the naughty puppy, that bottle over there for the cheeky kitten, this bottle is for Sally's eyes, her lips, her shoes etc. etc. Her little illustrated world with her toys and pets almost took over mine. I used to go to bed at night and dream of it.

Then after doing about thirty programmes, I got sick and tired of spending my days in a childish make-believe world. What I really wanted in those little jars of colours was red for the blood of the characters that would be spilled by Harry the friendly gardener with his axe and bright orange for the explosion that would destroy the garden I created for Sally and her cuddly toys (only kidding).

Truth was Sally's naughty puppy was taking me nowhere and it was time to look further afield for something more challenging and fulfilling. I had got off to such a good start with the industrial films but somehow was now stuck in a cul-de-sac, metaphorically and actually.

By 1977 I went into partnership with Jane Parnaby, a wonderful smart, talented and attractive young woman about the same age as me. I met her during my first year of college at Corsham but we were never close. Six years after Corsham we met up in Leeds at a college reunion party. We got on much better at the party and she said that she was thinking of going freelance and leaving her London design job. So we discussed setting up a business together.

She was soon up there and together we found a little place to establish a design studio in what had been stables at the rear of a large house in Chapletown, Leeds. Partnerships are never easy no matter how initially well intended. Ours lasted the best part of two years, during which we looked for and found design work of various types, had our scrapes with unscrupulous clients, went without pay every now and then and overall entered into a parallel marriage whilst my real wife at home was looking after our now two little girls.

Then into my sphere of the partnership came an extraordinary opportunity. Just as the year rolled over into 1978, we were joined by, of all people, Allen the former Executive Head of the Design Studio at Yorkshire Television.

He too had decided to go freelance and hearing about our place approached us for a room to sublet and moved in just across the landing. I met Allen several times at the studios, but I didn't know him that well, after all at the studios he had quite an elevated position. Now on the outside, he seemed a nice enough bloke and very professional. Jane and I both reckoned we could learn a lot from him and we were flattered that someone of his quality and standing would want to come and chum up with us. Added to that he still had his YTV connections and so we hoped we would pick up some work from him.

He told us that he'd had enough of corporate life and had decided to go his own way, but made it clear that there was no fall-out and had left Yorkshire Television on good terms. In fact, he said, he fully expected to pick up work from the studios.

Something didn't seem quite right. Although he said he decided to step out of the corporate structure for personal reasons I wasn't convinced he told us the whole story. After all he'd a plum job with what I imagined a great salary and benefits. If there *was* something else, he wasn't telling us.

Allen was older than us; in his late thirties and like Jane he'd never been freelance or worked outside a company. At first that showed; he was the proverbial fish out of water. I had the feeling he was let down that we didn't have a canteen and a bar with subsidised beer. But pretty soon he became used to the freelance way and take-away Indian food, and was nothing but charming and friendly.

Allen was already familiar with my illustration and cartooning as he had commissioned simple animated title sequences from me in the past through Dave and he said he liked my work. One day, not long after he joined us he stepped across the landing and into our room, coffee cup and cigarette in hand. Jane was out so he drew up her chair and sat next to me.

He explained he had a nice little job in the offing and there was work in it for me if I wanted it. He told me about a new mega light-entertainment show about to be produced, a quiz game the rights of which had been bought from a Spanish television company where it was a huge hit. He said the expectation was for it to be enormous here too and there'd be loads of work farmed out to freelancers during its production. He said, 'Fortunes would be spent by the producers to make it a ginormous hit.'

The new show was called 3*2*1. It was *the* hit light entertainment show in Spain where it had played for several seasons. Yorkshire TV bought rights to produce an English version. In Spain the show was known as U*n*Dos*Tres. The main attraction, resulting in sensational viewing figures, was the spectacular prizes, the most extravagant on television at that time.

But the catch, which kept the live audience, contestants and viewers on the edge of their seats, was that they could lose everything in a moment and go home with a booby prize instead of a yacht. A likely winner could go from riches to rags in a moment. That's what gave the show its hook and its teeth.

In Spain the booby prize was a squash, something so common it was of no value. The English show, explained Allen, needed something similar, but not a vegetable.

He told me how the show's ex BBC Producer, who was brought in specially, decided that in Britain an ordinary dustbin would make an ideal booby prize (a dustbin translates to a trash can in America). But a full-sized backyard galvanised bin wasn't much use, so he asked Allen to create a cartoon character, to become not only the booby prize, but the show's mascot.

He gladly agreed to take the development of the character as his first freelance project. But Allen was neither character designer nor animator; in fact he was one of those designers who could hardly draw a wiggly line. His talent lay in art direction and running a studio department not in artwork itself. That's why he said he was speaking to me.

It was right up my street. I loved developing characters for animation as all the dancing cavorting mushrooms and tomatoes for a recent supermarket commercial pinned on our walls attested to. It sounded like a great little project. I was hooked. Then he reached into his shirt pocket and took out a small piece of folded paper on which was a tiny stick drawing, a little sketch that the producer had given him. It showed a rectangle, with a triangular lid at the top like a Chinaman's hat, two stick arms and two stick legs. It was a simple thumbnail drawing with no hint of character or personality, but more importantly the producer had come up with the character's name.

When I heard it the first time it made me cringe but at the same time I knew it was perfect; *Dusty Bin*.

Allen said my job was to create a loveable and expressive character based on an ordinary dustbin that would feature in the show's animated titles and in the show itself in various guises and forms.

For me it was a great chance to design and produce something for national mainstream television, even if it was only a lowly dustbin.

Delighted at the opportunity I said I'd love to do it. 'The Bin' could be my first real break into television and out of obscurity.

He said he'd pay me five hundred pounds for the finished character, which sounded not over generous, but okay and to get me started there and then he gave me a hundred pounds in cash. So keen was I to take the job *and* so keen was he to give it to me, that I never considered where I stood when it came to copyright. I didn't really understand copyright issues at the time anyway.

However, Allen recognised that while Dusty Bin might be just a booby prize on the show, to the person who held the rights to it with all the potential developments that could spin from a nationally known character, it might just become a bin filled to the brim with gold.

Allen's intention was to keep me in the background. That happened all the time to creative people and I don't think he saw anything really wrong in this.

But as there was no order in writing or a deal between him and me for a buy-out (which means you agree on a price and assign all further rights and ownership to the person who's paying for it) any design or artwork I came up with would remain *my* copyright. Hmmm, but in the thrill of being offered the job I didn't think of that.

Creating a viable cartoon character doesn't sound difficult but if it has to have a personality, one that people can engage with, it often needs more than big feet and a silly grin. For the Bin to be engaging I believed it had to have a reason for its existence, and of course a personality, and it had to be loveable. It would have a story behind it, where it came from; it would be from the story that I'd derive his character and personification. So to get the story, I asked myself why and how would a dustbin morph into a humanoid character?

The designer's best tools are pencils and paper. That's where it starts, with drawing, always with drawing. That's especially true with animation art. So I started to cover sheets with ideas.

An animated character has certain properties, no matter what the final surface features might look like. Beneath the expression and costume, there's got to be a shape that can be animated easily, and that's where you start, the shape of the solid underlying form. Circular forms are best, and he already had those top and bottom. So beginning with the drum shape I kicked, rolled and bounced him (no longer an 'it') around on animation paper, squeezing, shrinking him in all manner of variable positions, poses and actions, like jumping for example, in which case the shape would stretch in the air and squash when it hit the ground; and this before he had any limbs or face.

When it came to his personality, I pondered where to start and began looking at dustbins outside people's houses and noticed something; dustbins (I'm talking about the old metal ones not the plastic wheeley bins of today) *did* have character, which to me they took on from their owners and what they put into them. In fact it was the 'rubbish that maketh the Bin.'

As soon as I got home I retreated to my personal think tank, the bath, and ran the water as hot as I could stand it. I sat in it and after many minutes of brain soaking, I had the bath-time bin-time break-through I was hoping for. The character's features would be made of things from *inside* the bin, from the rubbish.

It sounds obvious like a lot of good ideas, but it wasn't. Dusty wouldn't just be an inert blank empty character, he'd be a jester, a sad clown. He was after all going to be an essential part of the show, a sort of mascot, not the star, but he wouldn't be *just* the booby prize, he would be making personal appearances. Somehow I felt the character had to have roots and, as weird as it sounds, ambition.

Clowns dream of things perhaps unattainable. That's what this character had to be, a clown who dreamt of higher things. I came up with the idea that he wouldn't just be there from the start; rather he'd come to life every show from the front-end title sequence. It would be in the opening titles that Dusty Bin would make his first appearance and somehow come to life, but how?

I hadn't yet got the job to design the titles, but I thought the idea of the genesis of the Bin could be passed on to whoever produced them.

As I lay in the now lukewarm water that night pondering how the Bin might come to life, I drew lines in the soap bubbles on top of the bathwater. Yorkshire Television had a very strong logo, a symbol formed from the three letters YTV that simplified, made a pointed chevron shape like a big 'Y'.

Drawing it in the foam, I had a brainwave. I moved the foam around and saw that if the chevron pointed upwards it could be like a rocket or a jet plane. The idea for the birth of the Bin fell together in a second. I had the whole thing, not only the character design but also the show titles. I knew how to put it all together and as I lay back, submerged and closed my eyes, I ran the sequence through the camera of my imagination.

The next day I mapped the whole thing out and did several finished drawings of the Bin. Now that I had the story, I knew what the character should look like.

I showed Allen these first developmental sketches and asked if he liked them. Foolishly, I made no copies and when he asked to have them, I gave him my originals. But I did do one cautionary thing. I signed them and in a signature that was readable and up close to the character so that my name would be visible to anyone looking at them. Allen was pleased with the drawings and took them away with him.

A few days later, quite innocently, I went into his room to borrow something. He wasn't there. By now we were used to going in and out of each other's rooms. I needed a cutting board and knew he wouldn't mind me borrowing his.

On his desk I saw my drawings, now mounted as though for a presentation *minus* my signature, which he'd whited out. Why had he done that?

Fortunately as it turned out, I'd been so pleased to get the job that I'd made no secret of telling several of my friends at the studios prior to passing over my drawings to Allen. It was a good thing I had.

The next evening after discovering my drawings minus my signature on Allen's desk, I was in the bar at the television studios. I often went there in the early evening to socialise, to be seen and cast around for work.

A large man with heavy rimmed glasses who I'd not noticed before approached me as I stood at the bar and introduced himself as the producer of the new show 3*2*1. I almost bowed. He bought me a drink and asked me to join him in a corner away from the crowd.

'I hear you've been doing some work on developing the character of the booby-prize for my show.'

I told him enthusiastically and openly how Allen had asked me to come up with a character design and that I believed I created a viable character. I asked him if he'd like to see it. He looked surprised and said he would. I took a paper napkin and drew Dusty Bin, right then and there on the table. It took me about 15 seconds. He sucked on his cigar until the end burned bright red.

'Hmm,' he said. 'Very good. And that's the character that *you* created, without any direction.'

'Yes,' I said. 'Apart from a little stick drawing. I've got a lot of related ideas about the titles as well.'

He leant in on the table. 'Do you work here?' he asked. I told him I didn't and that as an illustrator, graphic designer and animator I often did freelance work for the studios.

Then he paused, thought and said, 'I'd like to have a talk with you. Would you be mind coming tomorrow to visit me where I'm staying?' I said, not at all.

Allen was out of town as it happened; otherwise I would have told him about meeting the producer and about his invitation.

The next morning I found myself ringing the doorbell of a flat on the ground floor of a rather grand detached Victorian house in the suburbs of Leeds, which stood tall, porched and pinnacled in red brick behind a large evergreen hedge.

I didn't discover until later that the show's producer, the man who asked me round, was a legendary figure in the industry. He made his reputation at the BBC and now he too was freelance. It was the golden age of British television and independent television stations were in competition with one another for the best people, best shows and the best ratings. Fortunes were being made.

He came to the door looking every inch the impresario. A large man in his fifties or sixties, with grey, slicked-back hair, he filled the doorframe as he puffed smoke from a fat cigar. Welcoming me in he explained as we went down the corridor that his home was in the South and that this place was an apartment rented for the duration of the production, for him and for his wife, who acted as co-producer. They worked as a team, he said.

I was more than a little awed. He looked for all the world like a successful producer and sort of played a cameo of himself with his wide black-framed square glasses, heavy double-breasted cardigan with collar and buttons, silk kerchief tied with a little flared knot at the neck and his cigars. He loved cigars.

Tony Simons was indeed the *real* thing, old school, with a history in television going back to the early days of the BBC; he was every inch the experienced old pro. I felt it was an honour just to be sharing his company but he was also, after all his years in show business, a wily and shrewd old dog.

His wife didn't display the same plumage. She was the organisational brain behind both him and the show and the first time I met her that morning she appeared out of the gloom of the commodious lounge in a pink dressing gown and matching curlers. Notwithstanding the curlers, it was obvious that they were a duo. She was responsible for organisation and cracking the whip. They'd worked together for years and like him, she knew the business inside out. And right now, though still I hadn't guessed, their well-experienced noses smelled a rat, well, if not a rat exactly, then definitely a mouse with a personal hygiene problem.

He showed me into their large lamp-lit sitting room, where I was told to sit upon a fat, worn and voluminous sofa. I felt nervous; the butterflies in me were tearing round my stomach and making little fluttery explorations in my intestines. I remember as I sank into the cushions feeling very much out of my league. After I was introduced to her she excused herself. That was something of a relief to me as after seeing her in her dressing gown I wondered what I got myself into. All sorts of weird stuff went on in Headingley (so I imagined) behind red brick Victorian facades.

After being asked if I'd like a drink, I said yes thinking of a tea or a cup of coffee, as it was only eleven in the morning. To my surprise a large scotch was thrust upon me. I don't know why I accepted it. Still, I was in awe and if he asked me to stand on my head in the fireplace I probably would have. I noticed that he wasn't having one himself. He was obviously intent on loosening me up.

After joining me on the sofa he said, 'I'm going to show you something and ask you a question and I expect an honest reply.' I thought if Mrs Simons comes back in a leopard skin leotard, I'm out of that window.

Picking up an envelope he produced a few sheets of drawings mounted in card frames for presentation. 'Are these yours?' he asked as he laid them out before tapping the ash from his cigar into a cut-glass ashtray.

'Yes, they're mine,' I said leafing through. 'I did them a few days ago.'

'And these?' he asked. They were ideas for how the Bin would look in different themed costumes. And then he produced the sketch storyboards I'd produced, done as my own proposals for the main title design, which I'd done off my own back.

'Yes, I did those for Allen. Apart from the title design, I did that to show the reason for the Bin to exist, if you see what I mean. I think he has to have a birth.' As I sipped the Laphroaig through a glacier of ice cubes I added, 'I signed them, they're all my originals, but they don't have my name on them now. Look,' I said picking one up and examining it closely under the table lamp. 'My signature has been whited out.'

The Producer, now standing, puffed thoughtfully on his cigar. After a pause he said, 'I see.' Then he poured a little more whiskey into my already heavy glass. It was doing the trick; I could feel it warming my brain. Easy John, I thought, take it easy, this is really important stuff.

'So,' he said placing white typing paper onto the coffee table in front of me, 'Would you draw the character again for me now? Here's paper and a pen.' As he put the virgin paper down he removed and replaced the originals in the envelope as though I might try to copy them.

Luckily, as in the bar the previous evening, I've never felt nervous of spontaneous drawing. In fact I love the challenge.

'Mind if I use my own pen?' I asked. I was having a love affair with a fountain pen at the time, with a nicely broken-in nib. To me it was like a magic wand.

His wife, now dressed, but still with her pink rollers, came back into the room and stood behind the sofa as I quickly drew the Bin in a standard pose but this time I varied the pose a bit and added some rough shading which made him appear more three dimensional. As I was drawing, I snatched a sideways glance at the producer. He didn't realise but I saw him wink at his wife from under a veil of cigar smoke. They were both smiling and looked on as though watching their galvanised prodigy come to life in front of their eyes.

Then I said something they weren't expecting. 'Would you like to see him do something, you know some sort of action?' The whisky was fuelling me with a risky bravado.

They looked at each other, not having expected the question. Then his wife, looking around the room said, 'Can you show him vacuuming the carpet?'

'Yep,' I said. It was one of those with a bag that hung under the handle, the sort you pushed with a little light at the front. I finished the sketch after about a minute and pushed the paper along the coffee table so they could both see it.

'How about waving his lid in the air?' asked Tony getting into the spirit.

'Okay,' I said. At that moment for me, the lid literally had come off the Golden Bin and Allen because of his transparent fraud, was in it. The producers were happy, impressed and smiling.

'Do you mind signing them?' asked the lady.

'Love to,' I said, and that's how I became the Bin, official.

'Have you got other ideas for the show?' Tony asked as his wife disappeared from the room again.

'Oh, yes,' I said now on a roll, 'a million.'

'Good chap,' he said sitting closer to me with a yellow legal pad on his knee and topping up my scotch once again. I was still sober enough to notice that only one of us *was* sober and it wasn't me.

I was there for another hour or so, pouring out ideas as he poured the booze. All the time he took notes. But I didn't care, I knew what was happening and I liked him, and I wanted to demonstrate what I was capable of. Besides, I gave him just tasters of ideas, not the complete things. I was getting a bit canny too.

Pretty well sozzled by the end of the session, I was nevertheless 'in' and onto the show team. Those sketches on the coffee table were my passport to be up-front and noticed. That's what I wanted, not to be hidden away in the back room. And if that meant the name on my passport was 'Bin Man' that was okay. I had to start somewhere. After all, Jack my scrap-man father-in-law had always said there was money to be made from other people's rubbish.

A weakness in all this on a personal level was something I've found to be endemic with a lot of creative types; deep down we're so bloody insecure, like some comedians I know who readily admit it; some of us put ourselves out there to seek approval. Sitting there with Tony on the sofa, I was in a classic situation, performing my tricks for a kindly (or so he seemed) and attentive older man.

The next day at the studio, I faced Allen with my whiskey hangover. He was not a happy bunny. He'd received a phone call from the producer and he knew that I knew what he'd done. He was very pissed off and it showed in his coolness, but what could he say? He blatantly removed my name from my work without coming to a prior agreement about what's called a buy-out and copyright, and reading between the lines he attempted to pass off the work as his own. I often wondered what he would have done if they asked him to sketch the character out in front of them as well.

Not much was said between us in the next few days. He left not long after to find another place. Funnily enough if it hadn't been for the intervention of Tony the producer, I'd probably have just gone along with everything. But as it turned out I learned I had some friends watching out for me at the studios and one of them must have told Tony that the drawings were mine and I'd created the character.

A few days after Allen's departure, I was called to another meeting. Not at all sure what to expect I wondered if something had screwed up, or maybe it was about more tests and more whisky. But it was nothing negative. Just the opposite for this time Tony offered me the job to design, direct and produce the animated titles for the first series of 3*2*1; a forty-five second sequence to original music. This would mean my work would be seen nationally, aired on the prime-time independent network, an amazing opportunity, beyond my wildest dreams. I was now a fully-fledged member of the show's production team and carrying more responsibility than I'd ever had before.

The original music for the show was to be written and produced by Johnny Pearson, an English composer who was famous for his television and film scores. Tony wanted a big orchestral opening piece to go with the animated titles and so my first job was to design a new storyboard. After it had been accepted the storyboard would form the basis for the title music. Instead of starting over from scratch, I decided to develop my original ideas, the ones I had already shown.

Composing music to accompany animation is a bit of a chicken and egg process. Musical ideas and timing can be based on the animation design or the other way round; generally it's a give and take sort of process.

A storyboard for animation takes the form of a sequence of drawings of the scenes and action and the backgrounds against which the action is set. The drawings are laid out in a sequence, usually left to right, showing key moments as they occur like still frames from a film, with approximate timings. The storyboard and drawn key frames define the direction of the sequence and are passed on to the animator; in this case a man called Ian Eames who I'd met at college. In a couple of days I had the storyboard worked out and coloured up and returned to the studios to show Tony. He loved it and approved it with just minor modifications. With my new portfolio tucked under my arm, it was off to the station again; only now I didn't have to buy the ticket to London myself; the studio covered all expenses. I was on my way to meet Johnny in person, one of the most successful composers and musical directors of his day, and, as I was to discover, a lovely fellow too.

I've found in my career that people of real talent and professionalism have no edge. The fact that I was this green kid with hardly a thing to my name meeting an older man with a credits list as big as a concert grand did not matter a jot to him. He couldn't have been nicer or more welcoming when I arrived at his studio where he did most of his composing. Of course, a big plus was that he liked my storyboard ideas straight off which I had to talk through as well as follow the action on the board. It was one of those creative opportunities where you fire off from each other's ideas.

As I stood there next to him he jingled a few notes on the piano, making little phrases. As I scribbled ideas on paper he was doing the same in sound. He played a chord here, a note there and already to my ear it sounded promising.

But the thing literally took off when I explained that when the titles open, the YTV chevron symbol (which took the shape of the three letters YTV) would shoot off as though from a usual station 'ident' blasting off into the sky like a rocket where it explodes into stars forming the numbers 3-2-1. That gave him his starting idea.

There and then he played three chords 3-2-1, which would ring out as the stars exploded. It was so simple. He got it all of a sudden. We had something very special.

After a meeting of about twenty minutes I left leaving him with a copy of my storyboard, rough timings and sketches of the Bin character, and headed back up north. I felt wonderful. I didn't see much of the by now familiar landscape passing by on the way up to Leeds because my eyes kept misting up. I have always been a weeper. I kept my dark glasses on; I just couldn't believe that this was happening.

The extraordinary thing about 3*2*1 and Dusty Bin, once the show was running the two went hand in hand; the Bin was as much a hit as the programme. For some extraordinary reason it entered the collective consciousness of the nation, where it still is decades later. Just everybody knew the Bin; it became iconic, kitsch but iconic. People either liked it or detested it, along with the show but for some reason it stuck in their heads.

While the Bin became an icon of popular kitsch, in truth, for years after once I got involved in the world of Cultural Heritage I never mentioned that I created him. I was too embarrassed believing that I would never be taken seriously.

The first programmes rocketed to the top of the viewing tables and stayed there for the whole of the first series. The Bin appeared during the show in various forms and costumes as a mobile robotic character, much, I think, to the chagrin of the show's host, the comedian Ted Rogers. Every week when the show titles started up, the Bin was born again as the rocket fell to earth exploding inside a dustbin outside the back door of the TV studio. (If you would like to view the title sequence and hear Johnny's music, look up the title sequence for *3*2*1* on youtube.com.)

Once the animated sequence had been completed, it was time to marry it with Johnny's sound track. I arrived at an imposing sound recording studio in London and was shown into the control room, from where I could just make out through the window lots of little lights on music stands and lots and lots of musicians; and there was Johnny standing at the front on a dais. Someone said I'd arrived. I was called out to stand beside him in front of a ninety-piece orchestra that was arranged beneath a huge screen.

He explained to the orchestra where he wanted the stresses in the score, and then he called them to attention for a run through without the animation on the screen.

I could feel the strings and brass and God knows what other instrumentation come to attention as he counted them down, raised his baton and launched into the first bars of the theme. I swear my body filled with the most astonishing orgasmic sensation of wonder as the collective sound hit me like an audible tsunami.

It was wonderful and fantastic to be standing there next to this incredibly talented man and his mighty band of musicians and this amazing sound. For the first time I heard the score played full-bodied and alive. It was wonderful. There was only 45 seconds of it, but it was a symphony to me.

After a few more run-throughs and adjustments as we looked back at my storyboard for points of emphasis, he was ready to put the animation up there on the screen. This is done so that the conductor and orchestra can play to the images and to the time clock that clicks away at seconds and fractions of seconds. To that moment I'd never seen something of mine blown up to feature film screen size. It was a humbling experience.

The countdown clock appeared and the animation played on the screen as the first chords of the music rang out like bells. The combination of the sound and the picture was astonishing as the whole thing married together.

I felt my eyes welling up, but thought bursting into tears in front of the maestro and ninety professional musicians would be somewhat inappropriate.

After a few run-throughs, they went for a 'take'. And that was it; ready for broadcast.

The walk-on, or rather roll-on radio controlled Dusty Bin who appeared on the show was designed, constructed and operated by Ian Rowley, of the Rowley Workshops, Leeds. It was quite crude really, certainly by today's standards thirty years later. It could move forward and back and lift its arms up but that was about it. It had a stuck-on expression and a big red nose. It was my character but it lacked a little in the expressive department. So to make more of him, I was asked to design different outfits that went with the different themes of the show. These were also produced by Rowley Workshops, for which the Bin became something of an industry. Ian travelled all over with Dusty and Ted Rogers, making guest appearances and live shows after the television series had come to an end. Ironically, the dustbin that wanted to go on stage became a star in his own right.

By the way, the pottery bins, the booby prizes 'awarded' on the show instead of the yacht that the contestants had just lost were made by a potter who had a place in the little moorland town of Kirbymoorside in the North Yorkshire Moors. He was already famous for producing those little teacups, eggcups and teapots with little fat legs, that's why we went to him.

Funnily enough show contestants who got the booby prize, if they didn't throw it away in disgust, ended up with something probably worth far more now than the yacht they lost.

Now with my head swimming in the starry skies of TV land, back home and down to earth it wasn't just the rocket that had crashed; it was my marriage.

Susan and I married so very young and developed into adults only after we took our vows. By the late seventies, we'd nothing left in common but our girls. We were both very unhappy. We discussed divorce and one awful day I packed a bag and left home.

Sue remarried and lived very happily after, and our girls grew up in a solid, secure and loving home. Meanwhile I floated about lost with my head still in the stars but my real life at the bottom of the bin. My sense of guilt morphed into severe panic attacks. They could happen any time and when they did, it was like a lift shaft opened up beneath me and I felt I was falling into a dark abyss. I was going through hell but on the surface I looked just the same.

My partnership with Jane crashed too. There was no work to be found for her in television or animation where my side of the business was now prospering. She felt out of it. So we broke up the business partnership as well, and she went back south to re-start her career in London.

It was a strange and bizarre time for me, one of great contrasts. At the show's first outing the audience response was hugely positive and we knew it would be a great hit. There had been nothing like it on British television. Its success rubbed off a little onto everyone concerned and I got an ironically apt nickname. Once we were into the production of the series, Richard Jarvis, the show's chief designer, started calling me 'Bin', which I took kindly to even as it was broadcast through the whole studios.

'If Bin is in the building, would he like to meet so and so in the bar?'

'Would Bin please go to studio three?'

The show stayed at the top of the ratings week after week. It was glossy, it was kitsch, it was glitz and corny and the public loved it. Seemingly nothing else in light entertainment at the time could touch it. In the process Dusty Bin became a national icon and like the show, you loved and hated him in equal measure. But from the hole of my self-pity and self-loathing I really couldn't give a damn. I continued to suffer with guilt, remorse and panic attacks for months.

Then one evening, midway through the first series of the show, I was standing at the TV studios' bar hoping that the now familiar lift shaft wouldn't open up in the floor beneath my feet until I got a pint or three down my throat, when one of the directors of the company came up to me.

He said something nice about the show and my work, adding that the Bin was going to be HUGE and that I should get in on the action. This man, who I shan't name here, was at the time one of the gods of the television world; why he should have given thought to my future I shall never know, but I have always been grateful.

I was too nervous and surprised to pick his brains there and then and had no idea how to go about 'getting in on the action', but I didn't have to ask as he gave me the name and address of his agent in London on a business card and advised me to get in contact with him as soon as possible. He said I could use his name as an introduction to his agent, Roger Hancock, and share what he had said to me.

I stood there after he went back to his table, pint shaking in my hand, trying to take in just what he had said. Did he really say his agent, acting on my behalf might be able to help me, as the creator of the character get some 'points' back from the merchandising and licensing of the Dusty Bin character?

What points were I wasn't at all sure, but they sounded important and I guessed were something to do with money. So it was down to Pall Mall to meet with the agent ASAP.

The last time I got on the train for London I still had a marriage, a home and in-laws I loved. Now what I had was weekend access to my girls, a crummy room in a little house in Headingley and terrifying panic attacks for company. I prayed to any deity listening that I wouldn't get one at my meeting.

Roger's secretary asked me to bring any original work I had to do with the creation of the Bin and the original storyboard I'd done for the show title. I bought a new folder. I thought I should look the part as his address was in a very stylish part of central London.

He was not what I expected. I thought he would be something like the producer of the show, but he wasn't at all and he didn't play the show biz part. In deference to that he was modest, charming, down to earth and welcomed me like I was already a member of the family. He was the brother, he told me, of Tony Hancock, the brilliant British comic actor. Looking after Tony's full-time neurosis and affairs was how Roger got into the business.

As I sat there on a dark leather sofa in his plush low-lit office listening to his introductory story, I wondered what they'd be charging me for this little meeting; but I needn't have worried. This was an opening consultation, no charge and no stress either. Roger was friendly and very much on my side.

He looked at my stuff and we talked about the origination of the Dusty Bin character and the contract I naively signed, which basically assigned all my rights away to the TV company. Even after almost being screwed in the affair with Allen, I screwed up on an even bigger contract, though not quite.

Roger said the objective would be to claim a small ongoing percentage (points) of the value of any future development of the character in merchandising, franchising, licensing and programme development, in which the character was newly featured. In other words anything that was not directly to do with what I signed up to do originally.

His reasoning was that my contract and the sign-over of rights to the character had been originally related *only* to the TV series, not a buy-out relating to possible merchandising and spin-offs. He reckoned there was a good chance.

It sounded wonderful. Could he really pull it off I wondered? And then when it came to the agency's fees, they'd take a cut of whatever they'd managed to claw back on my behalf, a percentage of a percentage.

He said I wouldn't be making a fortune but in the longer term the effort might be worth it. Especially as my angel at the bar back in Leeds had explained to him that Dusty Bin was going to be the subject of 'character merchandising' on a national and international scale and that the show was being sold overseas.

As points and the Bin went, nothing at all happened for a long time. Trident TV, the holding company, wasn't about to give away anything easily. In the end I got something as ridiculous as a half percent of a half percent of a fraction of a percent of something that in effect amounted to nothing.

I was a designer still new to the game and I sold the rights to a prospective fortune in royalties for a couple of thousand pounds in fees. It was a hard lesson to learn. But as they say, hindsight is twenty-twenty and anyway, I wasn't motivated by the money, never have been. It's always been the work.

There's no point crying afterwards. You might think you're the best thing since Leonardo, but to the client you're just a creative technician. Ideas are cheap, but some may be worth a fortune. The best advice is to get the best advice. That's what I was getting and it stood me in good stead when it came to swimming with sharks in the future.

There's something else about hindsight; it enables you to see how events shaped the direction of your life. I might have been talking Dusty Bin and a career in television, film and character merchandising. But as it turned out, the universe heard my 'eureka' moment all those years before and unbeknownst to me there were already Vikings crashing around in my own dustbin, and they wanted out

Dusty Bin, created by John Sunderland in 1978 for the Yorkshire TV hit game show 3*2*1

5   THE FUTURE OF THE PAST

I WAS WITH MY FRIEND and co-conspirator in all things animation in the canteen when the next lady of significance arrived in my life.

'This taken? No? Thanks,' she said sitting.

I stared at her across the vinegar and HP Sauce bottle. With distinct and attractive features, and a pageboy cut of blonde hair she appeared fit and athletic in a wiry sort of way. And she had the most amazing red-framed circular glasses on. She looked at me sweetly and flashed a pleasant smile. I nodded back and carried on talking across to Nigel as we cracked our usual juvenile jokes.

'Are you Bin?' she interjected. 'The Bin Man, you know, Dusty Bin?'

'Mmmm,' I nodded with a mouth full of chips. I wasn't sure where this might go. You could never tell where the Bin might take you.

'I'd hate to be called Bin,' she said. 'Couldn't stand it. Don't you mind? You seem like a nice man.'

That was an invitation for Nigel.

'He's not you know, not nice at all,' he said. She turned and responded with a withering glance that could have fried a snake.

'Well, it's a job you know. I don't mind. I'm glad of it,' I said.

Nigel chimed in; he wasn't the sort to be shut out easily. 'Better than being called Toilet or Cesspit,' he said nodding in my direction.

I laughed and spluttered some chips.

'Yes,' she said with perfect timing. 'Looks like the toilet just flushed.'

Nigel and I looked at each other. On some psychic level we both recognised we just encountered an elemental force, one that neither of us was entirely comfortable with. I saw him mentally take note of any nearby seats that freed up as he planned an escape. Then, after a pause and a blow of his cheeks, and after wiping up the last of the egg yolk on his plate with his finger he said,

'Well, I'll be off then,' with a knowing wink in my direction adding, 'Fancy a pint before we crawl back into the hole?' The hole was the rostrum camera room, where animation is filmed and where Nigel the cameraman lived his mainly nocturnal existence.

'Yeah,' I said pushing my chair back. We both thought this was a good time to escape. There was something intense about her. Anyway, we didn't want a girl in our gang just then.

'Nice meeting you,' I said standing. She wiped her mouth tidily.

'I'll come too,' she said with a bright and confident smile.

We were flabbergasted. Nigel and I gave each other a look, 'bugger', it said. They hadn't exactly hit off.

He didn't make it to the bar; he peeled off to safety before we got there with a pathetic excuse that he'd just remembered he left the camera running.

'Is he your friend?' she asked as she walked shoulder to shoulder with me escorting me to the bar. 'Dirty isn't he? Sort of goes with the Bin Man I suppose.'

'Yes, he is. And he does.'

'Scruffy and dirty, and smelly actually,' she said.

'Absolutely filthy,' I said. 'That's why I love him. We belong together.'

'Yes, I can see that,' she said. 'I'll have a spritzer.'

'Right,' I said. Lynda not only came along to the bar that day, she came along for the next thirteen years.

Nigel, Andy the animator and I worked together on various animation projects, titles for TV shows like O.T.T., various commercials and one huge project, a thirty-minute animated feature film for the British Cinema circuit. How I landed this was directly a result of the success of 3*2*1.

Roger Hancock had something else up his sleeve besides trying to land me some royalties. When he gave me a call the lads and I were as usual working on something in what doubled as Lynda's and my bedroom at night and in the daytime what we turned into a studio. This was much to the dismay of Lynda who was now the mother of my toddler son Tom, and my second wife.

He said he represented some people who wanted to produce an animated B film to go out on the circuit with an American produced feature film, *Can't Stop the Music* (which some people thought was so awful that we came to refer to it as 'Can't stop the Projector'). He asked me to come down to Hampstead, London, which I duly did.

The next day I met one of the producers there. I knew there was going to be some big name involved in the project, but I nearly fell through the sofa when in walked Kenny Everett, who at the time I regarded as God. The film they wanted to produce was to be called *Kremmen the Movie* based on a cartoon that featured in his hugely popular weekly TV show, *The Kenny Everett Video Show*.

I got the commission; and whilst I could easily write a book about the experience and another film to come with Kenny, Barry Cryer, Vincent Price and others, it really has nothing to do with Jorvik, not in the slightest, so we'll leave it there for now.

That epic over and done with it was time to get back to the bedroom and carry on with jobs as they arose. But Lynda had had enough of our working from home. Not unreasonably she wanted her bedroom back and she had enough of our putting a wooden lid on the still warm bed to make a platform for the two animation desks upon which Andy and Nigel worked.

'You have just produced a feature film, and by the way it was crap,' said Lynda. She was right, it was. 'If you can manage to do that and not do it here in our bedroom surely you should be able to find some space elsewhere to do a few commercials in.' There was sound reasoning in this.

We stayed on in the bedroom long enough to finish the show title for O.T.T., a late night no-holds-barred live unscripted comedy show which in its late night slot did its best to appear risqué. To get that idea across right at the start the titles featured a blow-up sex doll. I had no idea where to get one and didn't fancy the chance that it may arrive at our address under a plain cover, which would certainly have stirred my wife's interest. Luckily Nigel leant us his. He called her Mary. Once inflated in our bedroom studio she hung on a string as a visual aid to our animation. That was until my toddler son Tom got hold of her and launched her into the breeze outside one day thinking it was a 'bloon'. Subsequently Mary spent a partially deflated week waving to surprised motorists on Kirkstall Road from the spiky limbs of a blackthorn bush.

Mary was the last straw. 'That's it,' said Lynda.'I am not having my two-year-old playing with sex dolls. No more. Out you go.' And out we went.

But where? Where could I find a suitable and affordable place for a small group of animators to work? Then I had a brainwave. I would call the man who gave me my first film commission, Colin Pyrah, at the Wakefield Express newspaper offices. They were still regularly using our film, and I think he liked us; we were oddballs. I hadn't spoken to him in years but sure enough he was still there and had been promoted to the position of Joint Managing Director of the Group and created a media division within the newspaper company, which he was now in charge of. It was called The Yorkshire Communications Group. It offered services in promotion, public relations, printing and marketing. When I told him what we'd been up to since I last saw him he said what we did could be complementary to their services. Once again he came through for us.

He offered us the use of a couple of rooms to start with at a very reasonable rent. So we packed up, lock, stock, and animation desks (we left the bed) and moved back once again to Wakefield. Immediately it felt like we made a good move. It was, as things turned out, a bloody brilliant move.

We were soon in production again with a new television title sequence for a show called *Dead Earnest* and television commercials for a local supermarket chain. The client for *Dead Earnest* was a Midlands TV company called Central Independent Television and the job was urgent.

The show, a half hour comedy, ended up as another dead production too, but you don't know that at the start. Still as always, full of excitement and anticipation of a new job, I popped off to 'Brum' to get the brief for the job.

The Head of Design at the studios was an obnoxious little man full of his own importance (he's probably a lovely mellow pensioner now). He described what they wanted as he rushed down a corridor chasing a deadline for something or other whilst I, like a hungry puppy, notebook in hand, trailed behind taking notes as we went.

At the end of the one-way briefing he said over his shoulder as he disappeared, 'And we want it rotoscoped. You can do that, yes?' and then was gone through a door with a red light over it.

'Oh, sure, of course, yeah, definitely!' I shouted after him. 'No problem.'

Truth was I had no idea what he meant by rotoscoped. But the rent was due so I played it cool. I took the job on for a fee of three thousand pounds, very little money for a forty-second opening sequence.

No one back in 1979 had mobile phones and there were no phones on trains. A simple call would have alleviated three hours of agony and deepening anxiety. I would have called Nigel; he'd know. Good old Nigel would put us straight. He knew everything there was to know about animation. By the time I got back to Leeds I was just frantic to find out what I'd got us into.

Outside Leeds station I jumped in a cab and went straight to his favourite afternoon pub. Sure enough there he was in the snug coughing into his crisps already red-eyed from beer and smoke.

'Hi me favourite old pal,' I said cheerily, plonking myself next to him on the sticky bench.

'You're not going to force a pint on me are you?' he said. 'You know, compensation for the misery and stress you've brought into my life,' he spluttered as he gulped down the last dregs. Where he put all the beer I don't know, as he wasn't much bigger than a pint glass himself. But he was correct. He worked on *Kremmen the Movie* our animated epic produced under intense time pressure and now hated me with a passion. But he liked beer.

'Oh, you're just too generous,' he said when I came back from the bar. 'Crisps still available in the civilised world are they?' With him knowing by now that I was after something, I had to get him the crisps otherwise he might not tell me what I needed to know.

'Are we celebrating another commission, another gargantuan masterpiece before us wrought by the talented hands and brilliant minds of the on-top-of-the-bed team?'

'Yeah. I got us another job,' I said smiling like the cat that has the cream.

'*Us?* Aren't we already assuming a little?' he said. Actually I was getting a bit miffed. I had after all been keeping him in fags and Tetley's Bitter for a while. But he was on a roll.

'Another epic you've taken on for three quid then, to be completed the day before yesterday?' he said, swallowing the pint like a parched wildebeest on a drought-ridden migration.

'There's no point in being bitter about things. We have to look to the future,' I said trying to sound hurt and positive at the same time.

'You'll be needing someone to work out the moves then?'

'Yeah,' I said smiling and fluttering my eyelids.

'Talking about bitter as you were a moment ago,' he said. 'Going to buy me another pint?' as he slid his now part empty glass across the slimy table.

'You haven't finished the one I just got you yet. This is blackmail.'

'Yes, it is,' he said, 'but you know whilst I am a blackmailer, I am also cheap, dependable and professional, and I don't take up much room. So what is it?'

'It's about this dead guy who can't accept that he's dead and ends up in this sort off limbo place with all these other discontented ghosts.'

'Sounds like us. Did you say it was a comedy? Doesn't sound very funny.'

'That's their problem,' I said. 'Anyway, it's forty seconds, the music's done and all it's comprised of is this bloke.'

'The dead one?'

'Yep, the dead one, slowly going up this escalator towards a bright light.' I moved my hand upwards slowly over the table at an angle.

'Like to heaven?' he said.

'Well, limbo, not the dance, which is on his way to heaven, 'cause if he works things out for himself and others up there....'

'Or down there,' chimed Nigel.

'In limbo he can either come back to life or go on up to heaven, lingerie and sporting goods,' I said.

'What about hell?'

'Nobody mentioned hell,' I said. 'I'd have charged more for hell. Besides the head of design was a total pillock. You know one of those "cool" sods. He didn't say a lot about the job except...' I paused.

Nigel had a sixth sense, and put down his pint.

"Cept WHAT?' He looked into my soul.

'It's got to be rotoscoped,' I said picking up my pint and burying my face in the foam so he couldn't see my eyes. I thought I'd play it cool and not let him know that I didn't *quite* know what rotoscoping meant.

'You've got a problem there then matey,' he said taking a slurp then digging in his pocket for his packet of fags, finding a pre-smoked one and lighting it.

I stayed behind my pint, not wanting him to see the fear that was rising in my eyes.

'Why, what's the problem?' I asked matter of factly putting my glass down.

'You haven't got one,' he said.

'One what?'

'A bloody rotoscope.'

'I know that,' I said laughing. 'Thought I'd buy one.'

'Really?' He knew I'd *seriously* messed up now.

He got up and went to the bar and came back with a Jamesons. I'd never seen him buy a drink for anyone, let alone me *and* a whisky.

'Drink that,' he said seriously, pouring the shot into my pint. 'I think you could get a decent second hand one for about forty.'

'Forty quid?' I asked optimistically. 'That's all right then.'

'Thousand,' he said with a grim straight face.

I finished the beer-whisky pint quick. I could feel myself becoming the palest, most frightened mortal in the bar.

'You've not signed up for it, for the job, have you?' he asked. 'You haven't?'

I reached in my pocket and pulled out the order/contract and put it on the table. I felt it was an order for my own execution.

'Three grand! You must be bloody joking, you absolute f**king idiot,' he said. 'You've really screwed yourself big time this time; really done it, and if you think I am digging you out of a mess again for a couple of pints and a bag of nuts, you have another thing coming,' he said and meant it and muttering stormed off to the gents.

'Aw, come on,' I said when he came back. 'What about renting a rota-thingy,' I asked trying to muster some hope and optimism.

'It's forty seconds right? It's going to cost two grand to get it drawn up and I know for a fact that a rotoscope rental is about five hundred an hour.'

'Oh, heck.' Sinking my head in my hands, I wondered what I would tell Lynda.

At this point you might be wondering what this has to do with the Vikings of York. Well, the answer is it's about thinking outside the box. The thing about being creative and especially a freelance creative is yes, part of the time you make the completely wrong decisions for desperate reasons, usually because you need the money. But the other thing about being creative is just that – you're *creative*, you were trained to be a problem solver, to come up with *solutions*; that's what you do. As my ex-father-in-law Jack used to say, 'As one door closes another door opens.' One just opened in my head.

'I'll make one,' I said triumphantly.

'What?'

'I'll make a rotoscope thingy,' I said banging the table making the crisps jump.

He started to laugh and then spluttered, which graduated into a session of full blown inside outside lung coughing fit that had two or three regulars move to another room covering their glasses with beer mats.

When he quieted down and started to breathe again, he said with a very serious grim look on his face.

'It's a highly engineered sophisticated piece of machinery, a rotoscope. It's all about registration. That's why they're so expensive you idiot. Germans make 'em.'

'Well, sod the Germans. Look what happened to them.'

'Ya,' he said in a German accent. 'Ve own Europe.'

'Anyway,' it just dawned on me that I forgot the most important question. 'What does a rotoscope do?'

'Oh f**k me!' said Nigel slapping his forehead.

The real possibility of being sued by the television company for non-delivery was looming, so my outlandish claim to Nigel that I could make one had to be followed through. I had to at least try or answer to the wife who would not find the idea of selling the baby to fend off bankruptcy an attractive option.

Prompted into action, first I did some research into what a rotoscoper thingy actually did and how it did it. Once I got to know what the process was, I realised in essence, it's a simple process. It would be a bit like constructing a space-rocket with old baked bean tins and gunpowder. But no problem, I was sure it could be done.

Back in those days rotoscoping meant copying by hand live images first captured on film, frame by frame. First you shot an action sequence of the subject. Then each frame of the film, usually black and white, is projected onto paper or animation acetate cels and drawn (or painted) in by hand. And just like animation, for the smoothest movement, twenty-four drawings per second are required. However, as the technique is very graphic, for example drawn in wax pencil line or paint line or looser wash or a mixture of both, you could get away with twelve drawings, or even six for every second of film.

The cels used for copying could be paper or acetate. When you have the sequence copied say onto paper, they're re-filmed just as though it's animation. The result is a life-like image that mirrors naturalistic movement but with the interesting quality of a drawn or painted line. It was very popular. You still see it in use a lot, especially in commercials. The end result in fact often looks far cleverer than it actually is.

The difficult part is drawing each frame by hand from the film and the registration from one frame to the next. Unfortunately, I was faced with having to build one from scratch, which, as I am no German engineer and most likely the world's most impractical man, posed something of a problem. Still once again, needs must.

The title sequence already visualised by the television people couldn't have been simpler; a man, with his back to the viewer, slowly ascends an escalator towards a bright light at the top (limbo) into which he disappears.

What wasn't a problem was filming a man going up an escalator. Off we went to Manchester Airport where I knew just such an escalator. Once we got there and before anyone noticed what we were doing, we had the camera set up and Andy, who was going to be working with us again, stepped on the escalator as we filmed him; ascending not to Benidorm this time, but to limbo (same thing). That was the easy bit.

Back in Wakefield, Colin kindly let us use a second room to set up the rotoscope. I'm not a handyman; I am an 'artyman'. Therefore I thought about the rotoscope construction as a sort of art project like making a piece of sculpture. It didn't have to look German or act with German precision; it would be more like an arts and crafts *funky junky clunky* machine as long as it did the job.

So here then is how to make yourself a forty-thousand-pound rotoscope camera for, well, nothing. That is if you don't count labour or the market value of things you nicked, or the feelings of the upset people whose stuff you borrowed without permission.

First you need an animation desk. This is an angled desk a bit like a wooden wedge of cheese, with a large circular hole in it. In the hole a same size circular piece of board is cut and placed. The circular piece of wood can be turned three hundred and sixty degrees in the hole. Into this a rectangle is cut and into the rectangle a piece of heavy-duty glass is fitted. So now you have a see-through screen the size of standard animation paper set into a circular turntable that can be moved clockwise or anti-clockwise. Finally onto the glass you stick a metal animation registration bar for holding your animation paper in place; exactly the same place for every drawing. We had plenty of animation desks left over from the *Kremmen* movie.

The desk needs to be off the floor so that there's a space below to allow for the projection of the image, which is bounced off an angled mirror from a projector fixed above. To get the vertical height I screwed on four legs to the animation desk, just simple two by four pieces of wood. The image projection part was a bit more difficult. The 'scope required a film projector to project the black and white 16 mm film we shot frame by frame. As we didn't have a proper projector, a special one that advanced frame by frame, I acquired (pinched) my dad's old slide projector, one you could still get bulbs for.

The projector was mounted on a simple wooden frame and secured to the back of the desk with its lens pointing downwards. Where the slides normally went in was the place where the film would pass, one frame at a time. This was where a proper rotoscope would have calibrated wheels for the film sprockets and an electric motor to advance the film frame by frame through a fixed projection gate so the image would always be in the same position.

To achieve something similar but nothing like as precise, I rigged two broom handles, one at either side of the projector onto which I placed the spool of film with the broom handle passing through its centre. At the front was another spool. By turning this carefully we could wind the film by hand a frame at a time through the projector gate. Well, that was the idea.

It is essential to hold the frames of film in the same position in the gate. In a real machine this is done by teeth on a circular wheel corresponding with the perforations in the film. As I didn't have anything with teeth, I achieved the same effect more or less by friction using little pads of felt to hold the film in place. I'd cut the felt from the back of one of my grandma's old hats, which I hoped she didn't wear any more.

Projectors have to be cooled because they get very hot. The fan in Dad's old projector was bust and coming up with something like a fan was a bit of a challenge. It needed to be something capable of directing a jet of cooling air into the interior of the projector and the frame of film in the gate or it would melt under the heat of the bulb.

The solution came as I lifted my feet for Lynda to vacuum under them. A small portable vacuum cleaner, the kind that had a reverse action to the motor, making it blow rather than suck, would do the job. I found one at my mum's (a little more dust around the place for a few weeks wouldn't hurt) and rigged it on the supporting frame so its hose fed into the projector. (N.B. If you do this at home, make sure there's no full bag of domestic detritus in there first.)

The vacuum also cooled itself with its own fan so I could run the whole thing indeterminately. Trouble was the waste heat from the vacuum heated up the room and as there were no windows, it got terribly hot, as it had to run hours at a time.

I kept everyone away from my machinations whilst putting all the bits together, sure that my delicate ego could not stand the ensuing ridicule if the thing didn't work, which, as it started to take shape, looked very likely.

Once all those parts were wired, taped, screwed, strung, and coat hanger-wired and bolted together, and with the vacuum roaring, it was possible to wind the film frame by frame projecting it downwards from the back of the desk where the image could be reflected back up and focused on the rear of the angled plane of the glass in the desk, and the animation paper on the top side. When this happened it would be possible to trace off the image. One thing stood in the way of that; no mirror.

It had to be one that could be fixed in place on hinges and adjusted to the correct angle of reflection up to the underside of the glass. I found just the thing on my grandma's dressing table. She loved us so much I could have run over her with a truck and she would have died happy. Anyway, it was just a loan and, if she knew, she wouldn't mind us borrowing the mirror for a few weeks. Just as well the mirror wasn't there as she might have noticed the holes in her hat.

I hinged the mirror on the back in such a way at the bottom of the desk that it would reflect the projected image at the proper angle and managed this by hanging it by a chain (from a grandfather clock that had slept for centuries at my mum's house). At either side the chain was fixed on two hooks so I could vary the angle.

It may have looked like something from a mad-scientist's fantasy, but amazingly it worked, though it did sound a bit like a wide-bodied jet airliner was in the room with you. People laughed of course; they sneered and they ridiculed, especially Nigel, who nevertheless was big enough to comment: 'You're a f**king genius. You've got away with it again!'

So we got down to the laborious job of copying the film frame by frame with the vacuum cleaner blowing hot air into our dark little room. Every now and then querulous wide-eyed faces including Colin's appeared at the door, no doubt trying to make sense of what these two sweaty scruffy guys with their strange noisy contraption were up to.

In essence all we had to do was make a new and separate drawing for each sixth frame. In each the man on the escalator rose a little more towards heaven. Once we had the sequence drawn, the animation paper cels were filmed on the rostrum camera; the final sequence worked a treat. Just as well because my grandma had realised there was no reflection of herself when she sat down at her dressing table and Mum wanted to do a little spring-cleaning.

We met the deadline, just, and amazingly came out in front money wise, apart that is for the cost of a new hat for my Gran and a new vacuum cleaner for Mum. But there was another payoff. I think our crazy machine achieved for Andy and me a mark of respect at the newspaper offices in a curious sort of way and we became the bona fide geeky arty weirdoes in their attic.

As usual I never knew where the next project would come from and I got to the point where I thought if I had to draw another dancing mushroom I'd shoot myself.

3*2*1 had been a sort of career rocket. It had taken me to Kenny Everett after all, but then had sort of fizzled out, and Lynda and I were back to a hand-to-mouth existence. It had been okay living like that before I remarried, but married again and with a child, the lack of job and income security was a constant worry. And when you do get paid it goes out so quick. I wasn't charging huge fees and was still relatively new on the scene so kept my prices low in order to get work.

We were broke a lot of the time, and most months, now that Lynda wasn't working, it was a struggle especially with a toddler. Frustratingly I had friends in the film and production business that always seemed to be doing better, with money to spare. They were better at the business end than I was.

Mike Maloney was once such man; a successful cameraman come producer and a very nice chap to boot. He was a founder and partner in a local independent film production company that specialised in programmes about exploration, adventure and the natural world. Like most of my other contacts, I'd met Mike in the bar at Yorkshire Television.

One evening he called and said he'd like to come round and have a word; I couldn't say we were close, so I was a bit surprised. But as there was a chance he might be coming round with a job, Lynda and I tidied up the lounge and I popped down to the off-licence for a six-pack.

When he settled into the sofa with a can in his hand, he said he came to talk about a project. Great. *But* not one that existed yet. Not great. We had to make it happen. In fact we even had to create the opportunity to get it, but he said; it would be worth it if we did.

He handed me a small brochure, a twofold pamphlet. Before I looked he told me it promoted a project recently proposed for the City of York, something to do with an archaeological dig that was going on.

Apparently the archaeologists of York Archaeological Trust (YAT) were planning to build a museum or an exhibition or something and he thought they might be in the market for a video or a series of videos, the sort of production that chronicles the progress of a project.

These archaeologists were already in a race against time as they only had so much left to rescue finds from a rich layer of Viking age remains. It sounded like an exciting story to follow; but what was on Mike's mind for me?

Then he dropped a small bombshell having baited the hook and got my interest. He said he was off abroad to Borneo to shoot a documentary about bats. Whilst he was away he wanted me to research the project and come up with ideas, which we'd discuss when he came back. If he liked them, I'd be taken on to the production team. In other words he wanted me to do the up front research and concept development for the pitch for nothing in the hopes of turning it into a job for them, and me if I was lucky. Tough world. Thanks Mike. He said he'd be back in six weeks and with that he buggered off to Borneo and the bats. I never did see him again; for all I know he's buried in a cave under a million tons of bat guano.

Feeling that familiar disappointed feeling that there really wasn't a job after all, I put the leaflet down on the coffee table and as it was late didn't look at it until the next day. Fearing ridicule for being a chump from the missus, I first thought I should forget it.

The next morning, the York project was still in my head and hadn't gone away, so I picked up the leaflet out of idle curiosity and sat at the kitchen table to read it whilst I had another slice of toast.

I wasn't expecting to get excited, as I knew I was being used, not in a bad way, but still Mike was off chasing bats in sunny Borneo, whilst we were up to our knees in the West Riding in debt guano.

The pamphlet had an interesting picture on the front, a photograph of an archaeological excavation. In the hole you could see low structures of some sort. I opened it up and spread it out amongst the breakfast mess. It was about the Vikings of York. What Vikings of York? I'd no idea there were any Vikings in York. Weren't they always off raping nuns and pillaging monasteries in Northumberland? I read on. Apparently the archaeological site at Coppergate was unique and spectacular finds were being made, as the remains of a section of a 10th century settlement had been well preserved in a waterlogged layer of mud. Not just objects were being found, but organic stuff as well. This meant that when all the information was brought together, so I read, a virtually seamless reconstruction of Viking age York could be made. Their concept was to build an underground museum right on the site where they were digging and recreate what had existed a thousand years before, and to encapsulate this in a basement directly above the original dig.

I remember feeling something rising and buzzing inside me as I was reading. I was hooked. There wasn't much about the actual museum; that was still in the planning stage. But the overall concept was already defined. Inside as I recall was an illustration of reconstructed buildings and a schematic diagram that showed a layout in simple terms in four main sections. The first being the Time Tunnel, which led to a reconstruction of a section of 10th century Jorvik, this then connected to a section devoted to archaeology, next a museum display of artefacts, and finally the shop. Obviously they had gone a long way down developing the idea themselves.

Overall, the archaeologists wanted to give visitors an experience of what life had been like and believed that they would be able to 'bring to life' Viking age York based upon the information gleaned from the dig (a process which would actually continue for years after the opening of the exhibition in 1984).

Wow. I thought what a wonderful concept. Suddenly those bells that first rang in my head in the City Museum when I was eleven, the ones that had stayed mute for decades, were clanging away like fire alarms.

Lynda came in. Thomas followed on a little red fire truck.

'This is it,' I said excitedly, pointing to the pamphlet amongst the marmalade and marmite.

'Yes, I know it's serious. They're going to cut us off,' she said wiping Tom's face before slapping down the final demand notice from the electric company.

'No, not that. This, this *project*,' I said pointing to the leaflet.

'Oh, the thing that Mike Maloney brought. I thought you were miffed about that. Bats or something,' she said trying to excavate something from Tom's nostril, which could actually have been a small bat.

'Lynda, *look* at it,' I said holding it up, in front of her face.

She looked briefly as Tom broke free and scooted off on his truck up the hall, his little legs going like pistons.

'Looks like a dirty big hole in the ground to me. What films are you going to make about that? How are you going to make money out of a hole? He's disappeared off to Brighton or Bolivia, and you're expected to think about muddy holes whilst the electric is cut off. All right for some isn't it? We need a *real* job, John. Look at this bill. We've got three days left then it's darkness and cold and no washing machine. Come on John; join the living. We're late and you know

Mrs Wortley (our childminder) is a pain when we're late. I'm sure she takes it out on him.'

'It's not about films, Lynda, it's what I always thought. You can put people in it, that's what they are talking of doing.'

'In what? In debtor's prison?' she said as she grabbed Tom on his return down the corridor. Now he didn't want his hat on.

'In the experience, inside it like being in a film. It could be fantastic. It's what I've always dreamt of, and these people, the archaeologists, are dreaming of that too.' I picked up the leaflet again and gave it a second going over.

'Oh, please don't go off dreaming again.' She put Thomas down; he escaped and scooted off again. 'That is a child going off down the corridor,' she exclaimed. 'He is REAL and this inconvenient bill is also real. Everything in this damp freezing God awful flat is electric. If we get cut off, what are we going to do? Hey? You need new proper jobs with real *decent* money. No more working for nothing John, no more dreaming, no more "what ifs" and "wouldn't it be greats", no more fantasyland. Come back for once and live with me in reality. Tom and I can't live on fantasy-island with you. Maybe you could with Mike bloody Borneo Batty Baloney,' she carried on. 'Come here Thomas, NOW!' With that he stopped in his tracks and she stomped off up the passage.

I was going to have to dream in secret. I was back in the museum in Wakefield, standing on my satchel looking into the room with the ticking clock.

How I was going to get involved with Jorvik, I wasn't sure. One thing I was sure of however was that the Jorvik pamphlet left by Mike could be a gateway. I carried it everywhere, I couldn't stop looking at it and thinking about how such a revolutionary exhibition could be created.

I daydreamed constantly. If I got the chance, I'd design the exhibition so that visitors believed they were being transported back in time to the 10th century. When they got there it would be all around them, like I believed possible; a museum that was more like a film than a museum.

Me design a museum exhibit? Oh, oh, it was Doubting Dad in my head. He had a point though; I didn't have any training in museum exhibition design, but hey, that might actually be an advantage, if we were embarking on something revolutionary.

I was obsessed and couldn't stop thinking about it. When we went round the supermarket with Thomas crying in the cart I'd be thinking, 'The key would be to design the experience *around* the individual visitors, not around a collection of artefacts. In fact the *experience* of life in 10th century Jorvik would give more relevance to the finds.'

'Toilet paper.'

'What?'

'Oh God. Toilet paper, you use it every morning. Get the cheapest,' said Lynda, once more exasperated.

'Oh, right.'

I imagined the exhibit as being about a day and a particular time. There'd be people going about business a thousand years before and when you got there the clock would stop, freezing a moment. I saw it in my head.

'What kind of tea do you want?'

'Erm...' I said from behind the shopping trolley.

'John, do you mind my asking, are you still of this time, you know 1980 or have you sloped off somewhere to another dimension when we weren't looking.'

'That one, the bargain box; we always have those.'

Stop the frame. That's the answer. Just like now in the supermarket, everything stops. Then we'd hold it, floating in time, and when the visitors from the future arrive what they'd experience would be that frozen moment, get right inside it, be immersed in it. 'It would be *experiential*,' I said out loud by the shampoos.

'What?' said Lynda.

'Experiential, that's what it would be, experiential, being there in the moment.'

'Ha! That's a joke.'

Thoughts like these carried on even as I was driving. Like a private madness, I was talking to myself in my head. 'There wouldn't be just dumb dummies standing around like normal in museums. The figures would represent the population of that small section of the city, the real people involved at the moment when time stopped, going about their daily lives, lives reconstructed from the archaeological evidence. They would be believable characters, with names and families and histories *and* voices.'

'JOHN!'

'God.' I slammed on the brakes. An old lady with a wheelie-bag stood eyes wide in shock on the zebra crossing just in front of the car.

'You nearly killed her! Pull over. I'm driving.'

I got in the back with Tom in his kiddie seat; he blew bubbles and so did I, idea bubbles. 'You wouldn't so much see it as a visitor; you'll *experience* it through all your senses. Visitors will be like ghosts, and 10th century Jorvik will be tangible and real. The time machine will be . . . archaeological data, like a bridge from here to there. It's all in the numbers and charts, technical drawings and detailed site plans and under microscopes in laboratories, a tangible world that exists right now; all they have to do is turn that information back into a simulated "real" environment. So it will be as real a place as could be made.'

'Why did you do that?' Lynda asked in the kitchen in front of the fridge.

'What?'

'Why did you put the washing up liquid in the fridge?' I had no idea. She was right; I was in another place and time.

'And they say the buildings will be reconstructed exactly where they stood. And as you pass between them, you'll hear things, and smell things and see everyday life going on around you and someone will be telling you the story.' I was explaining this to Tom at the same time as attempting to get some mashed pear in his mouth. 'Isn't it great, don't you think my little man?'

'Truck,' said Tom. He didn't know how right he was, and neither did I.

I turned into an absolute bore. I didn't want to talk about anything else and new work just got in the way. Stupid really, for in reality all I had was a dog-eared pamphlet, let alone a chance to get my ideas across to the archaeologists who, anyway, seemed to already have most of it worked out. Why would they be interested? And, never mind Lynda; it wasn't unreasonable she was tired of my obsession. My mates were getting sick of hearing me going on too.

'Not bloody Vikings again,' said Nigel. 'Give it a rest.' I was in the pub with Andy and Nigel, as usual bending their ears about the old same thing.

'Yeah,' I said, 'but imagine if we could make a museum like a film that you could be inside of, like you were there.'

'Who's we?' said Andy.

'Well, I am imagining sort of being part of the archaeologists' team.'

'Oh, for God's sake John,' said Nigel. 'You don't half go on.'

'Yeah, great idea,' said Andy. 'You'd put us out of business.' Andy, who lived for animation was just as obsessed about it as I'd become about new kinds of museums. As usual he was sat head down doodling on a beer mat.

'No, come on, chaps,' I pleaded. 'It would be a start of a whole *new* business. We'd never be out of work. Imagine being known as the team who brought history to life.'

'But you make cartoons and stuff, not *museums*. I don't get it,' said Andy.

'I bet it was smelly,' said Nigel sniffing again.

'What was?' asked Andy looking up from his masterpiece beer mat.

'You know, a thousand years ago,' said Nigel thoughtfully sniffing again.

'That's a laugh coming from you.' I moved further away as he reached in his pocket. 'For God's sake don't get that out, you'll start an epidemic.'

'I think it's where I caught this from,' he said dragging out a grey piece of cloth whilst coughing all over my crisps.

'Well, anyway, Jorvik's not a job, not yet,' I said. 'I just wanted to show you it and thought we could talk about ideas.'

'Well, you've done that about a hundred and fifty boring times,' said Nigel. 'Thanks. Now get 'em in.'

'So why do you keep going on about it? It's killing us man,' said Andy turning the beer mat over looking for more space to draw on, and finding none, pinched mine.

'It'll cost you a pint to talk about it again,' said Nigel.

'Two actually,' piped in Andy.

'You're rotten swine,' I said. 'I'm showing you a vision of the future and all you're doing is ripping me off.'

'It's a cruel world,' said Nigel, 'as history shows.'

'Yeah, it is,' agreed Andy.

Really, I didn't know *why* I was putting all the time in sketching and making diagrams and visualising ideas for a project I probably hadn't a hope of being involved in and for people I'd never met and who I was never likely to.

Three months later, I was on my desk in the corner of our bedroom by the window still sketching out ideas. By now I had a sheaf of drawings an inch thick, all speculative concepts and ideas about how to do Jorvik, all just based on what there was in what was left of the pamphlet. I couldn't leave it alone. I thought that whilst they had the concept laid out, they would need someone, or some group to interpret their basic ideas and bring it to life.

I kept returning to the pile, going over the ideas and sketching out new ones. By this stage I even bought books on Vikings and followed all the news I could about the dig. The media loved it; Vikings were sexy.

Meanwhile thankfully, I managed to pick up some real work and the lights in our flat came back on. Then one day with Jorvik still on my mind, I sat on my stool by the window staring down across the green to the ruins of Kirkstall Abbey and tried to imagine the day Cromwell's men came to abuse, steal and demolish the Abbey down by the river. What was it like on that day? How could you reconstruct such a traumatic event, being that all that remained was a black and sooty shell of a ruin?

What if we possessed enough information, enough to form a complete sphere of knowledge about that day? Wouldn't it be possible to create a 'simulator of history' I mused, a sensory bubble based entirely on information of the organic, biological, cultural and practical world and put modern people inside it? It would have to be seamless, a complete immersive system. What you see and hear is not the world you came from but a world comprehensively reconstructed as it may have come across to all the human senses. What would you need to be able to do that?

I sat pondering and chewing the end off my pencil, and then I looked up at the calendar. On it I marked six weeks from when Mike went to film the bats and I'd heard not a word from him. I didn't even know if he was back, but I wasn't going to chase him. I came to a decision.

I put my hand on the sheaf of drawings and made up my mind to contact the archaeologists in York on my own. I wouldn't be going after the videos that Mike was interested in, although if some opportunity arose to produce videos I'd let him know. I wanted to be involved in the design of 'The Jorvik Viking Centre' as it was called in the pamphlet, some way or other. I so wanted to be part of it. I just hoped it wasn't too late to have a chance.

'Yeah, go for it man,' said Nigel. 'But you know what the problem is going to be don't you?' he said sounding sagely.

'Oh, bloody hell, Nige, don't give me any bad vibes.'

'They won't take you seriously.'

'Why the hell not?' I was curious and slightly offended at the same time.

'You look like a broke student. Actually worse; students have an excuse to be broke. *And* with no museum experience or success to speak of.'

I looked at myself in the pub mirror. He was right. Even I wouldn't give me a job I was totally unqualified for.

'That's not true.' I felt I had to defend myself anyway. I really wanted this to happen.

'Yeah, we know, but it's what you project,' said Andy.

'Yeah, let's face it. I wouldn't entrust you with decorating my rabbit hutch,' said Nigel.

'Thanks Pal!' I said. 'Hey, I'm nearly thirty with a wife and a child and some grown up serious jobs and some even more serious debt.'

'Exactly,' said Andy. 'Anyway what do you want to do for them?'

'I want to design it.' I said it out right for the first time.

'But you're not a museum designer,' exclaimed Nigel, 'and you did Dusty Bin and worked with Kenny Everett. You think they'll take *you* of all people seriously?'

'No, perhaps, okay I don't know. Anyway they don't need to know that,' I said. 'But I do know how to tell a story.'

'Granted, you do,' said Andy. 'You are a first class bull-shitter,' referring to *Kremmen the Movie* where I convinced them to sign on and then put them through hell for six full months, so they said. It was just before another round of beer was due.

'Come on chaps, that's done and in the past. I'm talking about *the future of the past,'* I pleaded.

'Yeah,' said Nigel, 'very sexy.'

'So how'd you do it then,' asked Andy, 'if you don't know the first thing about designing a museum?'

'I would tell a story and take people back a thousand years, just like the archaeologists want to do.'

'Alright,' said Nigel. 'Okay, let's be serious. To get this job, it could be a big one, I see that. They'll need security. You haven't got two pennies to rub together.'

'No 'cause I'm always buying you two your bloody beer. But, you're right.'

'He *is* right,' chipped in Andy pushing back his chair and gathering up the empties. 'Alright, it's my shout, a half?'

'Halves all round?' said Nigel.

'No, one to share,' said Andy.

'I'll have two halves please in the same glass,' said Nigel generously.

'I'm going to have to get a suit and a briefcase then,' I said looking down at my threadbare denim knees and seedy pumps.

'You'll look a right pillock in a suit,' said Nigel. He was right, I would.

'Okay,' I said, 'but I think I know someone who wouldn't.'

Monday morning at the offices in Wakefield, I asked Colin's secretary if she knew what he was doing at lunchtime. He had nothing planned. I knocked on his door.

'Come in. Oh, hi John,' he said. 'What can I do you for? Sit.'

'It's okay. I just wondered if you'd like to have a pint sometime?' Colin always made me slightly nervous at first; I think it was the fact he had a real job.

'Sure, are you buying?' he asked, 'Someone died and left you some money?'

'Yes,' I lied.

'Okay, when?'

'How about now?'

'Oh, I was going to see Donald for lunch.'

'It's about something really important, if you could I would appreciate it so much and I'm not wasting your time, promise. I'll throw in a bag of executive cocktail crisps.' He looked at me and saw that for *once* I wasn't joking.

'Executive *shrimp* cocktail flavour?' he said pulling his jacket from the back of his chair. I nodded. 'Go on then,' he said.

Colin's favourite pub was The Star in Sandal near where he lived. It was only a short drive.

'What's in the folder?' he asked as we were getting out of the car.

'It's what this is about. I'm going to show you.'

'Can't wait, is it another manic machine?'

'Yes, that's it. Heath Robinson was my father.'

'That explains a lot.'

I loved this kind of banter with him and it made him laugh to the point where I thought he'd have a seizure. We settled in a quiet corner of the darkly beamed and horse brassed pub.

Colin got the beer in, and a sandwich. He knew I was really broke.

I opened my portfolio and got out a copy of the Yorkshire Post and turned to the half page feature about the excavations in York.

He looked the page over and said, 'So are you suggesting I buy a pair of wellies and a wheelbarrow?'

'Funnily enough, you're not far wrong,' I said as I reached into my folder again.

I got out my Jorvik drawings. He seemed genuinely disappointed there were no plans for more weird and wonderful machines.

'So what's all these then?' he asked looking through the fifty or so sheets, which not unreasonably made not an iota of sense.

'They're ideas, for this,' I said, passing over the Jorvik pamphlet now held together with sticky tape.

He looked it over. 'That's quite something. I didn't know you were interested in archaeology. When's this going to open?'

'In a couple of years, maybe; maybe more,' I said taking back the folder. 'I want to design a new kind of museum.'

'*You* want to design a new kind of museum. It's not that virtual reality thingy again is it that you were telling me about before? Or something you're going to make out of old deck chairs and sewing machines like your rotoscope that you made for four bob and put your grandma in hospital?'

'No,' I said taking a sip and focusing. After all, he was the only 'suit' I knew. This was *the* all-important pitch.

'Have you got an introduction to these people then?' he asked. He would have been impressed if I had.

'No, but they're going to need lots of promotional print and graphics, and marketing and photography and lots of glossy printed Vikingy stuff. Yorkshire Communications could do it,' I said biting my pickle. 'No, I haven't fixed a meeting yet, but I bet they need someone to design it and build it.'

'But surely, to have got to this stage you must have been in contact with them?' he asked. I shook my head.

'What are you talking about then?'

'I want to go after the design and build, the whole job.'

'Hmmm,' he said unconvinced.

'And that's where you come in.'

'Why *me*?' he said.

I though honesty to be the best policy and gave it to him straight.

'Well, because you're the only person I know who owns a suit and besides you are a bona fide businessman who works with creative types. And because they'll take one look at me and think I'm just some scruffy aging student with bright ideas. But together they'll look at you and get a sense of reassurance from a man representing an established business and feel better about giving me, I mean *us*, the job. And besides, you like a challenge.'

'I do? How do you know what I like?' Then he said, 'Okay. Let me get another pint.' That meant he was thinking around what I just said. 'So what's your plan?' he said when he came back and sat down. I told him that I'd call the Jorvik people and try and get us an interview and that would be my first test.

'How do you know that they will want to see *us*, you an animator of dustbins and me a local newspaper and marketing man? Doesn't sound like we're qualified in any way.'

'I just have a feeling they will. And anyway, what have we got to lose?' Then he said something that changed both our lives.

'Well look, I'll tell you what I'll do. I'll call them, under the banner of Yorkshire Communications Group, agreed, okay? If you do land an interview, I'll come with you and we'll bring Donald from the office along for extra support. He's got a suit too.'

'Alright,' I said smiling. 'I'll get the executive crisps to celebrate.' When I got back he'd been thinking.

'But I can't imagine what my Directors would say about this. So if we get a meeting, we'll have to keep it quiet at first and simply approach it on a level of researching a possible opportunity.' Then he drank some beer and laughed.

'I don't know John, the stuff you get me into. Last week it was *Dead Earnest* and that machine you made out of your grandma's dressing table and a vacuum cleaner in the room next door. *This* week it's bloody Vikings.'

He went awfully quiet driving back to the office. As we pulled into the car park he said, 'Okay, I'll call them.'

I couldn't concentrate when we got back to the office from the pub knowing he was making that call. Lynda, who was there working part-time with me, noticed. She wanted to know what was up, and what I'd been talking about with Colin; she could read me like a penny book.

I made something up. I said we were discussing a brochure. I didn't tell her I was following up about Jorvik and attempting to get Colin involved. I thought she'd go crazy about it, Vikings and me daydreaming again.

I was in fact supposed to be drawing a storyboard for an animated commercial starring jolly mushrooms and happy carrots again only they looked more tense and nervous than usual. I hoped, and the mushrooms knew, I was destined for higher things and I didn't mean celery.

'So, come on, what's up with you?' she said looking down at my character designs. 'That's rubbish. That wouldn't endear me to a mushroom.'

'I know,' I said.

There was a knock. It was Colin's secretary, could he have a word, she said.

'Come in,' he said. 'Shut the door.' He looked serious. 'We're on.'

'Ecky thump!' I said leaning on the chair in front of his desk.

'This Thursday afternoon at three at their offices in Kings Square.'

'Crikey!' I said. 'I'd better get some things together then.'

'What *are* you getting me into?' He folded his arms, shook his head and blew a long sigh and then lit up an Embassy cigarette. 'Keep it quiet for now, alright?'

If you're a Yorkshireman or Yorkshirewoman then York is your capital city. It's in your blood. The ancient story of the city is *your* story; it's in your heart and most likely in your genes.

When we were kids we were taken there on school trips and for family days out. And York always delivered. Always special, it's a city full of history, stacked high and low with remarkable things, from the awe-inspiring Minster to the cobbled streets and gabled 13th century buildings of the Shambles – the tangible past.

It was the kind of place, especially outside the main tourist season, where you felt you might turn a corner and discover people from previous centuries walking about, folks who didn't know it was now the 20th century.

To me it was a place full of wonders; dusty shadowy ancient churches down hidden alleyways; the twisting streets lined with hunched and crooked medieval buildings with curious street names like 'Whipmawhopmagate', a street all of twenty feet long, which is thought to mean 'What's its name street'. The city was fantastic in a storm, wonderful in the slanting sunlight of autumn and winter, mysterious and spectral at night. The market, surrounded by half-timbered houses with bent redbrick chimneys that precariously poked from wavy backed red-tiled roofs, looked and felt like it had been there forever. In York you were always in the company of ghosts.

Since a little kid, York to me was truly like walking in history. And since I'd wondered about the ghosts in the room-set in the museum and how they could be brought to life, York felt to me as though the past *was* alive and in the present. And they were all there; The Romans, the Saxons, the Vikings and the Normans along with all the other generations who by turn had received incomers as their new masters. Those, like the Vikings, had come, seen, conquered, settled, interbred and left their indelible marks.

York was a 'pop-up history book' and crowning it was the soaring sculpted cliffs of York Minster, magisterial to a child, a glimpse of paradise to a medieval peasant. When the Minster bells pealed from the belfries it was as though the door-chimes of heaven were ringing along the cobbled streets.

The bells chimed the half-hour just as we parked the car, a short nervous walk away from our interview with YAT. Colin and Donald, both wearing smart business suits with matching dark blue overcoats and attaché cases, looked every inch like successful business people. I wore my uniform having taken Nigel's advice; a scuffed leather jacket I never had off my back since college, a frayed collar shirt, trousers pressed for the first time, and shod with shoes that had successfully avoided polish for years. I didn't want to give the wrong impression.

There were butterflies as big as Mike's Borneo bats in my stomach. As we walked my legs felt heavier and heavier. After just talking about it and dreaming about it, I was going to meet the people who were actually *doing* it, the real Jorvik people. We only had this one shot, and it was going to be a skin-of-the-teeth job; after all who were we really?

The address of the office was in one of those ugly 1950s buildings that fringed beautiful places in central York. Kings Square opens up at the end of the medieval street known as the Shambles. A doorway to the office address led up from the square. At the top of the steps we were met by a secretary who in hushed tones asked us to go into the room where she said the meeting had already begun.

Inside, several middle-aged men sat round a table. A large powerfully built man sat at one end. He asked us to sit on the three chairs by the wall. They'd be with us shortly he said. We obeyed and without a word, we sat.

They were poring over plans and a white card model, which I took to be a design for the museum. Opposite the big man was a smaller chap with a ruddy face and smoothed back hair, wearing a tweedy sports jacket, shirt and tie. He appeared to be absorbed and not a little frustrated in what was being said. I took the men at the ends of the table to be the clients and the other three to be the architects whom Colin had said would also be at the meeting.

Things didn't appear to be going well. The architects were having a hard time of it; all five around the table were grim faced.

Meanwhile, we sat like three naughty boys waiting to be spoken to. Without an introduction it felt as though we were being put in our place, as though waiting to see the Headmaster and his Board of Governors.

Ten minutes later we were still sat there and the meeting was not going well. The men at the two ends were not at all happy and I noticed that one of the architects, the younger one whose design I took it to be, was acting defensively. Then they went quiet as though they'd reached an impasse. Not a good situation for us I thought. Perhaps we should creep out now before anyone notices we were actually there.

The big man turned to Colin who he obviously took as the head honcho of our little band and asked him if we'd brought anything with us for them to see. He must have thought it was time for a change of mood and the cabaret. The big man still hadn't introduced himself, or his colleagues.

'Yes, Anthony,' Colin replied recognising his voice from the telephone. The big man nodded and half smiled. 'We have brought something.' Colin asked me to pass my sheaf of sketches over to Anthony.

They were the drawings I produced over the previous weeks during my mad Viking phase. They sat in an untidy and uneven pile on my lap; I hadn't tried to dress them up. There was no point; they were what they were, a pile of loose-leaf sheets of pencilled ideas based on nothing more than a schematic promotional leaflet. So in his hands my ideas just looked like a pile of old paper, hardly professionally presented. I should have thought better but it was too late now.

To make it tougher we weren't going to be given a chance to make any kind of presentation, I mean we hadn't even been introduced. Almost as soon as the pile reached the table, the heated conversation picked up again. We could see that there was serious disagreement.

Colin was as sensitive to what was happening as I was and wanted a fair shout, so he spoke up.

'Er, excuse me but, Anthony, wouldn't you like to let us tell you what our ideas are about?'

Anthony didn't look too pleased that one of the boys had had the temerity to speak up.

'We'll speak to you if we need to,' he said curtly and returned to the fray around the table.

Well, I thought, that's it, what a rude bugger. But never give up hope, especially when you believe in something.

I watched in despair as Anthony half listening to the others leafed loosely through my drawings, missing half, his mind obviously on matters at hand. He looked quizzically at some, screwing up his eyes and turning others upside down as though trying to make head or tail of what he saw.

Then he shuffled them roughly back into a pile and without comment passed them on to the two older architects who kept their backs resolutely to us. I could feel their resentment at our being invited to their client meeting and now in the midst of arguing their case we were in their way, and in danger, just possibly, of shining (or another word which starts with 'sh') on their parade.

I looked at Colin and shrugged my eyebrows; I knew he was thinking the same thing. We might as well go for a pint and a sandwich and a walk round York before going home. We had wasted our time and I felt terrible.

The architects were too busy making and defending their case to dwell on my ideas. In the end, they took the most perfunctory glances and passed my sad pile over to the younger architect who was now getting heated up in the defense of his own ideas. I could feel Colin bristling; I felt like throwing up.

The younger one didn't even look; he just put them down. Meanwhile, the other chap at the end of the table, in the tweed jacket who until now had said hardly a word, picked up my drawings. The first one must have got his interest because he cut himself off from the fray and slowly examined them. Looking carefully at each sheet, occasionally smiling or raising an eyebrow, he took everything in and became visibly engrossed. His interest had shifted from the discussion around the table. We could tell he was absorbed in what he saw. Colin gave me a gentle nudge in the ribs.

The others were by now really animated, going at it hammer and tongs. Though the big man was well in control, he looked as though he could easily throw all three architects out of the window in one go; I only wished he had.

Surprisingly the response came not from Anthony but from the man who I had taken to be the boss, the one in the tweed jacket, for suddenly there was a huge BANG that literally shook the room. We almost jumped out of our underwear.

He was indeed 'the boss', Dr Peter Addyman, Director of YAT. Though he appeared every inch the gentleman scholar, it had been his fist that had banged the table with such force that it made the model-building jump in the air shocking the architects into an immediate and incredulous pregnant silence.

'Gentlemen,' he said reverentially placing my drawings flat down in a pile on the table. 'There are more exciting ideas and stimulating suggestions in these drawings than I have seen from any other source to date. I have not been presented with anything that comes close. I suggest in turn *you* take a *good* look at them.'

He then turned to us. 'To our guests, thank you for your patience. You can see we have problems to sort out.' Looking at me he said, 'Would you be kind enough to leave your ideas with us? We're not going to have time to discuss them with you today. But I promise we shall take good care, and will shortly be in contact to arrange another meeting.'

Colin looked surprised and a little startled. Donald I think had almost wet himself when the table was banged and I thought I'd left my body and was somewhere on the ceiling.

'Yes, well, er, is that alright with you, John?' asked Colin politely. I would have left them in a chip shop if I thought it would do us any good.

'Absolutely, that's alright with me, as long as you don't pinch our ideas,' I said.

'We shan't do that,' said the big man. 'Don't worry.' Then he stood up. He must have been six foot four and fifteen stone, and towered over us. Standing up in a row we each shook his big hand.

'Thanks very much for coming,' he said smiling. Then he spoke to Colin as he shepherded us to the door. 'We will be in touch in due course.'

I looked over my shoulder as we left the room. The scholar was smiling absorbed in my drawings again, whilst the architects continued to argue amongst themselves.

We walked back across the square in silence. My head was spinning about what had just happened. Could I, could we dare to think that we did well? We were quiet on the way back to the car.

On the way west along the A64 in Colin's Saab he opened the window and lit a cigarette. He drew in a long drag; he must have been dying for one. I sat in the back.

'Well, bloody hell,' he said blowing the smoke sideways. 'What do we make of that?' I sensed it dawned on him that he might soon be going into the museum design and build business and that the thought was a little if not a *lot* scary.

Donald spoke up. 'Well, it could go either way. They might just want to pinch your ideas. No way of knowing.'

'I got the impression they'd stick by their word on that,' said Colin.

'I'm not sure about the architects,' I said.

'Especially the younger guy. He was well dis-chuffed,' added Donald. 'He seemed like he had his nose put out of joint.'

'We'll just have to wait and see,' said Colin. 'Well done John,' he said looking up in the mirror.

'Couldn't have managed it without you chaps. Are your trousers dried out yet? Mine aren't.'

'Mine aren't either,' said Colin. We all laughed.

By the time the adrenalin levels had fallen, we were back in Wakefield. I felt rather flat, after all they'd got the drawings and we came away with nothing, no assurances or anything. I called Nigel.

'That's great,' said Nigel on the phone. 'You're in with a chance then?'

'Suppose so.'

'Well, even if you just get the, what's it called, *The Time Tunnel* bit to do, it will be a hell of a job.' He was genuinely pleased.

Six long weeks passed during that time we heard not a word and I began to wonder if I'd ever see my drawings again, never mind a contract.

Excitement and anticipation gave way to disappointment and depression. Colin hadn't even mentioned it for a while. I reckoned our chance was gone.

Then one day as I sat at my desk, I realised the tomato I was drawing wanted to communicate, so I drew it a mouth. It had been some time since I spoke with a tomato.

'You've blown it you know,' it said, 'So, *this* is your great freelance career, bringing vegetables to life, producing below-the-line TV commercials for the rest of your life.'

'Shut up,' I said out loud 'or, I'll rub you out.'

'You going quietly mad?' asked Lynda from the other side of the desk. 'Yes,' I said.

Just then, there was another knock at our door, only more urgent than the first time seven weeks before. It was Colin's secretary again, Marjorie. She stuck her head round the door, whispered and motioned to me to come with her quickly. I got up.

'*They're* on the phone,' she whispered. 'Colin wants you to go in.'

'Who is?' I asked.

'The Vikings,' she whispered over her shoulder.

'Vikings don't have telephones Marjorie,' I whispered back.

I went into his office, Colin put his finger to his lips then gestured me to sit. I nodded and tiptoed over to his desk and sat. He was speaking in measured and falsely relaxed tones nervously laughing between puffs on his cigarette, the remains of the last was burning in the ashtray.

He wrote on the pad on his desk and turned it round. 'It's *Anthony!*'

'Anthony?' I mouthed. '*Oh*, Anthony.'

Colin went on, 'Well, of course we would. Yes, the *whole* thing, the *whole* project?' He looked at me with a look that said, Oh God. 'Yes we certainly could, right, right *and* the ride as well. Yes, of course, we'd love to handle the whole thing. Yes, and John will be the Head of Design, of course he will.' He looked at me and winked. 'We'll set up a special unit. Yes, okay then, great, thank you, next Tuesday same place, we'll be there. Oh, yes it is,' he said, '*very* exciting. Please pass on my regards to Peter, thank you.' He put the phone down and looked like he'd just been pole-axed.

His face was white as a sheet. I sat there with my mouth open. He swallowed deeply and loosened his tie.

'What?' I said. 'What!' My eyes were as wide as my spectacles.

'Christ,' he said looking up at me with surprise and panic in his eyes. 'They want us to do the whole thing!'

'Bloody hell,' I said, 'the *whole* bloody thing?' He nodded like a rabbit in the headlights. 'And what did you say?'

'You heard me. I said YES.'

'Oh wow!' I exclaimed. 'That's great!' I couldn't believe it. 'That's great!' I stood up and started jumping up and down.

'Bloody hell!' he cursed again. 'Oh, bugger,' he said with a sense of awful realisation. 'What the hell do we do now?'

'We're going to do it! We *can* do it Colin!' I stopped jumping and said slowly and assuredly looking out of the window to the horizon beyond the factories, the cathedral spire and the chimneys. 'Colin, we can. It's just a matter of talent, planning and management.'

'I've seen what your joinery and construction skills are.' With hands clasped to his head he said, 'We're doomed.' The enormity of his predicament fell on him. He was in shock; then another realisation overcame him.

'Oh, God,' he said rocking in his chair and lighting up again. 'What *am* I going to tell the Board?'

'You'll think of something,' I said. 'You're good at that, and if they don't like it tell 'em if they don't back you you'll send Eric Bloodaxe round with the boys.'

'Who?' said Colin.

I would be lying if I said that we believed we were technically qualified to take on a Museum project, we weren't. I was not a trained museum designer and Colin was not a museum producer. But design is design, (and basically it's problem solving) and Colin had been producing multi-media projects for several years, and so had I.

We might not have had the requisite technical skills at the outset, but we would adapt our independent professional experiences to suit. Combined, our skills covered a lot of ground. And besides, this was to be *no* traditional museum, and newspapermen and filmmakers are good at telling stories.

I believed my mantra *museums like films* was absolutely applicable to the Jorvik Viking Centre. The archaeologists had already envisaged some kind of immersive experience for the visitor and although words like *immersive* and *experiential* were not used at the outset, they were soon to appear as central in the developing brief and in our project proposal plan.

Our meeting the following week took the form of a briefing. This time we were properly introduced and the tone was completely different. As the Director of YAT, Dr Peter Addyman was a senior and highly regarded archaeologist. As such it was obvious right up front that he was putting his reputation on the line with this ambitious project, the likes of which had not been seen before anywhere. And he was not alone in that, I believe.

Richard Hall was also there at the briefing. He was the Director of the Coppergate dig and in the years following became the foremost archaeologist of the Viking age, for which he had a passion beyond his professionalism. Richard was responsible for the accurate detailed recording of the rich waterlogged deposits of Coppergate. I am sure he too was well aware of the possible pitfalls YAT might be facing in creating an archaeological attraction. And I must say, though I might be wrong, I always felt he was nervous about the undertaking. However, he was in a good position to ensure that our reconstruction followed the archaeological brief for accuracy, as it fell to him to oversee our work.

Another man that was there was Anthony Gaynor, the Project Manager of Cultural Resource Management Ltd., which undertook commercial and public affairs on behalf of the YAT. He was ex-army and built like a tank. He had been the youngest Lieutenant in Northern Ireland and, as we were to find out, was not an easy man to say no to. Actually none of them suffered fools easily. Together they made a powerful team and exacting client.

Other senior archaeologists of YAT took on specialist roles in the project. We had regular contact with Dominic Tweddle, Andrew 'Bone' Jones and Jim Spriggs, a specialist in conservation techniques (who by the way collected antique bicycles). I felt they all were putting themselves out there. It could have been uncomfortable for them, as archaeologists usually were to be found in a hole or in a lab, not on stage or behind a counter selling tickets.

They called the meeting to provide us with a background briefing to the project they envisaged. It was a hugely ambitious scheme. Truly there had been nothing like it; it was going to be a first, not just nationally but internationally.

What they presented to us was inspiring and spellbinding. The dig and subsequent study revealed such a comprehensive body of knowledge that a virtually complete reconstruction of the way people lived a thousand years before should be possible, and they intended to create it on the very site where the buildings had once stood and folks had gone about their daily lives.

Colin and I sat quietly at the table like we'd just been dropped into a degree course at Cambridge after failing our O-levels. We were riveted, excited, fascinated and daunted by the task we now found in front of us. And I should say not a little humbled that we should have been selected, subject to contract, to take on the job.

The requirement was that the finished exhibition would be an entirely fact-based simulation of the original settlement. It was fundamental that we as the creators of the exhibition should never step outside the data, which detailed and described not just where people lived and worked, but what they wore, what they owned, what they ate and drank and further *how* they lived and worked, how healthy they were, what their diet consisted of; in fact what life had really been like in the round.

It was essential that we grasped that the most sensational reality of our reconstruction would be about the ordinary everyday life of people who lived a thousand years before us.

This was not going to be some gory raping and pillaging story, all dragon ships and blood lust. The Jorvik story would be *more* sensational; a trip across a bridge in time constructed from scientific data to another era, but at exactly the same place. Their concept, deceptively simple, was of such brilliance it took my breath away.

That afternoon they told us what they'd discovered in the dig and what their goals were in presenting their findings. But what they couldn't tell us was how to bring the whole thing together in an engaging, entertaining and enlightening way that people would be prepared to pay to experience it. That was to be our job.

Why us? We couldn't help wondering; there surely must have been other individuals, companies and organisations out there that could have taken on such a project. As we later discovered, whilst they had searched at home and abroad for others to take on the role of designers and builders, they found no individual or business that got it like we had, that brought their concept to life.

My pile of drawings – done in the back bedroom and on pub tables over six weeks of concentrated inspiration alone and with friends based on that little leaflet fuelled by my passion to make museums more like films – in the end demonstrated that I did. With Colin in front of the team, they had enough confidence in us to give us the go-ahead.

And besides, I think they liked that we were from Yorkshire.

6   THE BEAUTIFUL BURP

YAT IS A NOT-FOR-PROFIT ORGANISATION. In fact, in 1980 as the new decade opened, they were almost broke and desperately needed to raise income to finance their future plans.

The Jorvik Viking Centre was a gamble, a huge risk for them. The project would cost millions of pounds to build, and then had to be expertly operated year in and year out, a colossal commitment for people who had trained to be archaeologists.

The JVC, as we called it, would have to be something very special indeed to capture the imagination of the public and attract sufficient numbers over the years to keep the project in business once it opened.

But it wasn't just about the numbers. If the project failed, careers would be tarnished, most likely ruined. There would be ridicule in the archaeological world. Colin and I soon learned that there were already whispers in academia that Dr Peter Addyman and his colleagues in York intended to privatise and commercialise the National Heritage. After all, Margaret Thatcher's government was all for private enterprise. Maybe the whisperers feared that, if we were successful and the Centre was able to support itself, government funding for their projects might come under scrutiny.

It was a very risky thing to take on, yet if it was a success and stayed in profit, YAT would own an income-generating business that could rid them of their financial woes possibly for good and allow them to develop other educational projects besides scoring a first in archaeological and museum presentation.

Many museums at the time in Britain were free admission. An independent archaeological museum charging admission would be something new. However, the ambition to finance and operate museum projects commercially and independently was already on the radar of the Conservative Government. If Jorvik could survive and finance itself, what about other public funded museums?

That idea itself worried the museum community, especially those that depended on local and national government sources for most of their funding. I believe it is fair to say that even in the early days of the development, there were those who would have been happy to see the JVC fail.

Whatever the politics, a fact of life for YAT was that once operational the Centre had at least to 'wash its face'. Only a small amount of initial financing would be forthcoming indirectly from government through agencies like the English Tourist Board, and that was not yet assured. The rest would have to be raised from commercial loans, like any other business. And, of course, those loans would have to be financed.

But there was a doubt whether that would be feasible. After all, the proposed museum was one of a kind, a new concept in every sense, not an easy sell. Imagine going along to your bank manager and asking him to cough up a couple of million quid to build an underground Viking museum *sans* rape and pillage. Who could possibly know if it would be a success especially without the horned helmets and screaming nuns?

So from the outset it was a huge risk. It's easy to look back and think little of it now, but the archaeologists really were putting themselves out there. At that first briefing meeting they didn't talk about such risks, but we didn't have to be clairvoyant to sense they were stepping way outside their comfort zones. *And* they had to work with strange non-academic creatures like us. I felt sure that this was one hole a few members of the archaeological team would rather not be in.

After their briefing, the spotlight fell on us. The core team of archaeologists invited us back to York to provide them with more information about Colin's set-up at Yorkshire Communications Group and how the design and build programme would operate. Not unreasonably, with so much at stake they needed more assurances about our ability to pull the whole thing off.

Colin and I decided we should be up-front; there was no point in kidding we had everything set up. We thought long and hard about it and developed an initial project plan. It formed the basis for our proposal to YAT. In it we expressed how we intended to establish a research, design and specialist construction team, locating and handpicking the members from various disciplines and specialist trades. But the most important and significant thing we said was that from the outset we expected to work hand-in-glove with them.

By the searching questions asked, it was obvious they did their homework and knew a great deal about Colin's parent company and so were even more interested as to just *how* we intended to deliver the project. After all, the Yorkshire Communications Group had its financial foundation in local newspapers, marketing and commercial printing and demonstrably had not the remotest experience of undertaking anything like this. But, as they discovered, back then pretty much no one else had either.

Colin handled the meeting well and with confidence. He told them we'd have a complete formal proposal explaining the whole of our approach and methodology within a couple of weeks. If they were happy, contracts and schedules could then be drawn up.

Though we didn't get signed up during that meeting, they did say something that was very encouraging. They told us that they *wanted* us to do it. They said they had searched high and low for a design and build company they could have confidence in and in the process had met with some very famous people and even approached the Disney Corporation. Yet in the end, they were delighted to come across a Yorkshire-based outfit, one close to home, to undertake the project. And we had demonstrated that we understood their concept and had a genuine enthusiasm for it.

As I heard these words, I thought about the enormous leap of faith these people were taking. It was all a little crazy; the archaeologists and us were an odd mix, untried, untested yet possessing a unique chemistry right at the outset.

Meanwhile, on my way to Jorvik, the clock was already ticking. And the opening date set as April 14, 1984 was just three short years away.

During those first weeks repeated veiled references had been made to a mysterious 'major player', an individual who was in at the inception and apparently someone who continued to be a driving force for the project, albeit from behind the scenes.

This mystery man's name was Ian Skipper. We were informed that he'd requested a face-to-face meeting with Colin and me the following week at a hotel in London. It was obvious he wanted to check us out for himself; so this was the next hurdle. It felt like it was going to be a big one.

Mr Skipper, we were informed, put great stay in personal contact and wanted to meet us to discuss our plans and ideas. We weren't told much more. But we had the distinct impression if he didn't take to us then Colin could continue his career in local newspapers and marketing and I could go back to animating dancing vegetables.

The Carlton Tower where we were to meet the mystery man is a very expensive and exclusive hotel in London. As we sat opposite each other on the train south we had no idea of what he was going to be like, but we did know that he held a special position in the hierarchy of the project and a powerful sway on its direction.

We were told very little so we couldn't help wondering how he could have so much importance and control over such a project. Was he an archaeologist? If he was how come he was rich? Had he dug up some treasure somewhere?

By now I'd retrieved my drawings from our initial briefing meeting in York and had invested in a smart new black portfolio to make them and me more presentable.

When we arrived at the Carlton Tower the entrance door was opened for us and the immediate whiff I got of the inside was one of serious money. We were expected, said a polite and smartly dressed man on the desk. We were ushered and escorted up several floors to the penthouse by another member of the lobby staff. Mr Skipper, we were to learn, occupied a suite of rooms there when in London and away from his home on Barbados. As we stood outside the apartment door on carpet which felt like walking on ten pound notes, I realised I hadn't been this nervous since our original interview.

A handsome bronze-skinned man in a white jacket with a black bow tie opened the door and showed us into a reception room. He looked like James Bond in a cocktail jacket and I thought he was The Man. I almost gave him an impromptu presentation on the doorstep. He turned out to be the butler who came with the apartment.

We entered a room like I'd only ever seen in films, where the baddy lived perhaps. Elegant, tasteful and beautifully furnished, its opulence had more than a tinge of artful decadence; or maybe that was just the effect of the overflowing fruit bowl full of shiny fruit. 'Eat me,' said the apples and grapes, 'but don't touch.'

'I could get used to this,' I whispered to Colin as we both sank just far enough into a deep green satin-covered sofa.

Mr Skipper, we were told by the butler, was on the telephone, and would be with us shortly. We waited, expectantly. He was probably weighing us up on a monitor somewhere.

'Hello, boys.' In he walked smiling and instantly the room lit up. He had that deep tan you don't get on a package holiday. He spoke slowly and deliberately with a slightly affected accent, like someone from a working class background who had attended a very expensive school and who now frequented the company of clever and well-educated people.

We stood up and he shook our hands. For a few moments he looked straight and directly into my eyes with such a piercing look that it felt like he was reading what was on the back of my skull and looking into my soul. It made me shiver inside. I thought there was something devilish about him.

He wasn't a large man, about five foot five, but making up for his small stature, he possessed this huge presence. I had never in my life experienced the force of such a presence. I thought of Napoleon Bonaparte, another man of short stature and extraordinary achievement. (Later I would discover he had a portrait of Bonaparte behind his desk in his Oxfordshire office.) In those first few moments of meeting I understood how he had become a multi-millionaire. And what a dynamic force and catalyst for the project he was.

He told us to sit. I watched him; I wanted to take him in as he made preliminary chit chat. He began smoking a cigarette that he held delicately in one hand whilst in the other he rolled over what appeared to be a small ingot of gold. It was a cigarette lighter, his familiar object with which he toyed; opening and closing it several times in those first few seconds and every time with a gold 'ka-ching' like the sound of a golden spur on the flank of a satin-black stallion.

He sat in a single chair at my side of the sofa and asked if we would like some refreshment. Yes, we would we said. He must have pressed a button on the table for the butler appeared and noted what we wanted. I think we settled for tea and chocolate biscuits.

There was a little quiet time, time to take him in further, time for him to do the same. He was wearing a discreetly expensive immaculate grey suit, white shirt and dark silk tie. His hair was black, as was his short well-clipped goatee.

I guessed his age to be perhaps forty-three, maybe older beneath his tan. His shoes were understatedly expensive, as was everything about him including his watch and his teeth. The only thing slightly over the top was the gold brick cigarette lighter. I realised I'd never met anyone quite like Mr Ian Skipper. He was one of those people who live on another strata, the nameless faceless, the ones who hold the power; the one percenters we hear about today.

He sat looking at us both but mainly at me, whilst Colin and I sat like expectant pigeons on Napoleon's window ledge. It was unnerving. Then he broke the silence and stood up.

'I've heard some very interesting things about you,' he said. 'You've made quite an impression on Peter and Anthony.'

'Gosh,' I said.

As he revealed this he picked up a crystal ashtray into which he tapped his cigarette ash. Then he took a tissue from a black onyx box, emptied the ash into the tissue, carefully folded it up and deposited it in a black lacquer bin near his feet. Then he polished the ashtray with a second tissue. He repeated the same action with practically each flick of ash, which was surprising and odd as he smoked almost constantly. It was as though he was cleansing himself from his smoking.

'So,' he said, 'I want to hear all about you and your ideas and not just about the museum, but what you are all about.'

Colin chimed in. 'Before we do that, I think we are both curious to know how did you get involved in a project like Jorvik; and if it's not too direct, why? Hope you don't mind my asking.'

'Not at all, dear boy,' he said. 'It's quite simple. I offered my services.'

'As what?' I asked.

'Well, as a digger or something like that, someone who carts dirt about on the site.'

It was hard to picture him in wellies carrying a bucket unless it was a gold bucket. I doubted the sincerity of this and wondered if he always liked to play such games with people.

'So, what happened then?' I asked.

'Well, I met them, in New York I think. They were on the radio and I gave them a call. They were looking for money to support the rescue dig. Anyway, we got to know one another and they seemed to think I could help them in better ways.'

Colin asked, 'What ways?'

'They thought I could be more effective advising them on how to make it happen then shoveling s*** in a hole.' Somehow that first swear word came as a surprise; there would be many, many more.

'So, how did you help them at first?' asked Colin.

'Well,' he said taking off his suit jacket, folding it and neatly placing it over a chair back, 'when we first met, they hadn't got two f**king pennies to rub together. They were up against it. To help them I went up there to York and the site – you know it I presume?' We nodded. 'They gave me a tour and I thought it was *so* fascinating. And I wasn't the only one. I saw so many people, passers-by, looking down into the hole watching what was going on. So I showed them how to make some easy money.'

'How?' asked Colin.

'I told them to build a fence with little teasy holes in it that would let people see a little but not a lot. And I got them to build a gate, solid like the fence, and told them to charge a pound coin for everyone who came in, saying the money was going to support the dig, which it was. I said they should make a little exhibit in a shed and put something around the hole that explained what was going on. That was it. They may have expected me to cough up some brass there and then, but instead that's what I told them to do.'

'There were gold in that there 'ole,' I said.

He laughed. 'Very good,' he said.

'So what had been free to the public, you got them to charge for,' said Colin.

'Yes, and it made them a lot of money, dear boy, in that first summer.'

'Brilliant!' said Colin. 'Just brilliant.'

At that moment a trolley rolled in pushed by the butler and on it there was a mini-feast.

'Dig in boys!' he said. 'Be a good chap Colin and pour the tea would you. There's a good fellow.'

Now with a face full of little sandwiches, he asked me to tell him about myself. I don't know what happened but as I started to speak I sort of ignited and his attention focused more intently.

He was genuinely interested. I told him everything, a sort of confession that I didn't make to the archaeologists. I went back all the way, *Dusty Bin, Kenny Everett* included and even further back to the kid in the museum and my *museums like films* idea, which lead on to my motives for being interested in Jorvik even though there was little chance of getting there. I told him about other ideas, for new kinds of virtual imaging of historic places and rambled away like there were fireworks going off in my head.

I was totally animated and felt like he was sharing the energy. I could see it in his eyes. For a several minutes we were on some kind of heightened level. Ideas and connotations I hadn't consciously articulated before strung together as if they were suddenly not crazy but achievable, like they made sense for the first time. I had a sketchpad out and my pen flew over it like an ice-skater on fire.

I showed him the drawings that the others had seen and newer ideas produced since the last meeting. He loved them. Then I drew more stuff and I drew as I talked. He was fascinated by the act of drawing, of making an idea come to life on the page before him.

The last time that happened for me was with the producer of *3*2*1*. This time though it felt like I was dancing with the devil. It was something I never felt before but Ian held our future in the project in his finely manicured hand. We knew it for sure that one negative word from him and we'd be out before we were really in.

The opposite happened. There was a resonance and a harmony filling the room that was explosive. Ian sat close and across from me, intense, watching, approving and sparkling. Then he turned to Colin and said, 'I hope he has a transferable pension plan, old boy.' Whatever that meant, I knew he was serious; this was a man who always got what he wanted. Colin gave a dry laugh. It seemed to Ian and maybe to YAT that I was an employee of Colin's rather than on the one-off special contract Colin and I had discussed if the job went ahead.

Later outside as we crossed the street the endorphins were coursing. I was high as a kite, and Colin was flushed with excitement too.

'Come on, let's go have a pint and come down to earth,' he said.

'Aw, really,' I said, 'let's not come down just yet.' It had been an extraordinary time and I didn't want it to end.

We sat in a pub nearby, still spinning. 'God,' said Colin, 'I think that went as well as it could have. Looks like we're on. That was great. He really took to you. Don't think he liked me much.'

'Well, you weren't the *cabaret*, but as far as I am concerned, we're a team. We're together in this or not at all,' I said feeling inflated with confidence and dangerously full of myself; but I meant it. I had nothing like the professional risks that Colin was taking, and I really did consider us a team.

A day or two later a call came from York confirming we had met with Mr Skipper's approval. We knew now that he was a successful, persuasive, dynamic and very wealthy businessman and it was he who provided the acumen, populist vision and much of the drive to get the archaeologists to this point. After that Colin had to face his still incredulous board to finally secure their solid support and backing. I wondered what *they* would ever make of the enigmatic Mr Skipper?

In the end, Colin swung his board behind him, a fact to be honest I've always been amazed by. They must have had incredible confidence in him. And they must have been impressed with Ian Skipper's involvement. I only wish I had been a fly on the boardroom wall when Colin first told them about the project.

The budget for the entire scheme, the interpretive exhibit and the Time Car system as well as the museum displays, shop, front of house, management offices, equipment etc. was three and a half million pounds, budgie feed as far as today's budgets go. Our part of the total was about a third, back then a considerable sum for a small local newspaper group to back.

Now, with our proposal submitted and accepted and the contract paperwork out of the way and assurance that funds were to come into the project bank account, it was time to face practical issues. The first thing to do was to find some place larger than the two rooms we occupied in which to house the core design and development team. Meanwhile, now that my fantasy had turned into a reality and there was going to be a steady income, Lynda was fully behind the project and me.

Back in 1981 York was too far away to travel to everyday from the West Riding. There weren't the motorway links there are now, so a place in Wakefield at least for the beginning period made sense. I told Colin we needed an open space more or less the same as the actual site where the exhibition would be installed, though I wasn't exactly sure why. It didn't take him long to come up with somewhere suitable.

We pulled up outside a new medium-sized unit on an industrial park just a couple of miles away from the newspaper office. It was just a big anonymous shed, with offices at the front and a large high ceilinged warehouse/workshop in the back. The industrial estate was new, and most units were occupied with the sort of businesses you'd typically find on industrial estates. Across from us was a cake factory; I wondered what on earth the workers from there would make of us. We definitely would be the black sheep.

The unit was perfect for our needs. We were able to set up the production offices in the front along with a small studio and build models and try-outs in the large open space at the back. I stood in there as Colin explored the offices and thought to myself, 'This is really happening.' The prospect was more than a little scary.

Now with an operational base in place we needed a production team to put in it. As I said earlier, there were very few specialist design and build companies around at the time, and neither were there many specialist designers or builders. We would have to create our own handpicked team.

This is where my previous freelance experience came into its own. There's talent to suit all over the place, if you only knew how to spot it and use it. I reckoned we'd find the people we needed very close to hand.

We needed a layered team on three levels. Put very simply, for the first year we needed a management, research and design team. They would be based in Wakefield. Then once we made the move to York and the Coppergate site when the building shell was complete and ready for us to move into, we would need the build and technical team. Lastly, we'd need the services of specialists, both individuals and companies.

I knew that we would find all the people and services needed within a fifty-mile radius. I knew this from personal experience because I'd searched for and found the talented people I needed for my previous projects.

They, the individuals at least, were all out there – the theatre set builders, the carpenters and plasterers, costume designers and sculptors, scenic artists and craftspeople of all manners and types. Most often they were freelance like me, coming together for one-off productions. I felt sure, as I had collected them for *Kremmen the Movie*, that the talent we needed would be local. I started putting out feelers, nothing too specific, confident that we would put together a great team. But before I could be sure just exactly who we needed, I had to develop a design concept with enough flesh on it to get a grip on the overall job.

Up to this point the architects and archaeologists had mapped out the main areas for the building and exhibition on three levels of the building. These were so far:

First floor – Administration

Ground Floor – Front Lobby and ticket sales

Basement level – Introductory walk-through

Basement level – Starting platform (where visitors would mount the Time Car vehicles for the ride around the main exhibit), which included in order:

— The Time Tunnel

— The Tenth Century Settlement Reconstruction

— The Archaeology Gallery

— Disembarkation

— The Laboratory

— The Artefacts Display Gallery/Museum

— The Shop

My job was not just to design the 'sets', build and populate them; I also had to come up with ideas of what the separate parts of the exhibition actually contained and what happened when visitors were in them. And finally, overall, I had to figure out how all those elements would mesh together as a unified whole, how they would work together to make a dynamic attraction.

If all the details of just what the visitors would see and experience had already been decided, we would have just been exhibit constructors. But with no detailed plan having been put forth, this meant there was a great deal of room for creativity in the presentation and interpretation of the whole project, as long as we never moved away from the factual foundations.

If we did stray and therefore made things up, we'd be in very murky waters. That's what the archaeologists were nervous of and what the detractors were already muttering might happen. It wasn't long before we heard the intentionally disparaging remark that we would be 'Disneyfying the archaeological heritage of Britain.'

Putting the initial critics of the project out of mind, I got down to work out the overall concept design based on the exhibition space already allowed for in the architects' scheme and the archaeologists' schematic concept. I started with the plans supplied by them for the basement in which the exhibition would be housed. I began by considering the layout as it had been handed to us. We were responsible for everything the visitor would experience on the ride. Everything that came before and after it was the responsibility of the archaeologists.

There was an awful lot to get into the relatively small space allotted for our side of things, approximately a thousand square metres by five high. I was just starting to figure out how to make the spaces work when Colin arrived breathlessly with news that he just learned that YAT, along with Ian Skipper, would be hosting a large-scale promotional event in York at the medieval Merchant Adventurers Hall and they wanted to present the scheme to the world. I looked down at my desk and an empty sheet of paper with not a mark on it.

In the UK, cultural and charitable projects such as ours did (and still do) their best to attract a patron, a figurehead of status, integrity and intelligence, and if possible, with real interest in the subject matter. Such a figurehead adds credibility. In this we could not have been more fortunate than having HRH Prince Charles as our patron. He studied archaeology at Cambridge and would be there to deliver a speech in support of the scheme to journalists and media people from all over the country. Even though this was early in 1981 when we were just beginning it was a splendid idea. Hopefully the media would drum up national and international interest that could be kept going through the design and build process of the next two years, right up to opening day. Problem was; what could we show them?

It's crucial that when you launch a project, you have to have something exciting to present (besides a member of the Royal Family). The launch was complete news to us and was set for two weeks hence. Truth was; I hadn't the confidence yet to let on that I didn't have the concept design worked out. I needed time for the whole thing to gel together in my head.

Still, problems breed solutions. The press and the Prince were no doubt going to be interested mainly in the reconstruction of the archaeology and we learned that the Prince was following it. With that in mind we decided to build a model that was limited to the reconstruction of the 10th century site and nothing more. As we only had a couple of weeks to build it, we had to get cracking.

I could easily do the sketches and plan drawings for the layout of the houses on the site. We would also show extra elements, like market stalls and carts. But we needed a model maker to make it.

Freelance creative people, in my experience, tend to develop a radar for others with talent. It's a survival thing; you never know when you might need the help. I remembered coming across a fascinating young bloke at the newspaper offices of all places. Derek, who I discovered when we were doing the rotoscope title sequence, was a very talented model maker and artist, totally wasted doing the paste ups for black and white classified ads for the newspaper. He kept popping in while I was doing the animation and was totally astonished and fascinated at what we were up to on the third floor. I got to know him and he eventually showed me some of his extraordinary creations, clocks I remember, and small mechanical devices he made, one of which was nationally famous. I believe it appeared in a Heineken commercial on national television. It was a snow globe, real size, in which the snowman, after the globe had been shaken, cheers himself up with a glass of beer, which his snowy arm lifts to his frozen lips. And there he was, Derek (not the snowman) sticking down pieces of paper with Cowgum advertising 'Bob's Cheap Tyres' for Friday's paper.

I filed Derek away for future reference and suddenly there was a role for him. He could make the model and was already on the payroll. But as I knew he was a key talent in the art department at the newspaper, that meant we'd have to kidnap him.

It took a little bit of skullduggery by Colin, but we nicked him from the newspaper and he joined us down at the industrial estate. Derek further confirmed what I anticipated; the talent was out there and in some cases very close by.

Whilst Derek was thrilled to join us, back at the paper, rumbles and grumbles accompanied the dawning realisation that our weird museum job was actually happening and it was going to have a real impact on the otherwise sleepy newspaper. If we could steal a star like Derek from under their noses, who next? Lure Margaret, the Head of Accounts, to be an axe-wielding Viking wench in a cardigan? Anything could happen.

So now we were three. And before we went a step further we needed someone to keep track of everything and keep the accounts. After all, the budget was a cool million plus, a lot of brass back then. Using the premise that I should always look close to home first for the bodies we needed, I thought of Phoebe.

Phoebe MacLeod had been looking after my books (such as they were) for a couple of years. She was a larger-than-life sweetheart and smart as a whip. She came to my flat once a month to make sense of my various piles of receipts, invoices and general chaos that I laughingly thought of as my business.

Originally from South Africa, Phoebe was a ball of fire, full of brightness, ebullience and efficiency and had a smile and a sense of humour that could have kept the Titanic afloat, or at least cheered everyone up. She was about as far away from an artsy crafty project person as you could imagine. Yet I had an instinct she'd be just right for our team and suggested to Colin that he interview her for the position of Comptroller. He wasn't that impressed with my description of her at first, but as soon as they met he was sold and offered her the job on the spot. Now we were four, and in the middle of our first week of production.

We were a bunch of individualists, but we gelled at the core. I felt instinctively that we had to keep building out from that core. Phoebe took to her new life and became the go-to person and, dare I say it, Matriarch on the job.

Derek was straight way into the model building so even without the rest of the design being worked out I felt confident to take another step with the team. I sensed that the archaeologists were nervous about us. So I felt we had a bridge to build from where we were to where they were on the other side of an intellectual divide.

I thought they'd trust us more and worry less about what we were up to if we had a qualified archaeologist on the team. Plus, there was the fact that half the time I didn't know quite what they were talking about as they used terminology that was sometimes hard to follow. The last thing we wanted to show was our ignorance. So far our contact with them had been on the cool and suspicious side to say the least. Thank god no one in York had yet discovered that I was the creator of *Dusty Bin* (even Mr Skipper kept quiet about that as far as I knew). I thought they would have had a collective seizure. To be honest, I felt the archaeologists that I met to date were rather stuffy and patronizing, but it was the early days. Later I found out how wrong this was, but at the outset that's honestly how I felt.

Our own pet archaeologist would help us understand their language and interpret our intentions in the appropriate way. Where would we get one? We didn't want someone from YAT; we needed someone we felt totally at ease with, and who besides being a go-between could act as an informed mouthpiece with the media and help us with presentations. We also thought, wisely as it turned out, that we should have an archaeologist who was young, open-minded, full of beans and would look good on camera. Colin placed an advertisement in the Yorkshire Post; we got responses straight away.

We decided to hold interviews in a luxuriously converted barn next door to Colin's lovely farmhouse on the outskirts of Walton just outside Wakefield. The barn was home to his neighbour who was abroad at the time. It was sort of like a bachelor pad and certainly not a business location, but very swish in the style for the time. It suited our purposes; we didn't want to have a formal setting, as we needed to see how the candidates reacted to a non-archaeological set up.

The Barn with its orange and brown shag pile everything was more like a nightclub or a porn movie studio, hidden away in the countryside. Anyway, we felt like producers and the over-the-top setting matched. It was going to be 'James Bond meets Archeopenny', if the candidate we settled on was feminine.

The ground floor of the barn where we planned to have the interviews was split level with a circular seating well that you stepped down into, about ten feet across covered in thick deep shaggy brown carpet like the rest of the floor and strewn with huge orange cushions.

The main feature of the room was one of those big rocky fireplaces built from boulders from which a missile could be fired. There was also probably a vast tank full of piranhas hidden somewhere, into which we thought we could drop the candidates we rejected, if only we could find the concealed button.

Colin wisely decided against a fluffy white cat with a diamond necklace. He said it might affect his dignity in the eyes of the interviewees, and anyway Colin was highly allergic to cats. And he also reminded me (as I couldn't stop laughing and cracking jokes having just seen the place for the first time) to take what we were doing seriously.

We saw several candidates, men and women and no one got to be a piranha snack. They were all well qualified, tweedy, serious and surprised at the décor. One went away, I learned later, believing that he'd just had an encounter with the West Yorkshire archaeological artefacts smuggling ring. We were beginning to get despondent by the time the last candidate arrived.

The one that jumped straight out at us as soon as she walked in was the delightful Carolyn Lloyd. Not because she was young, extremely attractive, blonde, blue-eyed, vivacious, obviously clever and wore a gold spandex jumpsuit. But because she was all of that *and* as an archaeology student, she'd worked for YAT, digging on the Coppergate site. She wasn't 'Miss Archeopenny', she was 'Carolyn Galore'.

In addition she spoke fluent archeo-speak. And although she looked about sixteen she came across with confidence. The other engaging thing about the lovely Carolyn was that she appeared as tough as she was smart and so she wouldn't be easily put down by her peers. I reckoned she could protect Colin and I as a sort of archaeological bodyguard, which was obviously going to be important, especially if the artefacts and the mud ever hit the fan.

And lastly but most importantly, we could talk to her about archaeology without feeling that we were being talked down to. In fact with her we could show our ignorance and not feel that we'd lose the contract in the process. She'd be our interpreter and at the same time coach us on how to stand up for ourselves with the diggers and sifters.

Colin offered her the job and when she left and was out of the driveway we cheered and jumped up and down on the sofas and threw the cushions about.

So now we had Phoebe, the real Miss Money Penny, and Miss Galore and our technical genius Derek who could be 'M'. Things were going well. And so was the model.

Next we needed a designer, ideally someone with set design experience to produce the measured drawings we needed for the construction of the exhibition. Everything had to be detailed, worked out and drawn up as plans and elevations to satisfy our archaeologist clients. My visualisation sketches would not be enough alone.

Again I thought I must know someone to fit this bill. Jonathan Bean came to mind. I'd met him at Yorkshire Television and knew him to speak to, well enough to know that he was rather tired of the politics and back biting that goes on in a television company and might be looking for an out.

Jonathan had a great deal of television design experience and when I bumped into him on one of my talent scouting trips I told him we were looking for someone like him. It was one of those fateful meetings as he was on the cusp of a career change.

Our warehouse may have not been glamorous; but that didn't matter. We were embarking on something new, a *film that was a museum*. We were pioneers. So I did my best to impart that idea to Jonathan. While he hummed and whistled and didn't get excited, he definitely got it.

Jonathan turned up the first morning on his motorbike and by the end of the second week we had, in essence, a small but complete production team. Unfortunately there was no complete plan to go with it as yet.

With all my focus set on creating the team, I wasn't in the headspace I needed to be in as a project designer to do my thing. I was at the front of my head where things get worked out in a rational way. I needed to be in the back where things bubble and gestate before making itself known out front.

While Jonathan and the rest were settling into their new home and working up the model, I crept away to try and figure it all out. Truth is, I am not and never have been a technical designer like Jonathan. I've gone on earlier about being a storyteller and that's an essential part of what I do. I lay out a detailed concept design by hand on paper, which becomes a comprehensive plan for the whole project. But I don't detail where the nuts and bolts go. In truth I couldn't sit down and produce final production detail drawings if my life depended on it. That's another training and another skill.

And I do something else. I look for that *fundamentally true* thing about a subject, which I call the 'heart' from which a concept design and the project's creation are based upon. My job is to give birth to a concept then a concept design, which has to be visualised. It's the unifying idea that gives the project its unique fingerprint and identity. Often finding the real heart of a project is something more intuitively *felt* than designed. It's those sketched ideas that allow a client to share the vision.

I know I've discovered it when I feel it first in my gut, rather than think it in my head. It's like being creatively pregnant. It's a mysterious process, a sort of mental alchemy. I put in the ingredients and hope and pray that a solution will appear, if not I rearrange those ingredients to find other connections leading to a different path to a solution. As time was moving quickly, with not a cohesive and complete picture to present to Jonathan who wanted to get on with the job, I was in trouble.

Back in 1980 I started keeping a daily work journal, and early on I realised just how important it was to use these journals to help gestate ideas and concepts, work them out on paper and keep them in one private place. Over the years those journals that began with Jorvik, now as I write, number 129 volumes.

The doodles and exploratory drawings, which are usually little more than nervous squiggles at first, would sometimes develop into award winning projects costing millions. Like creative worms coming to the surface of a lawn, ideas that are not the product of conscious thought come to light. A thrill for me now is to look back and see how those first thoughts rendered in pencil or ink were the first steps in the creation of a successful and enduring museum or heritage attraction.

Drawing is how thoughts become birthed for me; it's fundamental to my creative process. I find that after a time of doodling away, when I leave it alone and come back to it again, I get 'the beautiful burp', the sudden insight that's the key to the project. I hope that future generations of designers and artists don't lose the confidence or inclination to make marks on paper.

Having said all that, Jorvik was by far and way the biggest creative challenge of my life. Just about everything I had done until then had been flat, not three-dimensional. It wasn't an easy pregnancy and I still hadn't given birth when the Royal event came around.

17 August:

Note: Re Trevor sample background matrix for Time-Tunnel.

I think that the Drone and wind combined as they are, but in this mix are too heavy, sinister and overpowering — although I don't mind the form of the drone — *but* [we are not trying to frighten people.]

Overall it's too 'heavy' and dense. (wind and drone)

Very important (and working well) are the strip, and chatter of high frequency sounds — more of this and more of the way they travel about.

Love the smoothness, and 'flashes' — sounds like voices from a different dimension — heard on edge.

Can we build some this into the old tunnel — and maybe very remotely into the starting platform area.

torso and upper legs wrapped in blanket.

arched back head looks up and towards woman

drinking horn rests on knee.

Bowl on knees

Bread and porridge in bowl

Spoon half raised to mouth interrupted by speech

Feet wrapped in cloth to keep warm

Wattle Building ideas for old man.

Journal sketch of old man in house interior

7 INVISIBLE GUESTS

ON THE EVENING OF THE launch beneath the medieval timbers of the Merchant Adventurers Hall, fine speeches were made and Prince Charles gave the scheme his unqualified support. Champagne flowed, interviews were done, photographs and notes were taken and people studied the model of the reconstruction that Derek and Jonathan had completed just the day before.

Luckily there was so much glad-handing that no one prodded too hard for how the rest of the plan was going to work. It was a grand event, and only a stone's throw from the Jorvik site in Coppergate.

The event brought about a clutch of articles in the national media and the great British Public at large learned about the project for the first time. Vikings made good copy, as did Time Cars. This was going to be no stuffy museum project; this was Time Travel.

Construction work had begun on the Coppergate site and concrete poured where only weeks before archaeologists had still been digging. The Jorvik Viking Centre would have access from the square and run underneath the shopping development above. It was a great location and such an exciting idea.

I just knew that people would love knowing that beneath their feet another world from another time was taking shape and they'd be so curious. But first I had to see it all in my head and it still hadn't materialised. I had faith that the big idea that would bring all the parts together was coming; I just had to give it time. In the meantime there were the very real practical considerations of housing an exhibition and museum underground.

I never had to think about physical space planning before. Animation, film and television create their own virtual spaces, as I found in my kids TV series. Funnily enough, as it happened, *Sally and her Naughty Puppy* helped me come up with the final detail design for the layout of Jorvik, because doing those illustrations taught me how to create the illusion of space.

The overall design had to include many things that would not be seen by visitors, like the technical control rooms and where the Time Cars would be stored, charged up (they were to run on batteries) and serviced.

There was going to be a lot of technical stuff. The hardware and software that we planned to use was not yet digitalised. That meant the equipment for the multi-track sound system was large and clunky and needed a lot of cooling. Space would be at an absolute premium. Yet I knew for the exhibition to achieve its most powerful and memorable impact, visitors must be unaffected by the lack of space and practical constraints. Indeed once they stepped into a Time Car they should enjoy a seamless experience.

The cars had been thought of before we came on board yet in 1981 when the production began, they were still on the drawing board. The car system would transport visitors around the exhibition. In principle it was an ingenious and ambitious solution to what at first seemed to be an insurmountable problem. The Fire Officers from the City had never had to deal with anything quite like this and without their clearance on all safety issues, Jorvik would not be allowed to open. They put their foot down on one major issue; how many visitors would be allowed in the exhibition at any one time. Having done their calculations, the Fire Officer's department imposed a limit of one hundred. Not many people and not many tickets. So a solution was looked for that would allow for the upper limit, yet would control the throughput and flow to an hourly maximum. The ride system was an ingenious, bold and unique answer to the problem. And as with so many things about Jorvik, it was a first in museum exhibition design.

The cars would act as a 'conveyor belt' moving visitors through at a pace that would allow them to take in the exhibition and yet get enough people through to meet visitor through-put targets of so many people an hour, up to 400 people an hour on a busy day. Whilst at first conceived as a solution to one problem, the cars in the end provided a host of other solutions that weren't originally foreseen.

However, finding space for around thirty four-person vehicles that had to be stored, serviced and charged up overnight had been a nightmare for the architects. By the time we came on board a solution still hadn't been found. I knew that whatever the form of the final coherent design, the last thing I wanted was anything that would burst the bubble of 'the suspension of disbelief' that I planned to create, a goal that was used in radio, television, advertising, theatre and cinema but had never before been used in a museum exhibit.

I looked at the plans. How to fit it all in was a puzzle crossed with a conundrum wrapped in a potential quagmire. Yet I felt inside that there was a solution that would reveal other possibilities, but what was it? It was time for a bath.

I needed to think out of the box. So I locked the bathroom door and took a long undisturbed bubble bath. There I remained until seriously wrinkly, which was about when the beautiful burp burst upon the surface just like it did with the 3*2*1 title sequence.

My bathtub epiphany came as I revisited the idea I had as a kid about museums coming alive. Visitors wouldn't be on the outside looking into the glass boxes in old museums; they would be on the inside and like the pink stuff in the bath, inside a bubble. But what was the bubble, was it a real thing?

And then I got it. It sounds obvious thirty years on, but it wasn't then. The key would be the car; not only would it determine where people were physically in the basement or space but where they were in the *story*.

As I stood there, towel in hand dripping on the tiles I repeated 'story' out loud. Just like at the cinema it's the story that takes you out of your sense of present place to another, it's the story that makes the seats and the person sat next to you along with the screen disappear. The story takes you over. The story would be the bubble, and the car would be a moveable camera.

An audio commentary in the cars had been the discussed, but not a *story* as such. To me, that was a distinction. At that time in museum exhibition design, using a story to engage the visitor in relation to what they are seeing and experiencing was a revolutionary concept.

In my way of thinking, the ride experience would be *just* like viewing a film, each scene seamlessly opening and unfolding after the one before. We would transport visitors in their own personalised time machine to the same place but one thousand years before, where at the moment of arrival, life in the past goes into freeze frame. Visitors would be like ghosts from the future.

I thought to myself, what would the scene be? I got the idea of Mum's biscuit pastry cutters in the shape of a star. I imagined Jorvik one typical afternoon going about its business and someone comes along and stamps a pastry cutter down, literally a slice from life. It would be that, which we would freeze in motion. It would be 5:30pm on the 25th of October 975 AD. Why 5:30pm and the autumn time? Because it would be late afternoon light (dusk in the UK) and already starting to get dark, which would allow us to use lighting effects to advantage.

This was all very well, but I still did not have the heart of the project. I was still missing the key, the unifying idea. Besides which, how would we get all that we wanted into such a small space? Just then as Lynda was knocking on the bathroom door checking to see if I'd drowned or not, the second big idea bubbled up into my head.

Every visitor would have a *unique* experience (like at the cinema) and each individual would become his or her own *camera* mounted on a moving platform; the Time Car becomes a camera dolly. And because I'd know exactly where they would be at any given time, I could plan not only the story and its most effective way of telling, but the soundscape and lighting, and the way the scenes unfolded in tandem with the narrative. Fundamentally we would be able to create the illusion of greater spatial depth. That lead me to see that there'd be no problem with car storage and where to put all the control systems and workshops; everything could be hidden within the scenery.

On another level of consideration, it bothered me that reconstructions of historic events and places were often formal, cleaned up and sterilised. It was as though we culturally weren't willing to accept the past for what it was, messy and smelly. But at Jorvik, with the evidence that the archaeologists uncovered, we would be sure that Jorvik was true to itself, dirty and smelly, as the archaeologists wanted. The organic evidence, particularly the trodden earth floors, the spaces between the houses, the position of the cesspits to the wells and the remains of excrement would provide an honest version of history.

Before I unbolted the bathroom door, it came to me that each individual visitor was the only audience I had to think of. Whether the person was eight or eighty, Chinese, or French, British or American, what mattered was that each one would be like the little kid in the cinema, totally drawn into the story and the scene.

Even if there were four or five in a car, what mattered was each individual would use their own eyes, ears, nose and imagination. Through these thoughts I came up with a credo, which I have worked from ever since, three words that summed up this immersive and populist approach to interpretation: *Engage, Entertain, Educate.*

So now I had my cinematic story and camera and sound playing directly into the individual visitor's head as the roving 'dolly' in which he rides explores the scene from the inside. It was simple and it was revolutionary

I couldn't sleep that night; I kept playing the Jorvik movie in my head. Next morning I burst into Colin's office at the industrial estate. The surprise made him jump and half of his digestive biscuit disappeared into his tea.

'Bugger,' he said.

'I want to make a model,' I said breathlessly, waving the new drawings I just completed at home.

'We've got one,' he said.

'No, not that. It's too small.'

'It's very nice,' said Colin.

'No, I need a much bigger one, full scale. And I need some two-by-one timber. Lots of it.'

'Hang on. How big is big and just how much is lots?'

'Same size, same size as it will be,' I said exasperated that he didn't get it. 'Let's start with two thousand feet,' I said.

'What! We haven't got any money through yet.' The first payment from the clients hadn't come through by then.

'Then borrow some.'

'What's it for anyway?' he asked not unreasonably.

'I told you, a MODEL. So I can work things out,' I shouted over my shoulder as I went off to look for Jonathan.

'Couldn't you use spent matches like every body else?' he called. 'Honestly you will be the ruination of me,' I then heard him mutter.

'Jonathan,' I said as I entered the design office where he and Derek sat at their desks. 'Next job for you and Derek.'

'What's that then?' Jonathan approached me still in his motorbike leathers. I told him we needed a model.

'We've got one,' he said, pointing to the small reconstruction in its acrylic display case. 'It's only a part granted, but that's because you haven't shared the rest of the details of the exhibition with us yet.'

'No. Sized up a bit, actually, a lot. I'll explain. This is the idea. We have to see the whole exhibit from the point of view of the visitor who's sat in the moving car. Not from us standing or sitting at a drawing desk, or a visitor looking at "an exhibit". That's the old way, the conventional way. We have to view it and understand it from the *inside*. We have to plan from the actual individual visitor's experience outwards and imagine they are being told a story at the same time. That's how we'll get the immersion effect, see?'

'Right, I see,' he said. Then he started to do something; he rocked back and forwards and made a sort of whistley, breathy humming sound. I found it a bit off-putting at first, like he was totally bored or didn't agree with me. I got used to after a while.

'So,' I continued, 'to do that I want to make a full-scale model of the entire 10th century site. We'll start with them. Then go to the rest.'

He interjected. 'But you haven't told us what the *rest* is going to be like yet.' He was obviously and not unreasonably frustrated.

'Good point,' I said, 'but I shall very shortly. For now just map out the full scale available space from the architects' drawings, and of course all the exact locations and footprints of the buildings on the site.'

He nodded and gave a kind of half smile and continued the low whistle through his beard, which was probably the sound of his blood pressure rising.

'Right. Will do,' he said.

Now Derek spoke. 'Do you mean you want us to actually *build* full-scale buildings?'

'Yes, but only in outline,' I said, 'the corners and angles and interior spaces. And build them from two-by-one lashed together with string, so we can shift things if we need.'

'What, like the corners and the roof ridges?' Derek asked making lines in the air with his fingers.

'Yep, exactly. Okay?' I said. 'Then we can move around and plot what can be seen from the car, or smelled or heard.'

'So what *exactly* do you want me to do?' Jonathan asked a little more impatiently.

'You do the drawings showing us the lines of the buildings on the site.'

'What shall I base that on exactly?'

'Well, start with the layout we had for the small-scale model. But I want it more refined than that. That was a bit loose. So please work with Carolyn to get a finer positional fix on each building and the archaeologists' best guess at heights and so on to base the life scale model on.'

'And me?' asked Derek.

'I want you to go up to the newspaper offices and sniff around and borrow or steal one of those four wheel hand carts they use, the type that can be steered.'

'A hand cart?' said Derek.

'Yeah. We're off chaps, off at last. We're on the way to Jorvik.'

Even in those days, we could have constructed a simple three-dimensional virtual model on a computer that we could have 'flown' through. But there were two reasons I didn't want to. The first being we didn't have a computer or a programme to do it on and secondly and far more importantly, I wanted to travel in and through the model myself in real time and real space.

Next I went to see Carolyn.

'Carolyn, can you get on to those nice archaeological people in York and see if you can fix us up with a meeting with Dr Addyman next week sometime?' I was very excited about how things were unfolding in my concept design. What I wanted was a chance at this early juncture to bounce preliminary ideas off him, to make sure I was thinking in a direction that was okay with him. I wanted some feedback.

'What shall I say it's about?'

'Tell him it's to discuss time travel.' I was full of excitement over my ideas and forgot whom I would be addressing.

'Really? Oh, dear, you want me to say that?' she asked. 'That should be interesting.'

One of the absolutely astounding aspects about the Coppergate dig was the massive number of objects uncovered, over 40,000 from the period around 900 AD, which were preserved in the oxygen-deprived waterlogged ground. Many demonstrated striking evidence of a range of skills in their design and manufacture. What made the total spectrum of finds so exciting was that the collection included non-degradable artefacts like spoons, pottery, metalwork, brooches and bone combs. The archaeologists also discovered degradable items like shoes and other leather items, wood and textiles, which in many other conditions would have rotted away. Coppergate got its distinctive name from that time, twelve hundred years ago, because of the local production of wooden cups and bowls, 'street of the cup-makers'.

Another aspect was that the waterlogged ground had preserved environmental evidence like seeds, bones, shells, worms and parasites, even human waste. Data from this evidence enabled the archaeologists to envisage nigh on a totally complete localised world, in other words, a 3-D snap shot of daily life.

There were also the remains of timber houses and postholes where market stalls would have stood. All the timbers from these buildings had long since been removed from the archaeological site, which was now entombed in concrete beneath which a layer of sand protected the site for the future. This is what is done in rescue archaeology to protect the site for possible future exploration.

Most of the timbers, which consisted of uprights and horizontal planks, rose from the ground for a couple of feet or so and the floor plans which could be deduced showed that the structures were not much larger than the average garage today. The older ones were single story, a few, it was thought, might have had two storeys or at least a storage area in the rafters. And it was evident that they weren't all built the same. Carolyn explained further as we looked at the model that we based on the site plans.

'You see this one here? This one was semi-submerged, built in a pit. We reckon that was older. This one opposite was also half in a pit,' she said pointing into the model and referring us back to the site plan on the wall.

'Why were they sunk into the ground like that? They'd fill up with water, wouldn't they?' asked Derek.

'Well, we don't really know. Maybe they liked it, but it must have been flooded half the time because the rivers,' she indicated off the drawing, 'were just here and here. The Foss and the Ouse and they flood. Nobody really knows.'

'Ouse being the operative word,' said Jonathan. He went on, 'But these others were built up from ground level, that's right isn't it?'

'Yes,' said Carolyn, 'trouble is we don't know how high they were and we don't have any details for the roofs either.'

'Well, yes,' Derek interjected. 'But there are best guesses aren't there? And you know from the graves how tall some of the people were, so you're probably not far off in the model.'

'Yeah, we'll have to go with these projections, then we'll have to ask the advice of the experts,' I said. 'But for now, can you lash the frames together, don't put anything inside, but put the openings for the doors and make it so that the structures are separate and so that they can be moved.'

'I thought we weren't going to move them,' said Jonathan pointedly.

'Well, if it's down to a few inches we'll probably do it, if it makes the whole thing work better, hope not though. And anyway, we would have to check with you know-who-first,' I said.

I've always been fascinated with space and the way we seem to carry maps of things around in our heads. The buildings, represented only as lines made of wood and string, were constructed in the warehouse in a day. Immediately the effect was amazing. They were just outlines, but so much more, it was as though my mind filled in the voids. I could see the whole collection of buildings (there were seven as I recall) as though they were solid with small pathways between them.

After every one had left that night, I walked amongst the frames. It was already 'there' in this sparse and vacuous arrangement, a definite sense of place. I could almost hear the dogs barking and the babies crying. Then there was a noise.

'Got one.' It was Phoebe, wheeling in the hand truck. Derek had been a bit timid about nicking the truck. But if you asked Phoebe to go get a ballistic missile she would have gone out and got one.

'Great, right on time,' I shouted across the warehouse floor. 'Where'd you get it?'

'Don't ask, but it's only on loan.'

Carolyn came in. She'd stayed behind as well. Seemed they were getting the bug. 'Wow!' she said looking at the buildings. 'That's that then, it's done. It didn't take long.'

'Wish it was that easy,' I said.

Phoebe walked in amongst the frames. Looking round from inside one of the frames she said, 'It's funny, it feels like a place already but there's really nothing here.'

'Yes,' I said, 'it's peculiar. It's all in your head. I feel it too.'

'Well, it's six, we're off,' said Phoebe, 'and the others have gone.'

'Okay,' I said. 'I'll lock up. See you Monday.'

'Oh, before I forget,' said Carolyn, 'we're on with the archaeologists for two on Wednesday.'

'Was that plural? I thought we would just be seeing Peter? That's what I asked for.'

'Well, you know how he is. He said he wants you to tell his senior team your ideas. What could I say?' she said over her shoulder as she went through the door.

'Ah, right. Four days,' I muttered to myself. 'Okay. No problem.' I couldn't wait to tell them my ideas.

I stayed after the building emptied. I looked round the offices, checking that things were switched off. Funny, we'd just moved in a short while before but already the place was full of things our little team had deposited, creating their own spaces, colonizing the otherwise anonymous shed.

I thought, 'It's not going to be the buildings though, that will bring Jorvik to life. It's the things, the accidental things, the personal things, that will say 'people lived – or *live* here' like the full waste paper basket in the studio, the newspapers neatly folded on Jonathan's desk, the drying floral umbrella in the corner of Phoebe's room and the spare tie hanging from the coat hanger at the back of Colin's door, the ashtray emptied into his bin along with an empty pack of Embassy cigarettes. Little things, clues about the people who populate the place.'

'We're not that different today,' I said out loud.

I shut the door and went into the warehouse. The sound of my footsteps on the concrete floor echoed around the vault. It was getting dark so I switched on the overhead lights.

I walked around the outside of the frames and then between them. I looked at the angles from outside and in, imagined the solid walls and peered round corners as though I was travelling slowly in a car. It was surprising just how comfortable and familiar this small grouping of buildings felt. Maybe it was because we'd studied the plan and made a model.

What struck me was just how close the buildings were to each other. I wondered what it was like to live cheek-by-jowl like this with your neighbours, so close, just inches away. Did they all get on? How could they have had any privacy at all? What about when someone had a row with their spouse, or when they had sex, the houses were so small, and so packed together; it must have felt like one big family, like a shanty-town on the edge of some third world city, yet once here in York.

I wondered about the people and what they were like. How could we ever know for sure? We hadn't had the chance yet to be properly briefed by the environmental archaeologists, and they had to do that soon to help us understand better what daily life had been like based on the evidence. I felt like I needed to get close to the people of Jorvik and reach out to them, if we were going to bring the place to life.

What would they have been like? Would they have been like us? A thousand years isn't that long ago. Say a person lived an average of 50 years, that's only twenty lives. Then I imagined all those people holding hands in a winding line, stretching away across history. You could know all of them by name; they are your relatives stretching back or forward in time.

The hand truck was waiting for something to do. There was a stencilled sign on it, 'Property of The Wakefield Express.' I wondered if they knew Phoebe had nicked it. Sitting on one end I could steer from the back by holding the handle inching myself forward with my feet. I tried it out. I travelled at about the same rate I imagined the cars would go.

The placement of the buildings created a narrow alleyway between them. I knew from what Carolyn had explained that it was unlikely this gap had been a street, as we know it. Judging from all the remains of domestic waste that we knew had been found, it was more likely to have been a stinking rubbish pile over which people clambered to get to the well, the river or the cesspits. The average space between the buildings was only about four feet. What a filthy mess it must have been. There were no bin men to come round and clean up.

The cart was actually about the size I imagined the Time Cars would be. Slowly inching forward I spoke out loud to imagine passengers in the car.

'So here we are folks back in Jorvik a thousand years ago. Here on the left you see the launderette, and over there, the betting shop. And there in front is Tokis' Meat Pie Stall. Oh, and over here covered in embarrassment is old Tor on the loo recovering from last night's curry.'

I soon got an idea of the pace that the cars would have to travel, which I reckoned was about four inches per second, a speed that would not only match the pace of the commentary but the length and duration of the ride as well. This was an intuitive judgment and a good starting point. (It turned out to be exactly correct in the end.)

Because everything would be so close to the passengers, what was going to stop them from reaching out and touching and damaging things like the thatched roofs? It would be all too easy to grab handfuls of thatch and we'd soon have a bald exhibit. How could we stop them from doing that?

And then I stopped and thought; whilst I had been thinking of visitors being inside a bubble as a metaphor, in realty we'd have to make them feel like they *were* actually in a bubble to stop them from reaching out. Maybe we should make the cars like bubbles with a translucent skin. Then I said out loud, 'No, that would be putting them in a glass case, or rather the exhibit in a case. That's not what this is about.' Maybe, I thought, we could just have them *feel* like they're in one beyond the limit of which they should not reach. Okay, but how to do that?

Halfway down the alley between the houses I turned left and went through the side of the largest of the buildings. I tried to imagine what it would have been like to live in that small space. How many would have lived here? Where had they cooked? Where had they washed? Did the whole family live together along with the old ones and the babies? Did they have animals in the house with them? It was the largest, but still very small, about as big as a family-size frame tent.

I waddled my way through, getting a feel for the space, for the closeness and confinement. Would a family that lived so closely be *close* I wondered. They'd have to be. But no amount of evidence, environmental or otherwise could tell us that.

I thought we'd have to fill the interior space and the outside with everything the archaeologists could tell us had been there, but not in a formal sense. That would be ridiculous. For the visitors to feel a connection with the people we would have to model the reconstruction as though real people, not dummies, were living there. That frozen moment idea. Surely in such confined space life would have been messy, on top of each other, dirty, and smelly. Or maybe not, maybe in order to live cheek-by-jowl like this the inhabitants had to be organised and tidy. We would have to find out.

One thing I knew; things wouldn't be displayed, they'd appear to be where they would have been in a naturalistic way. It wouldn't be enough for us just to fill the interior with objects; we had to learn about the things that had been found and their uses so we could build them into the setting in a way that felt right to people of today. Fifty people away back in time was not so far. Had we changed that much?

What would it have been like to live with a grandfather who's deaf and complains all the time in such a tiny space, or worse who's demented and incontinent. All we really could do in the end was create a detailed and believably realistic setting and, with help from the archaeologists, speculate on what their lives were like, so that even the interior of this house would have its own story.

We'd have to create the people living their ordinary everyday lives. They'd be anything but stiff blank museum dummies; they'd look as though they had been stopped in motion, mid-sentence. Grandfather sitting over there (I imagined), his daughter and her daughter ignoring him as they sit cooking over the open hearth in the centre of the floor amongst the ashes, the smoke rising with the cooking smells and filling the roof-space with haze amongst the soot-blackened rafters.

Sound was going to be so important, a huge part of bringing this place to life. Our visitors would believe that these people were essentially like us, only in a different setting and a different time. That would mean that sounds would have to emanate spatially from their source; the chickens clucking, the fire spitting, kids laughing, granddad cursing, not just one generalised mixed track but specific sounds coming from specific things.

'We've got to think of you as real people,' I said to my imaginary company as I sat on the end of the cart. 'When I draw you,' I whispered, 'I'll draw you as though your lives are written in your faces and your hands. You will be characters with voices. You will have personality.' How to do that?

I'll write a screenplay, a plot for the Jorvik folks. I'll imagine what might have been going on amongst these houses and in the market at the end of the alleyway and down by the river's edge, and then imagine the people and what they were up to. Each would have a name and a family and things to do. I would write a piece for each describing who they were and what they were doing and their relationship to the other characters. That way they'll have intention.

More than dummies, they'll have lives and voices. Could I do that I wondered, give them all voices? There could be lots of characters. And then, I'd have to go further. What about the animals? What would they be up to? What about babies, what do babies do? They cry. What's more real than a crying baby?

'It's not going to be,' I said out loud to myself, 'just a reconstruction of a place, but a reconstruction of a community. Everybody here had a life, family, friends and enemies. This is *your* place; we're the aliens in this car, from another time, from the future. You can't see us, we're the invisible guests.'

Good job I was alone, I was talking to myself again. I was doing this more and more often in this planning stage.

I *also* had a life, though I was spending less and less time in it. And that weekend I wouldn't be a family man again. Now that I had the key and the perspective I was searching for and with a client meeting coming up in a few days, I had to stay detached, and 'in my head' as I used to say. Even as I apologized to Lynda for 'having to go into my head', it wasn't much comfort for her battling with the terrible twos all week. At least, with me under a three-year contract, we didn't have to worry about paying the next electricity bill.

There are many great things about being freelance and making your own way, but having to hide yourself away from a young family is not one of them. No matter how you spell it out, the emotional wrangle that goes on is hard on everybody. Worse than shutting myself in a room was that mentally I was already shut away. It's hard to describe what being in one's head feels like. But funnily enough both my first and my second wives described it as their husband having an affair with someone who lives in the house with you but that you can't scream at. What I didn't know and realised later was that I was developing an extremely valuable technique of envisioning.

When I was in that state, in my head, I was really in a different place, and not just focused in thought but with my own creative pregnancy. I'd almost got the whole thing down, but as yet hadn't got the whole. There was the Time Tunnel and the archaeological displays to work out. But I did have the central display, the core of it. I knew that, and I knew that the story would be the link from start to finish.

The worse thing when you are trying to stay focused is to have a row. But the worse than worse thing is to have a row *and* a migraine.

I used to suffer terribly with migraines, the killer pain sickening sort. My sight would become affected as the electrical storm in my head filled my vision with psychedelic flashing jellyfish swimming about and mutating. Then parts of my body would become numb or disassociated from the rest and then there would be an awful nausea. As bad as the attacks were, what made it worse was that they usually turned up at the end of an intense workweek.

I would invariably get an attack on Saturday morning. Somehow a change of pace and place would set the damn thing off, effectively ruining the weekend for everyone. Apparently this is common among migraine sufferers.

Well, luckily that didn't happen that Saturday, I was just too wound up to let the spring unravel inside my head. I sat in my room at home at my drawing desk and concentrated on the whole exhibition. What form would the Time Tunnel take and what would come after the reconstruction? It was all about time and its passage and being like a bridge. 'Going back in time' was a cliché, but no one had used it to describe a museum experience until we did. Or actually think of a museum as 'an experience'. You visited a museum; you didn't 'experience it'. A visit to Jorvik was going to change all that; it would be 'an experience' unlike anything else. What could we do to make it so people thought they were travelling back in time?

I sat there staring out of the window and wondered how far could *I* think back in time, back through the generations of my own family. I could get back to my grandma's older sister, kleptomaniac Auntie Annie who could empty a restaurant of its silverware before you finished your soup. And her husband Uncle George. After that there was a blank. I kept returning to that idea about the people holding hands, the fifty or so generation after generation, going back in time to York a thousand years before. That was it; so many Grandmas and Aunties connected us to the people who lived in Jorvik.

When I work and think like this I draw and write not in journals but on big, big sheets of paper, playing around with ideas seeing what appears creating a 'mind map' and if it's working, you see connections that you didn't see before. Drawing is magic and the pencil the magic wand sometimes. It's as though my subconscious has an outlet through the graphite on the white paper. Along with doodling I made lists of relevant things that might be peripheral, but were possibly and potentially connected.

My ideas sometimes appear fully formed in that beautiful bath-time burp, but more often I need to discover them on paper. Whichever way, the *obvious* ideas, the seemingly simple solutions, are so often the ones that took the greatest amount of effort to discover.

So it was with the design solution for the Time Tunnel; the answer was Grandmas. We're all linked and connected, the product of our time, our individual and collective past. Other periods before us can appear remote from our vantage point of the present, as though on another planet.

I felt it essential that our visitors should feel a direct connection with the people of Jorvik; that would make them more alive and real. The scribble on the pad suddenly became clear. The figures I was doodling for the settlement would be intent on their own thoughts and lives and interaction. Why not extend those people all the way back up the Time Tunnel to us, an unbroken line of people, from Jorvik of the past to York of the present. Realistically and naturally modelled, busy in thought and frozen in action and from different periods, passing through on their way to the future. And why not make an actual *tunnel* something that might actually run under a street and place with them in it; a conduit from the surface to the past, from the past to the present beneath the paving stones above? I knew it would work because it seemed so simply obvious.

But how would that tunnel begin? What would it look like? It's a metaphor, 'The Time Tunnel', like 'going back in time'; it could be awfully corny. How could the metaphor be represented without being corny? I didn't get the details, but I knew that once I had the other part of the big idea, the rest would come.

Okay, so that was two parts, the intro and the middle. What was the end? The missing gallery that the original schematic said would be devoted to archaeology.

I wrote on the sheet, 'Won't visitors want to know how Jorvik was reconstructed in such detail? Or would they assume it had all been made up, like a film set?' We have to show them how it was done, have to show them archaeology in process, and how information was gleaned from the evidence. Then another seemingly obvious thought popped into my head. 'We've taken them back in time. When we return them to the present we'll bring them slap bang into the archaeology, into the dig, where else? The archaeology is the portal!' It was so simple and it made sense. Well, to me anyway, would it to anyone else? That would depend on the story.

We'd make a reconstruction of the archaeological dig, the actual Coppergate dig, and create an exact replica with timbers, hearths and cesspits, standing sections, and also the equipment archaeologists used and the other stuff seen on a site, wellington boots and wheelbarrows. And wasn't there a Portakabin as well (a portable building hired by size and length of time you needed)? I reckoned that this in itself would be a fascinating introduction to the business of archaeology before going off the site and into the labs exhibit where the processes of conservation and examination were carried out. This then would create a natural link into the museum with its display cases of actual artefacts. It would be like having the two halves of the same nut in one nutshell. We would position preserved timbers where they'd originally been. The same as in the settlement; in fact we'd reconstruct every thing about the dig in detail. I slapped my pencil on the table; I knew I'd got it.

I sat there looking at the plan with my scribbles on it. It was all there; it had the perfect beginning and the perfect end. And like most stories, it had resolution, an ending where it all began, with science, curiosity and painstaking enquiry. I could see it all. Now I had to convince other people. What I needed now were the details.

Sunday lunch hadn't gone well. Lynda was tired and frustrated; it was the weekend and I was shut away again. Back in my room, the sounds of Thomas crying and Lynda's attempts to calm him played in the background through the door.

I was already deep in thought about how to make the reconstruction appear larger than what one half of the basement allowed for, when suddenly I heard Lynda's and Tom's voices in a different way. I imagined what they were doing and felt guilty about having to get back to work and my deadline when all of a sudden a vital connection occurred, one of those beautiful burps; their voices became the voices of Jorvik people. That gave me another idea.

The actual width of the entire reconstruction area was only about 35 feet, giving the false impression that this was a small settlement, complete in itself. It wasn't, because it was a neighbourhood, a small part of a much larger city with a population estimated between 10,000 and 30,000. Our reconstruction would show only a tiny fragment of Jorvik, the city that was at the heart of the Danish colony called the Danelaw.

The Vikings first arrived on the Northumbrian coast in the late eighth century and subsequently conquered a swathe of land and tribes from the east coast to the west of England. This was due to their ability to sail their shallow drafted ships in small numbers or in great fleets to the northern coasts or via tidal estuaries and rivers deep into the interior and turn up often without prior warning.

Eburacum (the Roman name for York) was well connected to the sea by river. Four hundred years later under Viking rule it became so successful a location that it became the capital of the Viking Danish colony. It became the main base for trade and communications with the motherland back in Denmark. The Vikings travelled by water in their open vessels from Jorvik along the river Ouse to the Humber estuary and then across the North Sea, a voyage that held no fear for such accomplished mariners.

As it thrived over time the indigenous Saxon people and the Vikings inter-married. It was a big place. How could I get over that idea, that such a large population lived cheek-by-jowl with each other?

I stood up by my window looking out over the expanse of the Calder Valley, over stubbly fields and flooded gravel pits. The wind was blowing hard across it as a few seagulls fought to make a headway.

How to create the sense of a much bigger place? The answer had to be in somehow fooling the visitor's perceptions. Beyond my door, Tom was crying because Lynda was trying to settle him down for an afternoon nap. They were two rooms away yet I understood what was going on even though I couldn't see them. As I listened I reckoned what I could hear suggested two things; the first was an emotional response to what was going on, and secondly, I had a sense of space and place. And there was something else; the wail of a young child *demands* attention.

That gave me the third great idea. We could create the illusion of a much larger space through sound – a dog barking somewhere distant, heard but not seen; seagulls, a cockerel crowing in a backyard, the sound of the breeze as rigging smacks against masts, water lapping by the edge of the river, pigs grunting and squealing, geese hissing – environmental sounds backed by archaeological evidence. Such sounds combined with human voices would create a sense of a larger community beyond what the visitors could actually see. We could pull the illusion off because visitors would be seated in the Time Cars, in their personal bubbles, not exploring on foot. Sound would contribute massively in achieving the *suspension of disbelief*.

As I looked down at the plan with these thoughts in mind, I kept repeating to myself, 'Remember each passenger is in a film, moving through it adding up everything as they go, building an illusion of greater space in their minds.'

It was falling into place with another breakthrough idea. The biggest, mind-numbing space-planning problem that had defeated the architects and everyone else up to that point was where to put the battery-powered Time Cars that had to be recharged every night. Besides that, there had to be a place where regular maintenance could be carried out and somewhere for storage of superfluous vehicles. Then there were the technical systems along with the security control station from where staff would monitor what was going on. All this was going to take a considerable amount of room. Up until now there hadn't appeared to be space for any of it.

But, with the notion that we could create the illusion of space and depth, I looked again but from a different perspective at the architects' floor plan that now combined the locations of the 10th century buildings. Picking up my pencil I laid a sheet of tracing paper over it and ran a curving line that I reckoned would be pretty much the route of the cars through the reconstruction. I had a feel for it now after my voyage of discovery on the handcart the night before.

Imagining what the passengers would see from their viewpoints in the car, I roughly calculated the viewing angles from the line of travel and did a number of little scene sketches at various locations along the route (in effect a storyboard).

The answer was there, the one that literally could not be seen. Roughing in a straight line through the buildings on the right-hand side of the reconstruction, the space we needed appeared. It was inside the reconstructed buildings. It had been there all the time; the answer was sublime.

Next I drew a long oblong corridor from one end of the exhibit space to the other, with access at either end through one of the riverside warehouses. The cars could shunt in at the end of the day after delivering the last of the day's visitors and shunt out at the start of the day through a disguised door in a warehouse that stood by the river at the other end.

The space in the corridor would be narrow but wide enough. With a little more sketching I could see that all the control facilities would also fit inside. I sat back, wishing I had someone to share this with at that moment. I have to tell you; when an idea works like that, revealing itself on the sheet at the end of your pencil and it all comes together, it's such a pleasure. I was cock-a-hoop. Another wonderful thing; my scheme didn't adversely affect the original archaeological layout. It was like having your archaeological cake and eating it too, only out of sight.

'I'm just going down to the warehouse,' I shouted to Lynda as I hurried towards the door across the hall with my sketches and a tape measure under my arm. Thomas was playing toddler football in the hall.

'We have to go to the supermarket,' shouted Lynda. 'We have friends tonight, remember?'

'Oh, yeah, right.' I was pulling on my coat and getting my car keys from the hook by the door. 'I'll just be half an hour, all right an hour. It's important,' I shouted back.

She appeared at the door, looked down at Tom who just kicked the football towards me.

'It's always important, John. But what's more important than this? Here Tom, kick the ball to Mummy. Daddy's busy again.'

I climbed in my brand-new bright yellow pre-owned MGB, looked at my watch and sped off. I said to myself, 'An hour, one hour John. Got to be back or I'm dead.'

It was 1:30pm on Saturday as I went to open the main doors at the warehouse. Surprisingly, they were unlocked. I went in.

'Hello, who's here?' I shouted.

'Hi, it's only me.' It was Derek.

'What are you doing here? It's Saturday, and how did you get in?'

'Oh, Sandra's taken the kids to her sister's for the weekend. I thought I'd come over and just finish this. I got some keys just in case,' he said lashing up another piece of wood to frame a window where it appeared in Jonathan's plan.

'I don't think Colin's paying overtime.'

'I don't care. This is more interesting than being stuck at home and there's only football on the telly.'

I thought, 'He's as obsessed as I am.'

'Well great! You've nearly done. Listen; do you think you could help me with something else? I'm trying to work out the route of the car.'

Derek was all for helping and being involved. He pushed and steered the cart through the buildings with me on top at a speed of about four inches a second as I focused on just what could be seen en route from the same height of the average adult. I noted exactly what could be seen of the buildings on both sides, and marked it down on the site plan next to me.

Every now and then I asked him to stop, pull me back and try a slightly different route. We could do that because although the buildings stood exactly where they had, we had some latitude in the movement and track of the car.

'Now, turn left here, keep it slow and go in through this wall.'

'Inside?'

'Yeah.'

'What, through the building? Great!' he exclaimed. It was just a bunch of sticks tied together with string but he was as excited as I was. Who needed virtual computer modelling?

By going over the route like this I was able to check the ideas for location of the 'garage' and confirm they worked. By the end of the exercise, I reckoned we could create an eight-foot wide completely hidden corridor, the full length of the recon-struction with a couple of small rooms. And, no one would know they were there.

'So, what are you doing on the plan?' asked Derek. I hadn't told him what I was checking.

'I'm just trying out a new idea. Can I tell you next week when I've worked it out? But,' I said with a big smile as I folded the plan, 'I think we've cracked it, mate!'

Then I thought suddenly of Lynda.

'Oh, no,' I said looking at my watch.

When the car slid to a halt on the gravel in the drive, I saw the note pinned to the front door. I was only ten minutes late and her car was gone. So that weekend I stayed well and truly *buried beneath the streets of York* and planned out the whole thing in detail.

At the beginning of the week I met with Colin and went over my new ideas. Thankfully, he liked them. We'd soon be ready to present the coherent plan. For that presentation, the big one, we needed to pull out all the stops and carry the day. In the meantime, we agreed it was best not to give the whole game away just yet because there were many details to work out and I didn't know if what I was thinking would in fact work. So for the earlier meeting I'd present only the concept for the Time Tunnel and tell them that this was a taster for the comprehensive presentation that was coming shortly.

Colin agreed, adding dryly, 'Don't forget,' as he lit a cigarette in that easy way he had. 'Peter doesn't suffer fools easily. Better have your act together, and try to stay grounded, will you?'

'Don't worry, Carolyn's coming,' I said. 'She'll translate me into "it-makes-sense archeo-speak". It'll be okay. Look, I've got to get them involved in the creative and theory side of this too. They've got to go with the ideas or what do we have? A bunch of sticks.'

He blew out the smoke. 'Okay, but for God's sake John, don't blow it. I've just got final confirmation that the shareholders are on board.'

'I'll stay grounded, I promise.'

'Go on,' he said. 'You'll be the death of me.'

I set Jonathan on doing more technical drawings of the inclusion of the hidden garage and workshops, which I explained to him. He liked the idea and I knew he'd improve on it, because as he might whistle and blow, he was a damn good designer.

Meanwhile Carolyn was busy keeping up lines of communication with the archaeologists open and along with Phoebe researching smaller artefacts and tracking down people who could make them for us. Every object, all the leather and the cloth, things like cooking utensils and personal things like bone combs and jewellery that could be incorporated and for which there was evidence, would be accurately reproduced. In doing this her regular contacts with the YAT team was building up a level of confidence that we were in fact applying ourselves in the right way.

She spoke up as we were driving over to York.

'Are you nervous?' she said adding, 'Hope this goes well?'

'It's going to be all right. Anyway we're not going to give them a presentation, we're going to talk about concepts for the Time Tunnel.' Carolyn turned to me.

'You know John, *you* might not be nervous, but I am and *they* are,' she said turning to me. 'They're not all sold on this job, *us*, or you! Some of them think it's just not what they should be doing. Some of them think that their careers are being put on the line.'

'It must look like they're going into show business,' I said by way of agreement. 'They'll think differently if it's a big hit and it makes lots of money.'

'See, the problem is, John,' she went on, 'some of them are nervous because if it fails, they'll all be laughing stocks. But equally they're nervous that if it turns out to be success, they may be screwed too because what will it do to the Trust?'

'Well,' I replied as we turned off the bypass, 'in that case we'll never win.'

'See if you can make sense today in terms of what they'll get. That'll give them confidence, you know, practical, factual and down to earth. That's who they are.'

I was so full of the rightness of the way I was thinking that I didn't heed hers or Colin's warnings. I was cocksure that I had it. I didn't have the details yet but I knew they were on their way.

I remember as we went in to the meeting that it felt like a courtroom with Dr Addyman sat in judgment. His senior colleagues, including Dr Richard Hall, who had been the Director of the Coppergate dig and who would now, we were informed, be keeping a very strict eye on what we were up to, came over as intensely serious and humourless. (He wasn't at all once I got to know him, but that's how I saw him that day).

All my cockiness drained away, as the archaeologists appeared like prosecutors grimly arrayed looking down on us. There wasn't a smile on a face in the place. I wasn't so confident any more.

'So, John, we want to hear your ideas,' Dr Addyman said. I explained we hadn't come to give them the comprehensive presentation; that didn't go down too well. Neither was my attempt to explain what I meant by a 'data bridge' and 'going back in time' and what the Time Tunnel represented philosophically, as I didn't have the physical design for the Time Tunnel yet.

If I hadn't been so bloody nervous and intimidated in front of scholars I would have had more confidence to pull off an explanation of the foundation for my design approach. Instead, what came from my lips sounded to them like complete twaddle. I tried to explain my concepts, how 'the bridge' made a type of time travel possible through information. I talked about how I would create a 'suspension of disbelief' and, not to mention, visitors being like ghosts and time standing still etc. etc. The more I talked about these concepts the deeper into a cesspit of my own making I sank. It's a wonder they didn't start throwing artefacts. They couldn't help but to think in concrete terms and they just could not wrap their heads around my creative abstract ideas, ideas that were necessary for me to establish the foundation of the design solution.

When Carolyn stepped in supportively with phrases like, 'What John's trying to say', and 'What I think he means is', she got verbally slapped down too, joining me in the mire. I could see they were each saying to themselves, 'We have employed someone who's going to ruin my career.'

After I dried up and after a short pause, an ashen-faced Dr Addyman spoke. 'I have never heard such unmitigated claptrap in all my life. We asked you here to give you the opportunity to present your concrete plans, not gibberish! Go away and don't come back until you have something worthwhile to tell us.'

It was awful. I knew that we had so much more to tell them, but I had promised Colin to hold it back till the big presentation. I went into that meeting full of the creative joys of spring and came out with my ego in tatters, designer tail between my quaking legs and completely embarrassed in front of Carolyn, and worse, wondering whether I'd wrecked the project for all of us.

There was silence in the car on the way back for a long while. My passenger sat in mute silence staring out the window at the scenery. Then she spoke up. 'That could have gone better.' A masterful understatement if ever there was one.

We were back in an hour, by which time Colin had had a phone call; he looked as grim as Peter Addyman had done.

'I've just had a call from Peter,' he said. 'To put it mildly you didn't go across very well and they want us to do a full presentation in two weeks. Can you do it? I must say John, I got the impression from Peter that if we don't carry it off, the whole thing's off, or, *you* personally may be out of it.'

'Yeah, we can,' I said. 'I was trying to explain the thinking behind the concepts, but they just wouldn't go there. They didn't understand or want to understand, Colin, that's what it seemed like. Look,' I said, 'it was a mess but I have learned a lesson. I will make it right for the next presentation.'

'Better bloody do! That's what you said before.'

Coppergate Dig late 1970s rescue archaeology underway by York Archaeological Trust

Richard Hall, Director of the Coppergate Dig at work on the site

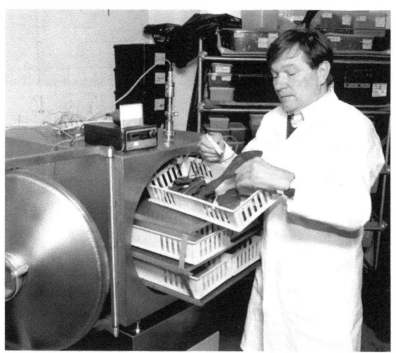

Jim Spriggs in conservation lab

Viking shoe

Anglian helmet found in cesspit after conservation

Dice

Wooden bowls

Viking comb, frying pan, dice

Images © York Archaelogical Trust

Design and build team in 1982, from left bottom - John, Carolyn, Phoebe. Top row from left Colin, Jonathon, Bob, Graham, Derek

Building frames with goose lady in warehouse

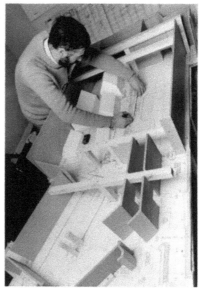

Jonathan at work on final model

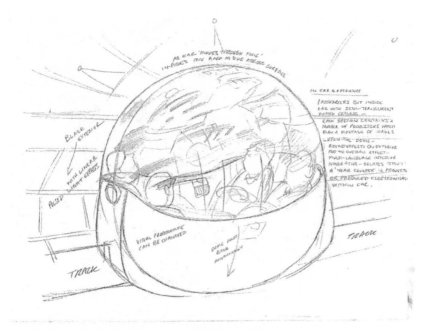

Early idea for Time Car design that puts visitors in a Sensurround bubble

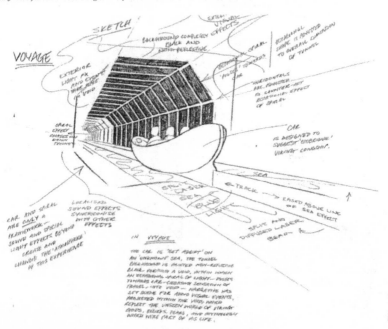

Concept sketch for tunnel made of ship timbers and Time Car designed as boat

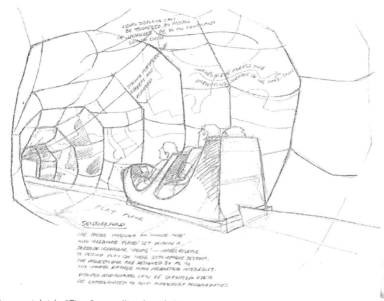

Early concept sketch of Time Car travelling through time

Early concept sketch of starting platform cellar

Foundations for dig site reconstruction

Dig site reconstruction with cesspit and original toilet seat in right-hand corner

Reconstruction of wattle and daub house with fireproofed thatch panel for roof in foreground

Wattle and daub house interior with family figures including old man from sketch

Wood and bone workers market stall with woman haggling over price © York Archaelogical Trust

Colin and wife Judy, son Mark and daughter Becky test driving a Time Car

8 MORE THAN A FRYING PAN

IT WASN'T ALL DOOM AND gloom. Before the presentation date came round we had other encounters with the archaeologists on their turf in York, some who had been there at the meeting who quietly on the side said they'd got what I was on about and liked it.

Hence when we went on our group visit the atmosphere wasn't as icy as it might have been, especially as we requested the visit ourselves. It was fascinating being guided around the conservation laboratories where they used sophisticated techniques for preservation of the large finds and woodwork from the buildings housed there. So were the environmental archaeology labs, where organic materials were under the microscope. All in all, a big thing for us was that for the first time there was a collective feeling among everyone that we were embarked on creating the most ambitious and pioneering exhibition; something truly ground breaking.

What we were shown that afternoon greatly affected us, as well as talking face to face with the archaeologists, who were as passionate about what they were doing as we were.

We took photographs to add to our own data bank for reference, especially small details that would make a huge difference to the authenticity of the reconstruction. We learned a great deal about the process of bringing the past to life through archaeology.

A big problem we faced in building the reconstruction was the restrictions on the use of combustible materials. That meant that the easiest option to construct the buildings out of wooden planks was not an option (not yet to mention the thatched roofs). So we discussed alternatives with the archaeologists and how we needed to study the plans and poles from the actual buildings so that we could find a way to replicate them.

Then we talked to them about the roofing materials. Seeds among the archaeological dig had been found to be attributable to reeds. Reeds would have been readily available growing in surrounding marshes. We had to find a modern source of the same variety of reeds and find a way of ensuring the thatched roofs wouldn't burst into flame at the click of a cigarette lighter, as people in the cars could easily reach out to the thatch from the Time Cars.

Such concerns aside, we were shown hundreds and hundreds of finds; leather shoes and combs made from horn, jewellery and coins, belts and buckles, pots and iron pans. There were tools and spindles, yarns and fragments of cloth all miraculously intact, just like out of your kitchen. That afternoon the distance in time between them and us shrank. The people of Jorvik came alive from what we were shown. Being immersed in the world of archaeology, we were not only learning how to work together with the archaeologists, but we were also learning how to relate with the people of the past.

Having said that, it was my job to take these things, macro and micro, out of the display case and bring their story to life. That would be a creative interpretive process.

The tour continued. From inside drawers and special storage boxes, we were shown beads and bangles, wooden trugs for making bread and torcs made of twisted metal for wearing around the neck. Then it was lunchtime in Jorvik, pig and chicken bones, oyster shells, dog bones and cows' teeth, seeds and grains, nutshells and fish bones. You could smell the cooking.

I was captivated by how some objects brought you, as it were, so close to the original owner. For example, the collection of barrel locks for securing chests. You had to wonder what was it they regarded as so valuable that they had to lock it up, their daughters?

But for me at least the most telling objects were the down to earth everyday objects like spoons and goblets made from horn and pottery jugs, and bone pins for fastening cloaks and leather pouches. And even remnants of the moss dropped into cesspits, the 10th century equivalent of toilet paper. Imagine going to the supermarket for half a dozen roles of double-ply moss.

Double-ply is one thing, but 'coprolites' (the scientific term for turds) came as a bit of a surprise. They had been preserved like everything else in the wet oxygen-deprived layers. We learned that 10th century poo spoke volumes about daily life, their diet and how healthy the individual was, for, as we were shown, the coprolites were loaded with intestinal bugs.

But wasn't there something missing? Where were the warriors? Had they disappeared completely from the culture? And then it appeared. The 'crown' of finds astonishingly recovered from the bottom of a cesspit was a warrior's helmet, what became known as 'The Jorvik Helmet'.

An extraordinary object, it was not quite complete and was undergoing restoration when I first saw it. But even in its damaged form, the helmet (which turned out to be 8th Century Anglo-Saxon and not Viking) nevertheless spoke volumes of battles and glory, machismo, muscle and murder. But why had it been thrown into a cesspit? I could just hear them.

'I'm telling you, if you go off raping and pillaging again Tor when it's your turn to baby-sit, I'm chucking your helmet down somewhere you won't want to find it!'

Unfortunately, we weren't allowed to hang onto the real thing. It belonged to the City of York and much to our collective chagrin was handed over to them for later display at the Yorkshire Museum. But before it was, our clever clients had a hologram made of it. Holograms were a novelty in themselves at the time; so rather than detracting from the real thing, in my view, the hologram on display at the end of the artefacts gallery served to enhance the power of the attraction of the original. I have often wondered if this was the first case of a virtual image hijack?

Of all the things recovered, the frying pan was my personal favourite, a beautiful iron object as blackened with use as with the thousand years it had spent buried. I was able to touch it and lift it up. It was really heavy with a long handle. Made by a skillful smith, it was an object used so often that frying breakfasts had worn a hole in it. And then it had been mended and used again. Such a pan had been a valuable domestic asset, so when it eventually wore through it had gone back to the smithy to have the hole expertly patched. When I first saw it I swear I could smell Danish bacon frying.

The archaeologists passed on their enthusiasm and their passion for their work as they explained their finds. They were the real 'Time Detectives' building that bridge in time from here to then. One that I met was really inspiring. He was about my age and a wonderful enthusiast. Dr 'Bone' Jones as he was known in archaeological circles was a populist too. He wanted to spread the word about the educational value of archaeology. Here was one archaeologist I found I could talk to on equal terms. Bones (as I called him) had been present at my roasting but had said nothing. Later on, on a one-to-one basis, I opened up to him and shared all my ideas. He loved the approach and got really excited. Bones was to become a friend and ally. Whilst some of the senior archaeologists could come over as being rather stuffy and reserved, Bones was totally approachable. And although he displayed a fabulous range of eccentricities in his dress, and manner and speech, he was as down-to-earth as I was. He loved to tell stories, share a pint or two and talk and laugh.

About this time an amusing coincidence occurred. The first Spielberg film, *Raiders of the Lost Ark* had been released starring Harrison Ford, who played the part of the adventurous and fearless archaeologist Doctor Jones. Though I never saw Bones being chased down the shambles by a tribe of blow-darting Amazonian pigmies, I imagined he had extraordinary adventures of his own, as both he and his cinematic alter ego wore bow ties. It couldn't have been just a coincidence. Sadly, I never did see Bones pull out his bullwhip.

With the presentation of the whole scheme coming up, I was now drawing up more detailed plans for the whole exhibition and what exactly each connected area would contain.

If the scheme was accepted as presented, then we were going to need a considerable number of life-size figures and animals; dogs, gulls, geese, pigs and piglets, which there was plenty of evidence for and which I intended to have in the reconstruction along with the people. Like them, the creatures would have to appear as though frozen in a stopped frame of life. The animals could have been modelled out of glass fiber or plaster, but I decided first to investigate the real thing – taxidermy.

One of the many great things about my job was the extraordinary people I got to meet. I was about to meet another. I continued to look for talent close to home. Here it's worth repeating that in the early 1980s specialised businesses that produced figures, costumes, props and reconstructed artefacts were very rare and, at that time, certainly not to be found in the North of England. What we were producing was new; we were creating an original genre of presentation. It meant finding uniquely talented people, like the taxidermist I was about to meet.

My search led me to a young bloke called Dave Astley. He was already quite famous in his own way in and around York because not only was he an artist whose medium was taxidermy, he was also the singer in a punk rock band. That's how he got the nickname The Punk Stuffer. I found his phone number, fixed up a meeting and drove out to his workshop in a little village just outside York

He came out to meet me at the gate. He wasn't a big man; he was quite skinny and wiry with really sharp distinct features, crow-like in fact, with a great tangled mane of black hair. When I met him face to face for that first time I realised I'd seen him elsewhere, on a poster on the wall of a café advertising a gig his band was playing. I remembered him because the poster featured a bizarre image, Dave naked but for a loincloth perched in a thorn tree.

There was something of the faerie kingdom about him in that poster. I imagined he lived under a rock in the woods, not in the very ordinary semi-detached bungalow in which he actually lived, with a shed in the back where he did his 'stuffing'.

We immediately hit it off. His enthusiasm was infectious. I think he was as close as a person could be to being a wizard. As I soon saw, he could take a dead and broken creature and breathe life into it. Once I saw some examples of his work I was convinced we had to have him on the team.

Dave was touchingly sensitive towards nature and wouldn't dream of performing taxidermy on animals which had been killed for sport. Nearly all of his subjects had been found or were accidentally killed on the road.

In his shed, he showed me a host of creatures stored in a big freezer, beautiful even in death. I wondered if he had a few Vikings in there amongst the voles and the owls, but didn't ask. Looking into a freezer full of dead animals was weird enough, especially as I couldn't rid myself of the image of him in a loincloth perched in that tree.

I hadn't been absolutely sure that taxidermy was the way to go; I thought there was something unsavoury and even macabre about it and hadn't at first seen it mixing in with everything else. That's not how I felt after my visit and once I saw how he treated his subjects. Not only did he skillfully put the fallen creatures in life-like poses in wonderful micro natural settings that he also modelled, but he somehow managed to capture the life-spirit of the animal itself. It was amazing. His subjects appeared so alive that I found myself whispering, not wanting to scare them. In fact his taxidermy further confirmed that the *frozen moment* approach was the right way to go.

There was one nagging question, however, at the back of my mind. The animals we were likely to include – dogs, cats, geese, chickens, pigs, mice and rats, where would he get them? On that first meeting in the shed I decided to leave that question till later. But still I couldn't help thinking how bad it would be for the project if some old dear from York on her trip round the exhibit came across her missing terrier.

Dave was very keen on joining the team and felt he could contribute, as he did, far more. Whilst I was marvelling at his taxidermy and the brilliant natural settings he created, I wondered what material he used to make things like the small wooden section of a barn on which a barn owl perched. Or the brick and broken plaster from which a mouse was emerging. It was so amazingly naturalistic. I asked him what he used.

'Oh, that's my magic material. It's a bit of a trade secret actually.'

The recipe didn't stay a secret for long. He was glad to share it with us once he was onboard. His magic mix used old newsprint first soaked in water then whisked until the wood fibers in it freed up. When it turned into a thick soup he added resinous fibrous plaster and stirred it all up again until it became a gluey shapeable mass with a consistency of bread dough. This could be moulded, shaped, cut into and worked on to produce surface textures. Then he coloured them with water-based paint that the material absorbed so it could be adjusted after-the-fact if needed. It was brilliant stuff, very strong and non-combustible even though there was the paper in it.

Our 'Punk Stuffer' was definitely a find. He was to stay with us all the way through the construction. Following the opening he was given a contract by the Centre management to take care of the exhibits. Ironically, he ended up making not tiny reconstructed worlds in which his creatures sat, perched, or flew, but one as big as a housing estate.

So that was that. The animals were sourced. What about the bipeds?

Finding the *right* sculptor for the life-size human figures was very much on my mind. He or she had to be in tune with the overall vision and work in a malleable style that fitted in with everything else in the reconstruction *and* be a team player. I didn't want a prima-donna artist on the job.

Instinctively I felt we needed a sculptor who expressed humanity or *human-ness* through his work along with a sort of earthiness. If there was such a spark in the figures I felt they'd be more realistic to our audience and not just a bunch of museum dummies. Up to that point I had never ever seen sculpted figures specially created for use in museum displays. They were almost always shop dummies in stiff unrealistic poses staring blankly from painted eyes like they were selling dresses in a Marks and Spencer window.

I came across the sculptor Graham Ibbeson by serendipity. Lynda and I with Tom, now a rambunctious post toddler, visited a gallery in Scarborough where unknown to us Graham's work was on show.

As soon as we went into the galleries, Tom yelled in surprise and delight and ran over to one of Graham's startling pieces standing in the centre of the gallery. The seaside was a good place for Graham to have an exhibit because it provided much of his inspiration. Graham, like me and most Northern kids of our generation, were taken to the coast for days out and holidays. I was going to use the word resorts but in the fifties and sixties you would hardly describe Bridlington on Yorkshire's east coast as a 'resort'. Back then it was a dump with sand and a bad smell of fish.

Bridlington, Scarborough, and on the west coast, Blackpool and Morecambe, all served up the usual seaside fare; lettered rock, fish and chips and amusements. Amusements of the illustrated kind came in the form of postcards. Shops lining the beach always had displays on racks with that salty blend of 'cheeky chappie humour;' little man looking around the beach says to shocked woman, 'Have you seen my little Willy?'

Graham had his fair share of exposure to the delights of northern seaside humour and it resulted in him producing three-dimensional versions in that postcard style but with his own storyline. The one that Tom ran over to and started climbing on was called *The Lost Platoon*. It depicted four plump rosy-cheeked boy scouts crowded on a little plinth, in the centre of which was a signpost that pointed to the horizon in four different directions, but still they were lost. The scouts were searching for the right way to go. Doesn't sound all that funny or charming written down, but it was really amusing to see and was created with a loving nostalgia. The other immediate impression was that it was so far away from the mainstream serious sculpture and rather than being abstract in form it was surreally humanistic.

Graham seemed to have combined the seaside postcard style with memories of his own childhood growing up in Barnsley, South Yorkshire. *Very Barnsley* was another life-size piece, a woman with pink rollers and pink fluffy slippers ironing her drunken husband on an ironing board with his arms and legs hanging over the edge, one hand still holding onto a bottle of beer. You couldn't take your eyes off it.

All the figures had a common and familial inbred look, as though they were directly related to their maker and each other. I liked that look; I thought that's probably how it must have been in Jorvik.

The gallery we were in had lots of serious art. But it was Graham's figures that were engaging because they were anything but serious; in truth they were a million miles away from Vikings and serious museums. But I thought, if he could step back from caricature and model figures for us that had that same earthy real-life family feel, then he could be the sculptor I was looking for.

Barnsley folk spoke in such a strong dialect it was as though they came from a different planet – Planet Barnsley, a town of strong working-class identity and still very much a mining town, at least in spirit. I could hardly understand Graham at first when I phoned to make a date to meet up. His speech was full of 'thees' and 'thous' and 'thissens'. I'd gone to school with lots of lads from there. Still, it was a long time ago and as I drove over with Carolyn to Barnsley for our first meet, I hoped not too much would be lost in translation.

His address was at the end of a terrace of large redbrick Edwardian houses and appeared normal from the outside; but that impression didn't last long.

From the gate we could see into a yard. Incongruously it was stacked with all kinds of fabulous junk; old prams, televisions, standard lamps, three legged wobbly chairs and pieces of weirdly strange un-completed figures that had never made it into a gallery. The sight was a cross between a funfair, junk shop, and one of those bad dreams where you are being chased by something very nasty with a big smile on its face. It was a drizzly grey day and cold. We watched as tears of sooty rain ran down the faces of the grinning clowns.

Ignoring the sign on the gate which read 'Beware of the Wolf' we climbed the steps to the back door and rang the bell, Carolyn is brave, that's why she stood in front. Graham soon appeared after shouting at a loudly barking dog. It wasn't just the dog that was intimidating. I saw Graham as he approached the glass-paneled door and he looked rough and tough too. I thought I mustn't get on the wrong side of this bloke or I'll be dog meat.

He was large and solid with an oily flat pancake cap and looked just like his figures. But for all his Bluto bulk I soon discovered that he was incredibly shy and self-conscious. He even blushed as he opened the door and stayed bright pink all the way through that first meeting with rosy cheeks like the lost scouts.

After pulling on his boots and an old jacket over his oily boiler suit he stepped out with me into the yard and into his weird and wonderful workshop. He unlocked the door as we went in and locked it again when inside. I stood there in the dark until he turned on the light; a neon strip flickered into life overhead.

I looked around. I was in a demented Santa's workshop full of finished and unfinished figures and parts of sets and moulds. Unidentifiable things hung in the shadowy roof rafters whilst below strange shiny fairground faces peered out of the gloom; like Graham, their fat red cheeks aglow.

At the back of my mind I couldn't help but wonder if I had voluntarily trapped us in a shed with a burly nutcase on the set of a horror film. Somewhat nervously I asked him about what he did and why he did it. His explanation made wonderful sense; he'd always loved the art of cheeky seaside postcards and childhood day-trips spent amongst rock shops and amusement arcades, and that had become his muse.

That day I trusted my instinct. There was something about his work and him. Though he obviously suffered from a terrible shyness, he nonetheless felt right for the project.

He was more relaxed in his local pub and after the first pint of Tetley's Bitter. Some of the regulars nodded as we went into the snug, Graham replied with a collective 'Eyupp'.

Though he didn't look out of place in his boiler suit and oily flat cap, The Oak was the sort of pub where you might be lynched if you ordered a Campari and soda. So I couldn't help wondering if the regulars had any idea of what he did for a living. He said he never had a problem (a vital necessity as he loved a pint or five at his local) because nobody had ever asked, most likely because he looked like a plumber and like the others he never took his cap off. And besides he smelled of resin and always had dirty hands and a big hairy dog that liked pork scratchings.

Once again I struck gold in the talent stakes; but would he be interested in such a demanding, all-consuming job? I assumed he might be struggling a bit financially as his workshop looked a bit run down. I was right. When I asked him if he could produce twenty-five life-size figures in twelve months (not an easy task), he thought for about a nanosecond then replied 'Alreet', and got a round in to celebrate.

At the back of my mind was the idea that we should commission him first to produce a trial figure, for which he'd be paid if he got the full commission. 'Aye, alreet,' he said again, scratching underneath his cap and passing some scratchings to his dog that still hadn't taken his eyes off me.

As we drove back over the border from Barnsley towards Wakefield I wondered if I was going too far out on a limb. I thought it unfortunate that he didn't have any more naturalistic figures to show; the ones in the workshop all looked like they belonged amongst the donkeys on Scarborough beach. So the trial piece was essential. I suspected our clients wouldn't approve if the population of Jorvik looked like characters from seaside postcards. I could see the headline:

'*Archaeologists of York Turn National Treasure Into One Big Joke.*' Plus, I only had his personal assurance upon which to base my own promise to Colin that one man could produce all our Jorvik figures for the reconstruction in time for the opening in the spring of 1984. It was a really tremendous amount of work for one person to undertake. What if he died? He did sweat a lot. Again, I trusted my intuition and hoped for the best.

There were just a couple of days left before the client presentation. Though I was a little apprehensive I felt I now had all my ducks in a row and a coherent master plan. This really was the big one; we had to show we knew what we were doing and get the client totally on board with our approach.

There were still areas I wasn't completely sure of. Still, I was more confident than before that the overall thing made sense and felt I was now ready to sell it to the clients. Armed with plans and visuals, I wouldn't make the same mistake I made just a couple of weeks before. My drawings would speak louder than my words.

Colin had also gone over the master plan and was happy, and so were Jonathan and Carolyn. Colin said that if we got the go-ahead to start the fabrication work based on these plans, I could give Graham the green light to start on the trial figure.

If all went well, then we'd move into the production design phase and start planning to make the move from Wakefield into the concrete box in York, which would be available to us by February of 1983, five months away.

9   SO MANY GRANDMAS

For the presentation, which we planned to stage on home ground at the warehouse, I swore on another stack of bibles to Colin that I'd keep to the plan and not wobble off into verbal quicksand. I intended to use story-telling techniques that involved a series of 'reveals' and engage my audience's natural curiosity, just like the visitors in the cars. This would also keep me on track.

I produced large black and white illustrations by hand that I covered with white paper and wouldn't reveal until my presentation was at that point of the story. This I expected would keep everyone focused and interested in seeing what would come up next. I figured that if the archaeologists couldn't relate to my ideas with words only, these visuals surely would help. Also worth mentioning is that this would be the first time members of my own production team would see the whole scheme laid out too. So, if it was a disaster they could all come to the stoning together.

On the day of the presentation, with the archaeologists and our team arranged around a display of master plans and covered visuals mounted on the wall, my aim was to tell them a story about *their* story, talking them through the plans as though they were visitors in the cars. My hope was to create pictures in their heads. This is how it went . . . .

'If it's okay with everyone, I'd prefer to run all the way through the plan and take questions at the end,' I said.

This was the first time I had put the thing together in one complete scenario and I felt that customary buzz of nerves. The same faces that had been at our last meeting were there with the addition of Anthony the project manager. Their expressions as I started were blank in a way that said to me, 'This had better be good.'

'The overall exhibition is divided into seven linked areas,' I began, 'which generally follows the pattern of your original schematic. But there are a couple of additions, which I'll explain as we go through. First, visitors enter from Coppergate Square and buy their tickets at the booth inside the front entrance. Then they descend either by the steps or by the lift to the basement level. From here, as you have already designated, they enter this small chamber where, if it's busy and let's hope it will be, a line will form.

'As you have already planned, the room has a divider and the queue will come back on itself. Along the walls is a display of illustrated panels describing what period in history we're looking at, what happened, where Jorvik was, who the Vikings were, and their origins and what happened to the population and the city following the attack on York Castle in 1069. People read these introductory illustrated panels as they go through. If they don't read the text at least they'll see and take note of the illustrations. They'll serve to provide a context. Next, they come to this small space, the Starting Platform, at the front of which is a large hole in a broken brick wall, which I think will look something like this (I revealed a visual mounted on the wall), the idea being that when the building was being constructed, the builders broke through into an underground chamber.'

'Oh, oh, he's talking fantasy and theatre already.' I could see it in their faces. 'There was no broken wall. What's he talking about?' Murmurs and quizzical looks circulated amongst the audience. Were their apprehensions going to be proved true?

I carried on in anticipation, 'Yes, it's poetic licence,' I said. 'It's also theatre. And it makes sense as you'll see in terms of the introductory story, if you'll bear with me.' I was determined not to come to a stop at this early point. I turned back to the plan.

'This is the starting point for the ride. The controls for the cars are mounted here in such a way that the attendant member of staff has them in easy reach as they stand at the entrance. These controls command a car to come to the platform from a position out of sight, so they'll glide in mysteriously, with no driver and no visible track. Technical details for such things as lighting and sound and so on will come later.

'Moving on, the staff member asks the visitors next in line, "How many in your party?" and makes up a group of four to share a car. The chamber in front of the starting platform where the cars will arrive and stop we call the *cellar*. It's an addition to the plan and the beginning of the Time Tunnel, and when the script is written will be the starting point of the on-board narration. In here there's a collection of old household junk (another visual is revealed), the sort that accumulates in cellars, garages and sheds, the kind familiar to everybody. This is more than set dressing; these things are archaeological remains of the future, material evidence of our time. Being in a cellar says that we're underground.

'As you will see in a moment, I've connected the past with the present, and the cellar is the high-water mark where the physical detritus of our present existence becomes stuck in time.' Colin shot me a concerned look but the faces in front of me were inscrutable; at least they were engaged because they were looking at me intensely. Only the smiling Dr Jones seemed to be willing me on.

'The cellar is dimly lit and monochrome, as though everything is covered in ages-old dust. In the ceiling there are windows made of dirty glass bricks set in the pavement above. Shadows pass over as though people are walking over them. Up here on the left-hand corner at the top of these steps, there's a small hatch. It's open. Daylight shines onto the wall and illuminates the steps. From up there we hear the sounds of the street, voices and passing traffic. On the steps going up to the street are two figures, children who are climbing the steps to the surface. The children are at the end of a line of figures we will meet on our journey back in time.' This was crunch stuff, mixing up fantastical theatre with history and scientific fact; would they buy into it?

'Okay, so visitors step into a car and off they go. The speed will be about four inches a second.' I demonstrated with slow footsteps. 'About that speed, slow enough to take everything in and yet fast enough to ensure our maximum hourly throughput on a busy day, which will be up to four hundred people an hour.

'The car sets off and the commentary begins. What people hear and what they see is now a unity. Leaving the cellar through another hole in the wall, we enter a tunnel (I revealed another sketch visual). The tunnel and everything in it is the same colour as the cellar and also dimly lit. It's circular and about eight feet high. Perhaps it was a sewer pipe or something like that. What it actually is, is not explained, but it is quite literally *a tunnel* and it looks real. The cars pass down it, about three car lengths between each. On board the commentary plays from speakers behind the passengers' heads. What is said throughout the journey is in synch with where the car is located. Other sounds, cones of sound actually, are directionally projected from the top of the tunnel above making those sounds heard only by the car passing under them. The looped sound tracks heard all the way down the tunnel relate to periods of York's history as the cars proceed through them,' (I revealed a series of sketches, one after the other).

'These are designs for what I propose is a line of monochrome life-size figures coming this way, towards the present day, our starting point. Here they are coming down this side of the tunnel. The figures are beautifully modelled and fully costumed, and they're all going somewhere, apart from the newspaper boy. All the figures are the same biscuit monochrome. They don't see us or each other because they're from different periods, they just keep on walking.'

At this point one of the previously blank archaeological faces spoke. 'You mean they're actually walking?'

'No, they are still, but modelled as though stopped in motion. Beautifully and realistically modelled in different costumes from different periods. These figures, like the sounds people hear, span a thousand years from our present to Jorvik. Whilst the cars and their passengers are going back in time, the figures are coming forward in time forming a human chain.' I looked around, they got it; it was history; the passage of time.

'Their lives are taking them into their individual and our collective future, all unknowingly linking our joint past to our joint present and beyond, ending back here where we set off as the children climbing the steps in the cellar and up to the daylight.

'What the figures are doing relates to what was happening in the city at that time. For example, there'll be one figure, very emaciated. She's bereft, carrying her dead baby in her arms, the plague was in the city.' I looked to Peter Addyman whose expression was giving nothing away. 'Just who all these people are and from *when* exactly is something we'll work on together.' He nodded a little nod.

Maybe because I could feel my stoic audience thawing a bit, I took a little diversion to tell them where I got the idea. Carolyn gave me a 'For God's sake be careful' stare. But I thought bugger it, she doesn't know what I'm going to say. It's a great idea and I'm sharing it.

'I got this idea from thinking about the passage of time, a thousand years back to the 10th century. To most people, that seems so distant, so remote, so very cut-off and unconnected with the present and our own existence. When I thought about how we could express the actual closeness of that time, I thought about my family and actually just how far I could go back in time, from generation to generation. I couldn't go back very far, only a couple of generations. That got me thinking about how to represent the passage of time as it effects humans and I measured it in "Grannies".

At that point I got a distinct 'Oh my God, he's off' from both Carolyn and Colin who were standing apprehensively together for comfort. But I was feeling confident even though the archaeologists seemed unmoved, one yawned. I continued.

'It's only so many grandmothers back to Viking times. When you think about this as a human chain it's not very many people really, not many generations and it demonstrates that we're connected absolutely with the past through this human chain.'

I saw Bones grinning and nodding in agreement, his gaze fixed on mine. 'Go on,' he was saying. 'Stick with it, don't be put off.'

'But these figures aren't Grandmas, they're all kinds of different people but all citizens of the city and characters in its story.' I went on growing in confidence and getting into my stride. If this were to be where I exited the project, at least I'd go out telling a good story.

'The sound effects I just mentioned relate to different periods from where the figures originated, starting out with popular music, say the Beatles *Love Me Do*. Then come the war years and Winston Churchill addresses the nation, and when we're back beyond radio we'll hear the sound of York's streets, musical instruments, market calls, bells, old songs, whatever's appropriate.'

The faces warmed. There was a distinct thaw, even nods and smiles. They liked the past. That's where they lived and worked. The design team and Colin sensed it and they all started breathing again.

'So the line stretches back a thousand years.' I pointed with my finger to the plan. 'Now in this area at the end of the tunnel, which is only about seventy-five feet long, we arrive at the sacking of Jorvik by the Normans in 1069. I wondered long and hard about the transition. How could we express it? This is the way to do it; there are historical accounts for the burning of at least one building. There are burnt wooden timbers in one of the buildings that visitors are going to see later. The narrator is going to point them out. So here at the boundary of Jorvik we're going to burn a building *backwards*.

'The cars enter a charred and collapsed building that smells of smoke. There's the crackling sound of flames and burning wood and smouldering glowing embers in the walls, here in this area.' I traced my finger on the plan. 'Ouch, that's hot!' I said but received not a smile in response apart from Bones who laughed out loud (I swear his bow tie started spinning). The others turned to look at him. Colin put his hand to his face and wiped his brow. I was actually making up the narrative to go with my visual presentation as I went along now. Then for a passing instant, doubt crept in as I wondered if I should have rehearsed.

NB. For those of you who haven't made a presentation or given a lecture, but may do so in the future, bear in mind that whilst you can be filled with terror and breathless panic, believe me that when it's going well you can feel the most alive you will ever feel. It's like your whole system is going 200%. It's a marvellous feeling, a natural high, as though a whole extra system of cogs in your brain comes into play, and little doors open in your sub-consciousness to rooms full of wonderful shiny things. Of course, when you screw up it's like being buried alive in wet sand head first.

But I didn't give over to panic and the doubt passed. I was feeling good.

'Then here, the clever part will be in making the building, the leather shop, change from a *burning* building into the structure and its contents *before* the fire.' (Buildings on the archaeological site could be identified with what had been left in them by the material that had fallen to the ground and stamped into the dirt floors along with everything else. Hence it was known that this was the leather worker's shop.)

'So as we come round here, we leave the charred and burning part of the building and it merges into the whole undamaged structure with all the appropriate scenic dressing and tools.' There were definite smiles and nods now all round. Even Peter was enjoying himself. I was on a roll.

'And here,' (I paused just long enough to emphasise the coming reveal) 'then we come through the doorway and into the street. The whole of Jorvik of 990 AD will open up, the whole panorama all the way down to the river, like we've arrived at our station in time.' I turned to face them.

'That reveal will be the most significant moment in the whole trip. At that point the imagination of the visitor will be ours, and we'll achieve the suspension of disbelief and we'll be able to hold our visitors in that spell for the next few minutes.'

I stepped away from the chart.

'The ride has already in itself given us much, transporting people and telling them a story, creating a sense of adventure and anticipation. But the ride gives *us* the opportunity to use the available space to the best advantage. Why? Because it's as though each person is a *camera* moving on a dolly truck. Whatever the camera sees is what it believes. And what the ears are taking in will construct in the mind of the visitor the space we want them to believe is there. The car ride is far more than transportation; it allows us to create illusions.' I left this statement hanging there.

Carolyn shot me that look again and waved her hand under the file on her lap as if to say, 'Cut it out, don't go there. Stick to fact and descriptions of actualities.'

It was, however, a key point, fundamental to the plan and layout. The space overall was not very big, and the question of where the cars were to be stored had not yet been solved, *until now*. Everyone in the audience knew that a solution to the car storage problem had to be found.

'So, into Jorvik; first the car enters the market area. At the speed it's travelling there's enough time to take everything in. Now we engage each passenger's sense of sight, hearing and smell. It's late afternoon. They catch a whiff of produce on the stalls in the surrounding market, like the fish and the apples, stacked in wicker baskets and crates. They can see close up the detailed craftsmanship of the goods for sale on the market stalls, like the bone combs and needles and brooches and horn goblets. Whilst all around them, Jorvik is filled with noise. Here are people haggling with the stallholders over prices. Seagulls circle over-head, a baby cries in a house, geese honk, dogs bark and growl and chickens cluck in a yard some-where. However, this picture, so alive to the senses, has been frozen in motion; even the out-stretched wings of the geese honking at the woman down the alley carrying water are held in a frozen instant of movement.

'Every living thing in the scene has this potential for motion, it looks so convincing, as though if the bubble burst everything would carry on going about its business, oblivious of us.

'The car moves on and passes down a narrow alleyway between the houses. On this side, the building is low, as you found it, half submerged in a pit. It's the same with the building on the other side. The car's close, so close passengers will reach out to touch the thatch of the low roofs. Below the car there's filthy foul smelling mud and rubbish in rank, dark muddy piles at the sides of the houses, flecked with rotting vegetable, shells, and discarded bones. Just here skinny dogs fight over a bone. Passengers on this side of the car can look down at them as the dogs growl through clenched teeth.

'Because we're in such close proximity every detail must be hyper-realistic. The grain of the wood, the wooden pegs that hold the buildings together, the look of damp and dirt and rot, the thatch must be perfectly realised. And importantly it all has to look lived-in. It's not that these things per se are on exhibit, on display; we're creating an illusion of a totally lived-in place. The mark of hand and foot and human intelligence and resourcefulness is everywhere, alongside the dog dirt and goose droppings.

'The next two buildings are the largest. They're above ground houses. Two mucky children, one on either side of the alleyway, are chasing each other and shouting. Whilst here a man, between the first and the second building on the left, carves a spindle on a foot-operated lathe. He must have worked there a lot on that spot as there are piles of sawdust and shavings all round. And now someone else is shouting from inside the house on the left, an old man's voice. He's calling to one of the children. Sounds and noises come from all around, from different directions, and near and far creating an illusion of a much larger community.

'As the cars get closer to the building on the right, they see it's festooned with shanks of newly dyed wool, hung out to dry. Colour from the dye stains the planks of the house and drips onto the mud below. Behind the shanks there's a shuttered window. We can see light through the cracks, someone's home, and there's a baby bawling its head off, in fact not just crying, howling. We wonder if someone's going to take care of it.

'Before we go into the building on the left, I want to break off from the journey for a minute. I said earlier that we have a practical solution for how and where to locate a garage and workshop for the cars.'

I scanned the faces of the clients and out of the corner of my eye I saw Colin smiling. He was intently watching the archaeologists. I moved across the wall to another plan, which was covered up. I pulled off the sheet. The plan illustrated the layout of the garage, the workshop and technical shed and a place where the sound-system would go and so on. I paused to let it sink in for a moment. This had been *the* intractable problem and here was the solution. I continued with the presentation.

'The sound from the house in which the baby's crying and the yard where the dogs bark and chickens cluck are audio illusions which will appeal to the senses of the passengers. They'll imagine houses with people inside, and yards and buildings way beyond the limit of what they see. The greater Jorvik will be in their heads. The sound effects will create an illusion of space. This house from where the baby's cries are coming from is where the technical gear will go.' There was laughter and a sense of relief.

'The garage is beyond, along here; it's a long corridor completely out of sight. We can incorporate it without losing any of the buildings that exist on the site plan, or losing any space, in fact we're gaining what would have been dead space. As far as the visitors know, all the structures are complete. I calculated this from the viewpoint of passengers traveling in the Time Cars. It can definitely be done.'

Smiles all round, including Dr Addyman.

'The car-storage corridor goes all the way from the end of the ride, just after disembarkation, to the wharf end where disguised double doors open into one of the wharf-side warehouses. Each morning after an all-night electrical charge-up, the cars will exit from here and join the track for a day's work. And at the end of the day, staff simply bring the cars round and shunt them in where they can be worked on by the night shift mechanics if needs be. We have allowed this space for a workshop and storage for all their gear. Otherwise the cars are shunted together to the bottom of the corridor and plugged into power sockets.

'We've even built in a space for the day shift security people to sit while they monitor the screens for breakdowns or problems. If there *is* a problem they'll appear like magic, from this secret door and then disappear again after they've sorted the problem. The whole thing works and with no negative effect on the exhibit, and no displacement of the buildings which remain in their original location. One thing though is we'll have to be careful of sound leakage, from the workshop for example. The walls and roofs of the Viking houses will need to be soundproofed from the inside.'

My design team looked liked cats that found a dairy full of cream, whilst the architect who'd come to check on progress looked a little put out. I continued.

'Back to the 10th century. The car travels on and turns here into the house on the left through the open door. This is a nice detail. At this point in the turn where the cars leave the alleyway, we can make piles of the kinds of things that would be outside; for instance, a woodpile of logs and kindling just outside the door here. This is important because it means we don't have to have the flat car track all the way down to the river. The pile here will break the view and that will help tremendously. Now we're inside the house.'

I uncovered another set of pencil sketches.

'These sketches give you an idea of what it could look like inside. The details of the interior are based entirely on advice from your team and from Carolyn who's been interpreting the environmental evidence for us. She and Phoebe are working on a list of all artefacts that could have been found in this interior. We shall have these objects reconstructed and dress them in. This will not be a formal display, it will be as close to real life as we can presume, as you can see from these sketches, same with the smell and lighting, which will come from the fire light and from the open door.'

At this point I asked Carolyn to fill them in further. She picked up the interior theme.

'There can be a surprising amount of objects in here and it's going to be an exciting process to actually kit out a Viking house of the period. Besides objects there are the people. We are presuming that families were nuclear and most likely the older relatives stayed with the family group. Hence the old man with the soup bowl in John's sketch. We'll only reconstruct domestic found objects and go to the environmental department for evidence of foodstuffs, winter feeds, cooking, ash from the fire and so on. We have already got a preparatory list to show you. All the objects like the firedogs and the pans and the trug that the woman is mixing dough in by the fire in this drawing, everything, will have to be reconstructed. And as he says, the objects cannot be perfect unsullied reproductions. The pan on the stove and the handle of the axe by the door, the stones around the hearth, must appear like they've been in use for years.'

I stepped back up. 'Thanks Carolyn. This is so important because seeing objects in real life use as it were will provide a context for visitors when at the end, in the Finds Display Gallery, our visitors will see the real things. This is what's going to be so powerful and I think in that alone we may pull off a first. Providing a context for things, people are going to be able to relate to the finds on a level of human experience they can identify with.

'There'll be winter fodder stored in the loft above the beams. That in itself at least for the first months following opening will fill the interior with a rich natural smell of straw that will mix with the smoke from the fire and the cooking smells. Oh yes, there will be smells.

'The inside of the roof will be blackened from the fire and cobwebs will fill all the corners. And actually, that's going to be a big point in the reconstruction. Things like cobwebs we presume existed. If there's no environmental evidence should we have them? For example we hear there's no evidence for the design or construction for the roof, whereas we do have environmental evidence for the type of reed used in the thatch. So that's an example of, 'can we assume, and how much do we deduce', or should we seek the best advice from the best source? We need your advice on that.'

I went back to the sketches.

'Incidentally, it's the old chap wrapped in a skin sat on the chest who was doing the shouting we could hear from outside. He continues to shout over the voices of the two women by the fire and the children in the next part of the house beyond the partition. Though there's the noise of voices overall, it'll feel small and cramped yet cosy.'

I revealed another sketch.

'There's a partition here behind which an older girl sits on a stool by a loom. She's holding a spindle whorl hanging from a length of yarn she's spinning. At the same time she's spinning 'a yarn' to her younger sister and brother. The chatter between the children, as with the crosstalk in the other room, will be naturalistic as though the figures are actually talking to each other. We'll achieve that by using individual speakers and individual soundtracks. We think there's going to be around sixty-five separate sound tracks. The speakers will be hidden inside the figures, in the fireplace, inside the chicken and the cats.

'Now as you can see from the projected route, passengers are going to be very close to the figures, so they need to be something really special. Most of all they have to look like characters, like individual people, individuals rather than the mass-produced dummies people are used to seeing. We see the figures as the cast in our film, and I think of them as *real* people. I'm happy to report that we believe we've found the right sculptor to produce them. Colin would you say something about this?'

Colin stood up.

'John believes he has found a sculptor from Barnsley who we could use to make the figures for the reconstructions, but not for the Time Tunnel. We want a different style of approach to the figures in the Time Tunnel. The Barnsley sculptor, Graham Ibbeson, has agreed to produce a trial figure for us. It's a large commission; we want to ensure we have the right person to create the people of Jorvik.

'Of course you'll see the trial figure, which will be the goose lady John wants out here and we will need you to approve all the design sketches he'll produce for all the other figures. We'll need your agreement to the designs and the trial figure before issuing Graham with a contract.'

Whilst Colin was talking I was looking at the faces of our clients. Now even the most doubtful of the group was spellbound as well as intrigued. I think that in their individual and collective imaginations, they were already *there* in Jorvik. The scenes I was describing had them placing all the things they'd found and studied into the overall puzzle, which as we spoke was changing for them *from* a puzzle *into* a living world.

After I finished the description of the interior of the house, I described how the car would leave by a door to the side and into the open. There the passengers would come across a surprising scene, one of the toilet pits that had been discovered next to an enclosure with pigs in it. The best way I could think of showing a toilet pit was to show it in use, and that's what I told them we planned to do.

The English are very sensitive about toilets, so showing one in use complete with a loo roll of moss to hand would, I thought, be memorable, as would the stink.

Unbelievably but true, just a few feet away from the pit there was a well, where drinking and cooking water was drawn. This was born out by the discovery of infestations of intestinal worms in the human faeces found in the pits from all over the site. So to make this point I explained how we'd have a person sat on a plank just as they'd found it with a hole in it, carrying out his business whilst not far away a woman with a bucket full of water, is seen leaving the well surrounded by honking geese.

This all seemed to be going down brilliantly as the archaeologists who'd been stoic before were now nodding and smiling. Bones was positively beaming.

Pointing at the plan with a pencil, I took them round turning right and along a section of riverbank levee.

'Next we come to the river. There's a ship pulled up along here. Men are unloading it into the warehouse.'

I explained that as the basement floor was flat concrete how at first I'd struggled to find a scenic solution to creating the illusion of a river with a full size vessel floating on it. I explained how the breakthrough came once I started designing all that can be seen from the visitor's point of view. I continued.

'Along the river bank there's the levee, built up on the visible side with wattle fences. The river can't be seen but it can be suggested. On top of this there's the walkway, beyond which there's the full-scale reproduction of the ship, fresh from Denmark. We can hear the sound of the water against the boat and the voices of men on board, each voice coming from individual sources, so there's a tremendous audio spatial sense.

'The top half of the body of the ship is visible as is all the rigging and sail. As it's tied up to the bank and being unloaded it would be listing to the bank side as the cargo is being transferred. That's great as the angled deck will mean the deck and what's on it will be visible.' I turned away from the plan on the wall to look at my audience. 'When it comes to the design and build of the ship we'll need your advice on dimensions and materials. For example, how was such a ship constructed, what kind of rope was used, what kind of material was the sail made of, how was it held together, what kinds of smells could be expected from the dockside? And just what was their cargo likely to be?

'Okay, carrying on, from here the car continues along the riverbank for about seven metres before entering into another riverside warehouse. On the way we'll pass a small group of figures sat on the levee drinking and exchanging jokes. Passengers will hear them laughing before entering the warehouse. It's dark in there.'

At this point I described that we are coming to the end of the 10th century reconstruction and how important it was to make the most effective return to the present day.

'There'll be no second Time Tunnel,' I said. 'But it is so very important we repeat the same kind of dynamic and arresting *reveal* we gave them on entering Jorvik. Visitors must have no clue as to what's coming next.' (I knew that the archaeologists in front of me had no clue either.) 'So the car enters the second warehouse, then turns sharp right; at which point double doors open in front of them to reveal a completely different brightly lit scene. The cars have made a leap in time and landed slap bang in the middle of the Coppergate dig in the year of 1978.'

I paused for that to sink in.

'Rather than display larger materials in a formal way as might be expected, I think it will be far more effective to reconstruct the actual dig and incorporate real objects. For example, here's the cesspit as you found it and over here timbers of buildings in place just as they were discovered, and the hearth, as well as all the paraphernalia of a working dig, including diggers and sifters. Being down in a dig will be an experience too for most people. As the cars enter the dig the onboard storyteller explains how they are now travelling through the Coppergate excavation exactly as it was and that it's a *mirror image* of the Jorvik that they've just visited.'

I could see from the archaeologists' expressions that this idea was so unexpected it was really hard to take in and I was talking about incorporating real finds in it. I was glad I'd asked to keep questions to the end.

'Everything in the second reconstruction, like the first, will be based on evidence, right down to the mud on the wellies lined up outside the Portakabin.' I showed them photographs taken in the site and said we needed donations of all kinds of used archaeological equipment including more personal things like mugs and boots. I asked them to think about all the little details of life on a dig that we could show, as this wasn't just about the process and the science, but about them in the process and what they do.

'And of course, who is seen working on the site is something you will have to decide amongst yourselves.'

I further explained with the aid of a sketch. 'One thing that won't be based on reality is the ditch in which the cars travel through the site; but so then was the car track in the 10th century reconstruction. Having the cars travel *below* surface level brings passengers' eye-lines closer to the surface and allows the cars to travel through minutely reconstructed standing sections, so they can see close up how waste stuff from everyday life got swallowed up into the ground.

'We believe that passengers experiencing the site in this way will find the experience a double revelation; firstly being on a working excavation and secondly being able to relate it to the reconstructed houses and hearths, middens and wells they've just seen. And of course, bear in mind that all of this is explained by the narrator.'

For some in my audience this idea was a leap of imagination, totally unlike conventional methods of presentation and interpretation. But it was obvious from my point of view where I was standing that the idea was meeting with general approval.

There was, however, a persistent little bee in my bonnet. I wasn't absolutely sure if we should put the archaeology before or after the reconstruction. I wondered; weren't we putting the archaeological chicken after the egg?

Intuitively I knew now was the time to ask the question of the group. 'At this point, playing the devil's advocate, I'd like to ask, wouldn't it make more sense to put the archaeological site *before* the 10th century reconstruction? Don't you think that way round we'd show, this is what we found, and this is how we know what it was like?'

Dr Addyman spoke up for the first time and put his foot down. He was adamant that the archaeology *had* to come after the reconstruction, his reason being as follows:

'Presenting the archaeology after the reconstruction adds emphasis to the *value* of the archaeological process.'

And that's how it stayed. Just as well really because switching it would have meant radical changes to the design of the Time Tunnel and car storage, so I didn't push it. Besides which, he was the boss.

I continued, 'But of course the story doesn't end here on the site,' revealing the last plan and visual as I spoke. 'Now we enter the cellars of Craven's sweetie factory.' It was made into a dig crew room, the place where crew members had a cup of tea and a cigarette. At one side of the actual dig were the lower walls and cellars of an old sweet factory that they had managed to commandeer as part of the dig. I had spoken to the original site workers and they agreed with me that leaving the site that way would make a fitting exit from the excavation and would make a great link to the environmental laboratory, which was coming up next.

'We'll dress it up,' I explained, 'with all the daily detritus; remains of chip-butties, damp socks and coats, helmets with their nicknames, gloves and newspapers, half-filled mugs of cold coffee and so on, such as on a real dig, cigarette ends included along with racks of plans on the walls. It would serve to remind visitors of those unknown souls who'd done the grunt work, enabling this unique excavation to be carried out against the clock.'

That went down very well.

Finally I explained how the car travelled on for about three metres further coming to a halt at the disembarkation platform where an attendant would see the passengers safely off, directing them to the Environmental Laboratory display and the museum beyond. And there my presentation ended.

There were at first no questions, just a pause, a pregnant one. The archaeological team looked to Peter to speak whilst we on the design team held our collective breath once more.

'Well,' Peter said smiling. 'I think with a few small reservations, that's all *very* marvellous and inspiring. Congratulations!'

10   HISTORIUM – WHERE HISTORY COMES TO LIFE

We passed the crucial test, and now the real work could begin. We were in the Production Phase, and there were an awful lot of things to get organised on multiple levels.

Up front every detail for every square inch had to be researched, designed and checked by the archaeologists. Each artefact had to be reproduced so they were drawn or photographed from the originals. Carolyn and I worked together on the details relating to the archaeology before we submitted them.

It was an intense and in its way a magical period of work, a special coming together of her knowledge and experience and my skills visualizing with a 2B pencil. Whilst writing I asked her what she remembered. Here she is in her own words,

'I sat next to you at the drawing board with lots of reference material and info, I talked/explained details while you sketched, refined and revised to get the details as authentic as possible. We did this day after day after day until late in the evening often. We had photographs of the dig, examples of other types of evidence and very dry excavation reports to go at so it was quite a labour of love. We discussed endlessly the importance of showing the different kinds of buildings.

'The houses had workshops behind and "shop fronts" on the street with little alley ways or ginnels running between just as we created. Being a student and digging on Coppergate with Richard Hall was really helpful as I'd seen many of the finds and handled the real material. It meant that between us we really focused on the detail of authenticity as much as we could, with the support of YAT and I think it was why they trusted the YCG team (eventually!).'

Once this was done, specialist artisans had to be found to produce the hundreds of things we needed for inclusion in the reconstruction. Also every figure before being sculpted had to be visualised and sketched, including what they wore; every item of clothing from shoes to hats had to be based on finds. Here Carolyn was an invaluable asset, not that she knew everything, I'm sure she'd be the first to admit it. But besides her first-hand experience on the dig she had that so important line of communication with the archaeological team.

Besides the smaller world of details, what we needed was a subjective experience of what it might have felt like to live in those times. How could we get that? Again here's Carolyn,

'Remember the wonderful trip to Aarhus and Moesgard and Roskilde to see reconstructed Viking longhouses, "living history" places; that incredibly evocative boathouse on the shoreline that made the hairs on all our arms stand on end? It was so magical and felt like we had stepped into history, the house with its eye-watering smoky and dim interior but cosy. It was a real inspiration and everyone was so helpful. The international dimension in terms of academic support was amazing. We often referred to experts in Scandinavia. They were brilliant.'

Back in York on a more technical level the lighting had to be planned and designed. We had to work out how best to make everything fireproof. We had to ensure that the multi-track, multi-speaker audio concept that would play throughout the reconstructions was practically feasible. At ground level we needed to find out how best to reproduce mud, muck, mess and animal droppings (believe me goose droppings are a piece of work). And as we planned to use smells, we had to find someone to make them. There were other sculptors to locate and contract to create the additional figures for the Time Tunnel as I felt those passing figures required a different stylised treatment, not like those in Jorvik, which would have a mucky kind of down-to-earthiness and sort of inbred look. And last but not least, there were set builders to locate and sign on before we moved into the basement in York.

All this and then the myriad of organization details felt as daunting as having to knit a Fair Isle jumper without a pattern and no knitting needles. It was obvious that there were multitudes of interrelated items of planning. It became very clear that an interconnected schedule that would bring the enormous number of strands in the production together on time was crucial. To say we were learning on the job is an understatement.

However, before detailed scheduling was possible we had to get a grasp on all that the project entailed in a global view. More accurately, I needed to be able to see the whole thing but in depth. Fortunately, having pulled off other jobs that required multi-level planning and scheduling (like producing an industrial film or planning a promotional campaign) we realised that in order to achieve our end result on time and on budget, there were two main steps to begin the process.

Step one:

An overall production plan was necessary which accounted for and identified all the multiple levels of production and ensured authenticity. This fell to me to envisage. I had to grasp all the areas of action and the pathways to that action. For example, how would we end up with a basket full of apples for the market area? What questions would we have to ask? What evidence would support the choice of fruit? Would apples be available at the chosen time of year? What did they look like? Then, what kind of basket? What type of design for the basket? So, that's research. And then what specialist would make the apples? This kind of envisioning was a real test for I had to see into the future of that basket of apples along with hundreds of other such items and develop the master plan based mainly on foresight. So I had a serious word with my brain cells about how to work it out.

Once again I turned to the pages of my current journal to explore ideas. My journals were to become the exterior mirror of what was happening in my head; scribbles, dots, unidentifiable squiggles, often abstract, reflected the formulation and the birth of a concept into a tangible and realisable form. It was like a private, creative dialogue with the paper where the marks were a graphic record of what I was exploring in my head. The best journal records that I made were like a route map from a single little line more felt than thought to a full blown sketch of a project. The other thing about journal writing was they enabled me to keep track of things. We didn't have laptops or PCs back then. My journal was my laptop. Over time journal writing became my daily habit.

Moreover, I developed the ability to intuitively or 'remotely view' a finished project while I was designing Jorvik. The completion might be three years away, but with only the most basic initial outline to work with, I needed to 'see' the end product in my head. Doing this allowed me to create action lists.

Once I honed my ability to do this, it became a valuable career asset. It was why in the early stages of considering and planning future exhibitions and museums, clients and project managers were surprised that I could estimate a global price for the production early on within 10-25% of the final budget. Of course, anyone in the business could say reasonably, the more jobs you do the more you get a sense of costs, say, per square metre. But there was something more than just budget matters in this for me. It was also about being able to see the entire *design concept* – not the final nuts and bolts of a detail design, but a working scheme realised as a whole. I call it *foresight envisioning*.

By the time Jorvik was completed and I developed confidence in my foresight technique, I discovered that I was able to take a mental virtual-reality walk-through of a proposed scheme. In fact I could switch it on and off and start from whatever part of concept design I wanted to start from, eyes open or shut. I could sit at my desk and tour a finished project in my head and draw out and describe what I saw. I could also go to a location we were considering for a scheme, whether it was in the open or inside an existing building, and envisage a plan in 3-D in my head and walk and talk myself and others around it. Talking about being crazy, I certainly looked it sometimes as I madly described things to my colleagues and clients by drawing in the air like a demented windmill.

I wouldn't have the smallest details but I would have a vision that would be at least ninety percent of what would finally come to be. In fact as my ex-colleagues would attest, I think, I used this technique with two projects that came soon after Jorvik, the Canterbury Tales and the Oxford Story. It allowed the executive team to share a vision of the completed project before a mark had been made on paper, or more importantly, a penny spent. (Ian Skipper who would also be on these trips looking for new project opportunities, would say, 'Come on John, tell us what you see.')

Another example from the early nineties was a fantastic project I won for Dover District Council. The project manager, Mike, was an extremely capable, level-headed and down-to-earth manager of complex projects. He and I on the surface seemed as different as chalk and cheese but we got along like a house on fire. I'd spent some time researching the subject range to be included in the attraction. After my initial visit to the open site before the architects had even planned the new building to house the yet-to-be-named attraction, I told him I would come back after the week-end and meet with him in London with the design concept for the completed scheme.

I think Mike thought the process would take weeks or months. What he didn't know was that by the time we walked over the bare ground and viewed some Roman excavations on the site and with my background mental notes on the subject, I already had the plan in my head. I knew all I had to do was to draw them up. It was Friday afternoon and he looked at me incredulously but said nothing. I was in his office in London by Monday lunchtime and unrolled several sheets of plans titled *The White Cliffs Experience* that I'd written across the tops of all the sheets. He looked at the drawings, sat back and said, 'I never would have believed it.' Those sketches not only formed the basis for the exhibition content but also for the shape and form of the building and became the foundation for the architects' brief. It saved them months. I had developed the ability to produce a holistic workable plan, not just the ideas, the story, the exhibits, but how all the practical and physical elements would work together.

Incidentally, those plans also added a word to the lexicon of interpretive exhibition design: *historium,* a place where history is brought to life.

But I digress again, sorry, let's get back to the job in hand – Jorvik.

Step two:

Produce a combined multi-track schedule which laid out the multiple lines of action against time, bringing them all together by the beginning of 1984 ready for the soft opening in March and the formal opening in April, which was now just 17 months away.

At this point in my career with my first major exhibition, it was a challenge to draw up such a detailed and lengthy schedule that covered a two-year period for a project the likes of which no one had ever tackled before. But Colin and I did it using common sense, combined experience and a lot of imagination. While bathtub soaks and 'the beautiful burps' that they percolated had their benefits, here I managed the exhibition planning using A1 sheets of paper, a ruler, an HB pencil (harder than a 2B) and an occasional slurp of lager, not, by the way, in the bath.

I created all sorts of basic block plans, flow charts and schematics some of which looked like interconnecting railway lines. Others were groups of circles and balloons connected by dotted lines and then there were the floaty amoebas of possible ideas swimming in a Sargasso Sea of 'maybe ifs'. Then I would take a bundle of these and plop them down in front of Colin to discuss. He was a great straightener of my mental spaghetti.

The knack in doing this was to shut myself away in my study at home, close the door on the world and cast my mind into the future through as many aspects of the finished project as I could envisage down to the smallest detail manageable. I had to see it as real as possible in order to chart it.

This reminds me of another planning tool that I didn't use specifically for the JVC project. But it was an important one that evolved from my JVC experience and assisted me for the rest of my career. It was a technique, which like foresight envisioning, spoke largely from the subconscious.

It was a creative catalyst technique that I perfected and used to develop original concepts for projects (some very expensive ones). In one example, I remember using it as a key to unlock a uniquely challenging and complex conceptual and practical problem for Madame Tussauds, a major tourist attraction in London. I'd been headhunted to come up with an original idea for this already established and hugely successful venue (but don't worry, you won't find my head on display at Madam Tussauds).

The problem was difficult for three reasons: firstly, it would come at the end of an extremely popular exhibition that already drew over two million visitors a year. People had to leave on a high. So, how do you top that? Secondly, it was in the basement where the Chamber of Horrors had been housed until it was relocated in an updated form elsewhere. It was a very restricted and restrictive physical space, which limited what could be done there. The other challenge was it had to connect with the existing attraction and – something else I felt from the outset but was not in the brief – it should connect with its location, London.

The technique I used to crack this challenge and come up with a solution began like this: I'd start with a big piece of paper and write on the left-hand side letters of the alphabet. On the horizontal axis I would write a series of passive, subjective, descriptive and active words relating to the main object of the client and the type of project he or she was after.

In this particular case, I remember there was one phrase that stuck in my head after my initial briefing. My client, the managing director of Madame Tussauds with the most appropriate name of Mike Jolly said, 'I'd love to have everyone leaving the place whistling our tune'. That was all I needed. The implications of that comment, what it meant – for instance, obviously there had to be music – I entered into my creative matrix. The word 'music' would be one of many I entered on the horizontal axis.

I'd written the letter 'A' on the top of the vertical axis on the left-hand side. I then went along the horizontal line below the words from the letter 'A' and would think of any words, no matter how seemingly disassociated, which started with the letter 'A' that popped into my mind. Soon, additional words for the horizontal axis came into my head and I would add them to the horizontal axis.

So, for example, in the instance of 'music', at the intersection of the letter 'A' and the word 'music' above it, I'd come up with associated words, like 'acapella' and 'amplification.' These would be loose associations and not over-thought. So I would get a collection of words in boxes, some passive, some descriptive, some actionable and at the end I'd start with the next letter down. As I went down the alphabet axis believe it or not, embryonic, original ideas relating to a solution would start to appear through patterns I learned to identify. Now I am sure that cleverer people than I would recognise this as some existing word association tool. But for me it was a unique and personal way of cracking creative puzzles. And it never failed.

Think of it as something like this: onto this chart you enter ingredients, not all of which have obvious connection. Mix them together and put them into the pan of your subconscious, put the gas on low, wait a bit and let it bake while you go to the supermarket, make love, walk the dog and/or bath the baby (not all at once). If it works out right, out pops a fabulous cake, a bubbling mix of interconnected ideas that you and no one else thought of before.

For me, sometimes the result would be surprising and often quite amazing. At the beginning of the exercise I would never have thought to have come up with that solution, which often seemed so very right. This was the case for Madame Tussauds. After completing the matrix, the content of the new attraction was revealed and even its name popped out appearing in pink icing on the top of the cake: *The Spirit of London.*

The matrix told me that as a foreign tourist, rather than just gawping and taking photographs and doing the normal touristy things, part of you wants to feel connected to the essence of the place. In other words, you want to feel you're not an alien but a part of the whole circus of life. That's what The *Spirit of London* expressed.

The title I roughly and expressively sketched on the top of my ideas sheet was even used on all promotional material as the banner title for the new show.

I often wondered what Mike Jolly would have said if he had seen me working with only my bits of paper, ruler, eraser and trusty pencil. As it was, what he did say when I arrived with the concept design four days later was, 'It knocks my socks off'. He subsequently spent 16 million pounds building it. (Well, maybe it was a bit less, six million perhaps. It was a long time ago. Anyway, it was a lot.) I should add it was a huge and lasting success. And he was able to afford a new pair of socks.

Time flies from day one on a big production. On a personal note, over the years to come after Jorvik, when I landed other design and build exhibition and museum projects, time itself seemed to change. Days and weeks would be one continuous merging of travel, meetings, motorway food, brief respites in bars, problems, resolutions, conversations and calls which focused or revolved around the project. Not to mention being prepared to meet many, many new people for fleeting business engagements in all sorts of different locations and from different professional worlds. Hotels seemed to be the same soulless places, waking in sterile rooms not knowing one bathroom from another or where I was. I became a travelling salesman of ideas, visions in my bag that some mornings didn't seem as great as they had the night before.

Then there was what I used to call *car life*, living in the back of the car. For a few years I was busy all over England and northern Europe travelling thousands of miles by road as well as rail and air. So many jobs were easier to reach door to door by car. I couldn't handle all that driving so I employed drivers. One of them packed it in because he developed driver's elbow; such was the mileage we did.

I worked in the back of the car during journeys that often took five and six hours one-way. Trouble was, I got to know the back of my drivers' heads better than my young children's changing faces. Motorway service stations became as familiar as our dining-room, along with the girls who served the meals; meanwhile my wife was two hundred miles away, putting the kids to bed and reading them stories on her own, again.

And whilst time speeds up with the constant race, there were times when it dragged in the bedroom of the hotel, strange and without comfort. These were times when I wondered what the hell I was doing it for, making these things. What monstrous ego was causing me to take these monumental risks that ate up my life and stressed my family life for two, sometimes three years at a time.

Then the phone would ring and it's someone with a proposal for a new project and they're thinking of you to design it. That's the spark that ignites the fire again as your mind starts racing. Sometimes I was working on two and three multi-million pound design and build projects at a time. I used to view this kind of professional freelance life as living in a series of my own time tunnels. Land a project, get a contract and go into the tunnel until opening day; that's what it felt like.

Meanwhile, back in the warehouse in Wakefield we were all in it now for the very first time.

The design team, complete again as we smuggled Derek back to the warehouse, jumped to their tasks.

Meanwhile, based on what the production schedules called for to be achieved by the end of that week or month, I had some interesting tasks of my own to undertake. Those other sculptors had to be found and Graham Ibbeson needed a design for his trial figure. Then there was the design for the Time Cars, and we needed a musician who ideally would have expertise in designing and producing audio environments. Besides which I had to find the builders for the exhibit. And in between there was the all-important narrative script to begin thinking about.

There must be, I thought, other people, professional museum and exhibition designers in Britain that already used multimedia. After all, someone had to design the Festival of Britain type expos. If I had been in the business for years and not just a few months, I would have already come across a famous English designer, James Gardner, or simply 'G' as he was known. It was he who originally took the exhibit out of the box and made the exhibition environment a place where extraordinary things might just happen. By the 80s he was already a senior figure in the museums and exhibition field, having completed revolutionary exhibition projects since WWII (during which, by the way, he was the Chief Deception Officer for the Camouflage Training School, a place I'm sure that was hard to find) that were to set him apart *and* set him up as the go-to man. He designed the British contribution to the World's Fair in Brussels in 1958 and, my favorite, the Museum of the Diaspora in Tel Aviv.

I was called the *Father of the Heritage Industry* several times in the press after Jorvik opened (and by the way so was Colin). Well, if I'm the Father (or even the Godfather as stated in one article in the 90s), James Gardner is the Grandfather and I mean GRAND.

I don't know why YAT had not approached him for Jorvik. Or perhaps they did. He had a reputation as a non-conforming, strong-minded idiosyncratic and talented problem solver. He created extraordinary immersive and monumental exhibits. His designs were always fresh and surprising. Whether his style would have suited the Jorvik project I'm not sure. His approach would most likely have been different from mine.

As G designed many famous projects at home and abroad over decades, I thought surely he would know the sort of talented specialists we had to find now. So I called him at his studio in the London suburbs and got to speak to the great man himself. He was nothing but charming and helpful and didn't mind my calling, adding that he would help us all he could and would love to meet up.

When we met in his pipe-smoked unassuming studio I explained what I was doing and showed him my drawings, which he delighted in. Drawing was his primary tool as well. I asked about sculptors and he gave me several names and numbers straight off, saying it was all right to use his name as an introduction. At the end of the visit I suggested when we were closer to completion up in York that perhaps he'd like to come and have a look at what we'd been up to. Face-to-face, he in his mid seventies and me just beginning my thirties, it felt like I, the apprentice, was asking Rembrandt to come and check on my Paint by Numbers effort. When he later came to see Jorvik in person, he was thrilled by what we'd achieved. He was enchanted by it and told me he liked my thinking. It seemed we both thought 'out of the box' only I was on the other side of it.

The first name he gave me was Freeborn. G said the husband and wife team specialised in beautifully modelled and costumed figures and high quality props. Like other similar specialists Pat and Derek Freeborn were based close to the centres of the British film industry at Pinewood and Elstree studios. Usually, he said, their main line of work was producing 3-D special effects for film and television. But he thought they could be tempted out of that by an exciting and interesting challenge. When I called them they too were extremely charming and I felt were genuinely interested in what we were doing 'up north'.

They invited me down to their workshop. I was beginning to love these trips, which had begun with my first visit to the Rowley Workshop in the days of Dusty Bin. They were so exciting you never knew what you were going to find or what geniuses you might meet. It was like looking behind Alice in Wonderland's mirror seeing how things were done; a privileged view really.

I went out to the workshop on an empty mid-morning commuter train from Paddington. Their business occupied a small group of single-storied buildings that wouldn't have been out of place on an army base. A very nicely done hand-painted sign at the gateway spoke of quality and taste; the rest of the campus, painted dark green and cream, arranged around a central courtyard looked as low-key and muted as the sign.

Pat met me at the door. She and her husband Derek founded the company and though they both were getting on a bit were still at the heart of the business. Derek was the sculptor and prop maker and Pat was the costume designer. Besides the two of them, there were other technicians and artists at work in the background that I met on a walk-round, including their son who would later take on the business. They didn't need to sell me on anything, as they and the things I saw in production were simply wonderful.

My impression was that I was in the company of consummate professionals, very much of the same generation and quality as G for whom they'd produced lots of work. And like him they possessed the same calmness and manner of people who know and love what they're doing and have made a lifetime's living from doing it.

When I met them on that first exploratory trip (I was to work with them on several future projects beyond Jorvik) they were already close to retirement age. They had no conceit about their wonderful work, which they talked of in a matter-of-fact way as we leafed through piles of bound folders of their work.

We sat together over a pot of tea and digestive biscuits (they had the job right there and then). I was blown away by their range, finesse and professionalism. People like them were the genius specialists of the film industry who worked the magic in the background before the age of digital effects. They created convincing illusions that transported the public to other worlds. I'd never before had the opportunity to work with artists of such experience and quality.

As they turned another page in their folio I could feel my eyes suddenly widening to the size of saucers. 'You worked on *Alien?*' the extraordinary and innovative sci-fi film directed by Ridley Scott.

'Yes,' Derek said with characteristic understatement over the rim of his teacup. 'We made the space suits and some props.' I was astonished to be looking at images of things I recognised from the film.

I asked, 'What was your brief for the suits and the helmet?'

Pat said, 'Ridley wanted them to look real and used. We've still got the moulds of the helmets. Would you like to see them?' It was like asking if I wanted to see the Holy Grail.

And there they were, not the finished things but the moulds for the helmets. What made them look so convincing was the way they had worked circuitry into the surface making them look real and practical. I asked them how they had shown the suits to Ridley the first time.

Pat answered again. 'Well, we took one completed set, suit and helmet to the studios and at first intended just to show them as they were, you know flat without anyone wearing them. But we were close to one of the sets outside the ship and caught sight of him. I think they were setting up the lighting. They had the smoky atmospherics working. It was a fantastic scene. So Derek had the bright idea to put on the suit and present it in that setting.'

Derek took up the story. 'So I put it on and turned the light on inside the visor and walked slowly into the scenery.'

'What did he say?'

'Oh, he was delighted,' said Pat. 'Just as well because we put a lot of work into them to get them just right. He said we'd brought it all to life for him.'

Crikey, never mind the biscuits. I felt like I was in the company of gods.

Of course, I was sold and I hadn't even seen a figure. They showed me loads of other exquisite things they'd made. Then Derek, warmed by my genuine enthusiasm, went on to tell me about how they loved making and costuming figures.

They showed me some. They were superb with beautifully detailed custom-made costumes. Many of them were a light beige coloured monochrome (which is just what I wanted) and some were in full color. These were no dummies. They looked alive and their eyes glinted. Exactly what I was looking for.

The costumes were very much part of the overall presence of the figures. Pat's technique was to create them, as she would have for the theatre. Once completed the whole finished thing, the figure dressed in its costume, was dipped in a bath of special resin that soaked into the cloth making it hard, durable and fixed in a certain position. They described how they started developing their techniques when they worked on projects for James Gardner.

It was time to tell them about Jorvik; I got out of my sketches a bit apprehensively, after what I had just witnessed. Just as happened with G, both immediately lit up. 'Oh! You can draw,' exclaimed Pat adding, 'Oh, these are lovely.'

I think I must have grown six inches in my chair when she said that and so did my 2B pencil. Looking back with less and less people doing free-hand drawing to describe their ideas and designs, I realised by those drawings I was joining an old-school club, which was soon to be taken over by new technology.

I explained the whole scheme and then my concept for the design of the tunnel. They were totally taken by it; they loved the concept and what I was

JOHN SUNDERLAND

trying to do in a different kind of museum. For them it was a new and intriguing challenge. God knows they didn't need the work. They said they'd love to be involved in part because they wanted to share my enthusiasm for a job. It's one thing to be brilliant; it's another thing to be nice, and they were just lovely. Thank you G.

Having expressed their very real interest in the project and how much they liked my sketches, I got them to give me an idea of what the figures would cost approximately. There were to be about fifteen altogether and as it was for Graham, this was a large commission for them too, all of which had to be produced to their usual high standard in a relatively short time. I wasn't surprised that their prices were dearer than Graham's; that was only to be expected.

Armed with a glossy Freeborn brochure, I shot off back to Yorkshire. Colin didn't take much convincing. But he was a bit apprehensive about the price.

Within a week I made a series of sketches of all the figures we decided on with the archaeologists' agreement and sent them down to Derek. Within days, they faxed back a hard price. They were indeed expensive but Colin agreed with me that it would be well worth it even though they were over our speculative budget, and so they were commissioned.

With the Freeborns in the bag and started on the work, it was time for me to turn my attention to other design matters.

First, I wanted to get to grips with the sound. I had in mind that I should look for a composer who also created audio environments. It was an idea to use music in the pre-entry area as we called it, before visitors mounted the cars. I thought it would be great if that person could also design and produce audio effects for other areas, like the Time Tunnel. I asked around and found the person I was looking for, amazingly a stone's throw away, a short walk from the Coppergate site. He was currently employed as a part-time tutor in the Department of Music at York University, name of Trevor Wishart.

Trevor, his wife and two young daughters lived in an unprepossessing 19th century brick terrace villa in York. It was a small place made even smaller inside because Trevor had turned one of three downstairs rooms into a recording studio and editing suite. It's where he took me after answering the door.

The room was absolutely stuffed with wires and boxes bristling with switches and dials, microphones and mixers and in the middle of it all sat Trevor, small of stature with a bald head, a thin face with pale skin and sprigs of hair at either side of a large cranium. He looked like an elf caught up in a great ball of string.

Though he was intense, Trevor was modest about his work and himself, yet struck me straight away as possessing a brain the size of a small planet.

His creative enthusiasm and passionate interest lay in the human voice and in the creation of compositions using the voice as an infinitely variable instrument. In fact I was to discover, he was at the cutting edge of experimental vocal music and world-renowned in his field. He told me the Japanese were big fans. Yet he came over as a totally unassuming, totally dedicated gentle man devoid of any ego. I was also to discover that the Wishart household simply resonated with intelligence; even the rabbit in its hutch in the little backyard had a PhD.

He played me samples. To be honest I found his music a bit difficult at first, but understood his aims when he explained them. But it wasn't long (second packet of tea biscuits, not digestives this time) before we found common ground in my plan for a Jorvik environmental soundscape in which all the single audio strands work naturally together, like the common sounds you hear in a market place.

By now Colin had become used to me introducing some pretty exotic people so I wasn't nervous about introducing Trevor in person. In his own quiet and slightly eccentric way, Trevor was no less exotic than the rest. In fact when you saw and heard him whooping and howling into the microphone, he was exotic on steroids.

When he came over to the factory to meet Colin we first walked around and through the full-scale model. I showed him where the figures would be and my ideas of creating a greater sense of space through sound. We got on famously as I pushed him around on the trolley like a bald baby in a pram doing my best to bring the scenes alive for him. The project was as much up his street as it was down my alley.

I now noticed that following the presentation to the archaeologists, whenever I talked about the exhibition, the more real and fleshed out it became for me. I could visualise the place in depth and detail and weave such a convincing story for visitors like Trevor, that the vacant lashed together two-by-one structures came alive for them too.

Colin took to him after our meeting especially after he played us samples of his work, which I thought might come as a bit of a shock to Colin, who was more of a Beach Boys fan. But that didn't happen. Colin the Producer continued to surprise me. So I thought it was all over barring the shouting, or in Trevor's case, the shouting, screaming, wailing, humming and whistling. But I thought too soon.

Someone must have mentioned music and sound to Ian Skipper. He missed my presentation but had obviously heard reports from Peter and the archaeologists on our progress and amongst other things that we were searching for someone to create music and sound effects.

I wanted Trevor, but before I could get him signed up, Colin got a call saying that Mr Skipper would be arriving with a musician who he rated highly, and who he would like us to use.

A couple of days later Ian arrived in his chauffer-driven black Rolls Royce. It was like receiving a visit from Royalty; we even bought some chocolate biscuits. After chats and descriptions of our progress we asked him who the musician was that he recommended and where was he? It turned out he was about to arrive.

'I think that's him now, boys' Ian said as he looked out of the studio window. 'Let's go and meet him.'

Outside the leaves and litter started to blow furiously about and a line of faces appeared at the cake factory canteen windows opposite, eyes raised heavenward, mouths-open as the musician in a helicopter descended like an angel landing in the car park just outside 'Binghams Plumbers Supplies' next door. Out came the rock-star, golden locks blowing in the downdraft to be met by copious hugs from an open-armed Ian. I was beginning to realise that arrivals are important, if you want to make an impression.

I shan't say who the rock-star was just in case I ever want to go to a concert of his so I'll refer to him as 'J'. But believe me this was pretty heavy stuff; I had several albums on which he appeared in my collection at home. I wondered if Trevor could manage to land in a spaceship because that's what we might need for him to create the same entrance. We were all suitably impressed. I now reckoned Ian might turn up with Jesus if we ever needed a miracle.

Anyway we all trilled on and made a big fuss. It seemed like J got the idea of the project and what we were looking for pretty soon before ascending and returning to the ethereal other-place that Rock Stars go to. Ian likewise, beaming after an afternoon with a star and his Yorkshire 'boys' purred off in the big black Roller and into the gathering twilight.

It had been a strangely surreal afternoon and not just for us. That night as I was leaving I got some curious looks from the girls leaving the cake factory.

'What are you lot up to in there then?' asked one as she got on her bike.

'We're making a James Bond movie in the back,' I said.

'Bloody looks like it!' she said. 'And who are you, the head of MI5?' she giggled.

'Yes, can't you tell I'm a good guy?' I said.

Her friend butted in. 'Well lad, I don't know who you are or what you're up to but you're no James Bond.'

To cut this part of the story short – rock star and helicopter versus Trevor and his front room – the idea was that J would compose some ambient style music inspired by Jorvik in some way as a sample before we gave him the job. But in truth it seemed pretty certain we'd *have* to take him on, whether he was any good or not.

But I wasn't going to give up on Trevor. I called to explain what was going on with the rock star whilst at the same time, off my own back asked him if he would make us a sample of music, which I wanted to have in reserve. He was happy to oblige.

A couple of weeks went by until time was pressing on the audio production schedule. Then we heard literally and metaphorically from Ian's pet-rock musician. I still wanted Trevor to do the job, as his sample was already on my desk and right on key; but the man who pays the Piper was playing the tune. Eventually a tape arrived via special delivery.

Colin and I wanted to hear it first, so we played it in his office, all ninety seconds of it. We looked blankly at each other and wondered if there was something we'd missed. There wasn't.

Colin looked at me and said, 'What do you think?'

'I expected something better than that. It sounds like 10th century lift music.'

Colin agreed. It was, shall I say, unsuitable for our purposes and didn't come close to being what we wanted, or what we expected. I think J didn't get it; or more likely just wasn't that bothered. Perhaps after seeing the stick village and us in the warehouse he wasn't inspired and to be fair to him, probably felt more at home in a rock stadium. Trouble was Ian seemed to want him, and we had the idea that what he wanted he usually got. But on this we were adamant; sound was going to be very important.

So we had to make a stand. This would be the first time we would go against Ian's wishes and we were more than a little worried, knowing just how important he was to the whole of the project. Yet so was the sound and we wanted to have the best, or at least what we felt was right.

Colin and I decided that the way to broach this was to send Ian a copy of J's demo tape, tell him what we thought of it and then hope for the best. That's exactly what we did.

We shouldn't have worried. You don't get to be super-rich without being super-smart as well. Ian agreed with us after he listened to the tape, using two well-used Anglo-Saxon words to describe what he just heard.

We got back to Trevor, who quickly finished off the piece with a few extra bits. We rushed it to Ian with our thoughts. It was great he said. So, much to my delight, Trevor got the job without the spaceship or the golden locks.

Every detail of the production for me, Colin, and I'm sure for the rest of the team, just had to be right. For all of us now it was more than a job, it was personal and we were inspired. Making the right choice meant, for example, that Phoebe and Carolyn scoured Britain for not any old blacksmith but the *right* blacksmith, the *right* woodworker, just the *right* jeweller, just the *right* leather worker and so on. Second best just wouldn't cut it.

And as with the musician it wasn't just about getting the best craftspeople to make a particular item. They had to make objects that had a semblance of having been used. It was a simulation in depth. Everything had to have a patina that came from use and age. It was essential that they *got* this, that they understood what the project was about, 'bringing history to life', which meant everything looked as though it had already lived a life and had a story to tell that was part of a whole larger one.

11   BACKWARDS IN TIME

IT WAS NOW LATE INTO the autumn of 1982 and time to start work with another specialist, again introduced by Mr Skipper.

Peter Millward was an engineering genius and inventor. He had already made his millions through inventions and patents and now amongst other things he ran a company that bought, sold and hired out helicopters. It seemed that everyone had a helicopter but Colin and me. Peter's task was to develop the Time Cars for us.

Initially, the concept for the exhibition had not included robot vehicles, rather it was thought that visitors would explore on foot. But during the early planning stages before we came on board, it became clear that fire and safety regulations would restrict throughput on foot. A better means to move people in and around had to be found. Whilst ensuring that the one hundred visitors at any one time limit established by the Fire and Safety Department would never be overstepped, the cars were a brilliant solution.

However what wasn't understood was just how important the cars would be to the design of the exhibition, as I've already explained.

The system by which they would guide and steer themselves around was known but not in museum circles. It was a system in use at the Fiat automobile factory in Italy, where special automated robotic rafts glided around vast warehouses taking car parts off racks. Whilst Peter had so far completed the technical design, and was constructing a prototype, the chassis hadn't been designed yet. That was my job.

The cars were another unique feature of the project. Looking back from the advantage of thirty years, I'm made to think what a fearless bunch the whole team was. We needed robot vehicles, about thirty of them and they didn't exist anywhere. We had to design them from scratch and then build and test them as well. It was the nature of this project, like so much of Jorvik; it was another first in the world of museums.

Peter Millward needed to meet with us and I wanted to go over my initial concept designs for the style and look of the chassis. Once again, I thought that touring the stick village in the warehouse would be a useful way to do this, even if it was a bit low tech.

So the day came when it was Peter's turn to pop up to see us, in *his* personal helicopter. We suggested he should come up to Rose Farm, Colin's house, and we'd take things from there.

Colin had plenty of lawn space for a helicopter. And besides which a helicopter landing on his back lawn would impress the locals (his locals being sheep and cows).

How do you give directions to someone flying a helicopter? Turn right at that little grey cloud? We weren't quite sure how to explain where Rose Farm was. In the end it was sort of, follow the M1 up to almost Leeds, then turn left and watch out for two blokes waving like crazy from the rose beds and a flock of impressionable sheep jumping up and down with excitement.

Colin had a better idea. He planned to lay out white sheets on the lawn in the shape of a big H for 'helicopter' that Peter would be able to spot. But, unfortunately on the day of his expected arrival it started to snow and soon the white H was lost in a field of white.

No matter. Colin, a decisive man of great initiative, jumped onto his motor mower and started to carve a swathe in the snow on another lawn forming a giant green letter 'H' in a field of white. I was so impressed.

Once done, whilst Judy, his beautiful wife, collected the damp sheets, he and I put our heads into mugs of coffee and cigarettes and discussed things for a couple of hours whilst waiting for Peter. Suddenly Colin's young son, Mark, came running into the barn to say that there was a helicopter hovering not far away looking very lost. Surely, how could he be lost? He must have spotted that great big H on the lawn.

I went to the window. The sun had come out unnoticed by us and melted all the snow. Gone was the H. In the end it was two blokes, a boy, his sister, two big dogs, Judy and a flock of excited sheep running in circles that brought Peter down onto the lawn.

Peter was a shy man, very softly spoken with a little ginger beard under his chin, which made him look a little like a leprechaun (come to think of it now, we had quite a few characters that looked as though they lived in fairy tales). We talked for a bit, breaking the ice, as we hadn't met before. He was another unassuming intellect, totally confident that he could make the cars work.

This was an important meeting for Colin, because Colin was now the client, not YAT. The cars were something we were responsible for delivering within our budget. Yorkshire Communications Group was contractually bound to produce the cars without which the Centre could not function. And it was going to be a huge outlay. We drove down to the warehouse for the handcart tour, which gave me a chance to explain what we wanted the cars to be capable of doing.

Though very low tech, that handcart tour of the life size model was once again proving invaluable. On return to the farm we went over my first tentative sketches for the chassis that showed two bench seats, one behind the other; restricting bars to reinforce the idea for passengers that they weren't to get out of the vehicle; speakers, four of them in the hand rail bars, and generally a muted sci-fi look.

Peter wasn't one for small talk and he didn't want to hang around too long, as he wanted to fly south in the remaining daylight. So off he went, disappearing over Colin's roof.

A short while later he invited us down to his place for a demonstration of the technical prototype. He lived in a lovely stand-alone cottage somewhere in one of the Home Counties. To get to his place from the road, we had to drive down a long private lane through thick black forest. He obviously liked his privacy and, as we soon discovered, speed.

When we pulled up it was obvious that here was yet another very wealthy man, judging by his toys; for standing in the driveway was a top-of-the-range gold Mercedes, a bright red Ferrari and round the back, a helicopter or two.

I'd never known really well off people and all this was a revelation, a far cry from Mum and Dad's semi-detached bungalow, our half-timbered Mini Traveller and a caravan on Yorkshire's East Coast.

Here I was hobknobbing with the super rich. It took a bit of getting used to. But Peter couldn't have been more down to earth if he'd been an earthworm, and a nice guy with it, no attitude, no edge. He was so softly spoken (like Trevor) it was really hard to hear him. When he spoke it was barely above a whisper. We soon came to learn that he didn't waste words and when he did speak it was usually and brilliantly to the point. I wondered whether he wondered why we stood and sat so close to him all the time. It was because we didn't want to miss a word.

He directed us to the side of the house where there was a gravelled area. There was the prototype Time Car. It was an exciting moment. Here was the real thing.

It didn't have a body; just four squat little tyres and an oblong frame, supporting the technical guts that made the thing go. It actually looked like a small metal bed frame covered in cables, batteries and electric motors.

Across the gravel was a strip of copper foil which had been laid flat. The copper strip followed a curving path and was connected to a box. Peter explained that to steer, the car had a device at the front end that 'sniffed out' a special pulsing signal coming from the copper strip. When the sniffer antenna found this signal it followed it. Peter said we'd be able to lay the strip along any path we liked, the only restriction being the minimum turning-circle of the car. He said that the strip should be set into the last level of concrete that still had to be laid in the basement and would be completely invisible to passengers.

Peter held a control box that was connected to the car by a conduit of cables. When he switched on the power off it went, looking for all the world like a dog following a scent with an antenna for a nose that swung left to right. This, he explained, would be out of sight. There would be no cable either as the cars would operate on batteries.

Amazing. The demonstration was a big hit. Afterwards inside, we spent another hour or so discussing the ramifications of the design and the cost and so on.

My mind wandered a bit. I stood outside watching Colin obviously delighted to see the thing moving around, like a big kid with a new toy. I remember looking at him in a slightly detached way and thought how much I admired him for his courage in taking on the risk to do this and stepping outside his safety zone and wondered, how on earth could he ever sleep at night?

So apart from the engineering technicalities that Peter had yet to work out, the cars were in every sense 'a goer'. It was time to design the bodywork, ironic for someone as unpractical around machines as I am. But I shouldn't have worried. All I had to do was produce sketch design concepts of how the vehicle should look and function from a visitor's point of view. Peter would enlist a car designer who would do the rest.

The basic factors affecting the design of the cars were practical ones; it had to be rechargeable, easy to use, clean, and service and carry at least four adults, or two adults and two kids. And something in the design had to restrain people from getting out during the ride.

Overall the size was small at around two metres long and just over a metre wide. Weight didn't really matter apart from the fact that occasionally the cars would have to be manhandled off the track during opening hours in order not to bring the whole ride circuit grinding to a stop.

A potential problem that hadn't been thought out before was the possibility that someone could have their ankles crushed by a car if they got trapped between two of them, after a breakdown say. There was sufficient weight to the cars to do some real damage to a person even though they'd never be travelling at more than four inches per second. We told Peter we were worried about that so he quietly said he would engineer a solution that he promised to demonstrate the next time we had a group meeting.

A week or so passed when he called me up in Yorkshire. He wanted me to visit the car designer he lined up who would make the technical transfers of my sketch ideas into a model for the car bodies.

All this was great fun for me. I am the most untechnical person you can imagine, but as with the rotoscope fabrication, I'm all for having a go as long as there's plenty of string and wire coat hangers available.

Here I was in the company of people who were way beyond string and coat hangers. It was a thrilling experience as was my trip with Peter to meet the mysterious car designer. He turned out to be one of leading designers of Aston Martins, James Bond's favourite toy. In fact, the whole experience of visiting him was like being in a Bond Movie. If only the girls from the cake factory could have come along.

I hoped we would drive to the meeting in his red Ferrari, but no, he said, it would be quicker by helicopter. I gulped; I'd never been in one especially one that wasn't much bigger than a bumblebee.

We went round to the back of his house. When I got up close it really was a toy. It was tiny, with a glass bubble at the front into which we only just fitted. As I reluctantly got in I could feel what little courage I had in me dissolve into my shoes. I wasn't that keen on flying then, especially in a lawnmower with a bubble on the front.

It was an odd sensation, going straight up and no lift buttons to punch. Once we got up travelling over the Home Counties at a height of a few thousand feet, I found it wasn't so bad as long as I kept my eyes closed. But of course, I couldn't do that especially when Peter kept pointing things out to me, things a long way down between my trembling knees.

The flight mercifully didn't take too long when Peter announced through the headphones that we were nearly there. We dropped in height. Beneath us the countryside turned into a vast green expanse of perfectly laid out landscape, one I suspected belonging to a stately home no doubt. But a stately home wasn't our destination.

We were over a park. It had a lake, quite a sizeable one, in a mini valley with woods on both sides and a higher section of shoreline, which, as we skimmed the edge, rose up into a rocky cliff. Perched on top of the cliff was a beautiful modern house partly cantilevered over the edge. No doubt this was indeed where Bond lived when he wasn't off on Her Majesty's Service.

Peter pressed the 'Lobby' button on the helicopter dashboard and down we spiralled, coming to a soft landing on a broad green lawn edged with tall elegant conifers quivering in our downdraft.

The door of this beautiful house opened and a beautiful tall blonde-haired woman in a one-piece trouser suit appeared and waved. She obviously knew Peter and gave him a sweet little kiss on his red-bristled jaw. I got to shake her lovely hand. This was the designer's wife, and his professional associate.

She wore something on her hip in a holster that caught my attention. This was 1982; there were no cordless phones available to the public yet, never mind mobiles. But that's what this was, a cordless phone with a little silver antenna.

I thought I'd better act cool, as though this was my everyday experience. Nothing would surprise me. I am sure I could have carried it off being cool if only I'd been able to close my mouth.

After walking down a softly lit corridor with rooms off to the right and views out over the lake, we entered the studio. By contrast with what I was looking at as I stood at the door, in my dark and tiny studio I worked on a piece of plywood that I've had for years. And, though to date I have conceived and visualised many, *many* millions of pounds and dollars worth of international exhibitions and their contents, no matter how I romanticise it, it's still just an old piece of board, taped over the front edge so it doesn't snag my jumper.

This was *not* that studio. For a start it was large and the windows looked out over the lake, as the studio was in the cantilevered rear of the house hung out over the cliff. We could have been on another continent, on another planet; there was no sign of England out there.

The other beautiful thing about the room and its interior design was that it was circular. There was a continuous desk, like a flat doughnut, running all the way round the room. In the middle of it stood a stately refined middle-aged man dressed in fashionable casual clothes, the man we'd come to work with.

As with all the people I was meeting at this time he was courteous, pleasant and professional. I wondered how Peter had come to know him? I asked him once. Peter obviously loved fast and powerful stylish cars. But he was vague about anything other than the job. I gained the impression over time that he knew the car designer from his motor-racing days. Peter was, as they say, 'a dark horse' and kept his private life private.

We spent a productive time over my sketches and ironed out a few details. It was very professional and there was no small talk. After a while he said he would work from the initial design. I got a personal thrill out of that. In the final version the Time Cars (much to my disappointment) didn't have rocket launchers, ejector seats or bullet proof glass. Well, you can't have everything.

When we were done we said goodbye and climbed into our helicopter. There are times when you really want your mum or your best friend to see you, knowing full well that you would never be able to fully describe the scene or event apart from saying you spent a day in *Thunderbirds*. Climbing up into the helicopter seat in that extraordinary place was one of those moments.

Work over for the day, Peter had it in mind to scare the effluent out of me. He slung the engine into gear and wound it up so the little insect shuddered and screamed with excitement.

I felt like I was in a food mixer as my face turned the colour of soy powder. He threw out the anchors and up we went vertically very fast; like in a glass lift only there was no building. Up, up, up we went then he slung the little chopper over on its side and we shot off over the house, plunging down towards the lake. I screamed internally.

Quiet, shy Peter my foot, this guy was a crazy man. We hung a curve round and down towards the shining water, then just in time he pulled out of the dive. We skimmed across the surface of the lake towards the other side scattering the ducks and where a bank of dark conifers rose up like a wall on a small hill. It looked to me like I was about to become one with the squirrels and pinecones.

As I was visualising my epitaph and the fun people would have at my wake, as the trees and certain death loomed closer, Peter pulled back on the stick in the last moment and up we shot again. I kept thinking, 'It's just an average day's work, but next time I'll take the train.' All I remember about the rest of the journey was trying to keep my bowels to myself.

Next day back at the factory Dave Punk Stuffer Astley came in with a sample of fake wooden planks with joints that he made for us with his magic material. The effect he achieved was simply astonishing.

A specialist company in Leeds produced the latex moulds of four of the original conserved Jorvik timbers. Into them Dave poured his mix. We were able to refresh and enhance the surface effects such as knotty details. Since we only had four original planks to work with, Dave showed how with a wire brush we could make every plank individual by working the grain slightly differently and adding details, like heads of the wooden pegs that the Vikings used to hold the structures together. The beauty of these plaster-based materials was that it was absolutely inert and totally fireproof. Jonathan, who came up with a great plan to use the four basic planks in different orders was delighted with the effects we were able to achieve on his buildings, which helped make them convincingly real.

We were now into production mode and working productively as a team as we approached Christmas 1982. After the holiday it would be time to begin to make the move to York.

My last task before the move was to help Colin find the construction team for the exhibit. Again I asked myself, 'Who do I know who knows set-building for theatre and television?' That's when I thought of the lovely Bob Wood the carpenter who I commissioned to make the animation desks for the animators to work on when I made *Kremmen the Movie*.

Bob would build you an airship from two plastic carrier bags and a rubber band or two. He was incredibly positive about everything, including his wife's fecundity. He had loads of kids, all mini-Bobs and mini-mams all blonde and mucky. They were really scruffy, happy wellie-ringed kids, with scabby knees and knotty hair, and they were always around their dad who they obviously adored. Bob also had a big hairy scruffy shaggy dog that looked just like him. It was a big untidy mutt and incredibly intelligent. He could ask it to go down the fish shop and bring back cod and chips twice with scraps on and it would and count out the change when it came back. That dog hung around Bob all day, and moped around when he wasn't in sniffing range.

I think why Bob Wood came into mind at this time wasn't just because he was a more-than-competent set builder; he actually looked just like a Viking. Bob was the chap; I was suddenly sure because he also knew lots of other suitable people, and I knew him and liked him, that was if I could get him away from the kids and his dog long enough to build our exhibit.

There was only one slight problem with Bob; he was essentially an anarchist, a free spirit who lived his life outside normal rules. Could he actually take on such a large part of our job without conflict with schedules and prices and deadlines and Colin? The two were poles apart, yet we had already gelled a team from a bunch of out-of-the-box individualists. Perhaps Bob and his band of merry men would fit right in. I reckoned it was worth a try.

I found him in his favourite pub in Leeds, performing a one handed roll-up from an old tobacco tin that was never far away from his leathery hand. He was as surprised and chuffed to see me as I was to see him. Over a pint or three I told him about the job and asked him if he could get a crew together. Without being over excited or committal he said he'd get back to me real soon. Bob was not one for pressure, but he was one you could trust.

Christmas and New Year came and went with the wrapping paper. We were on schedule to move into the exhibit basement by early March. Most importantly that space had to be dry as a bone before we could move in. I remember going down and seeing the place shortly after the concrete slab had been poured.

It really was just a big box, like an underground car park and with as much character. But that was okay; it was after all just a container. The extraordinary thing though being that the floor slab had been laid directly over the excavation and in-filled with sand to protect the site as is usually done in rescue archaeology. Our reconstruction would sit where the original features of the site had stood. Still, it was daunting to think that in a few short months in this concrete windowless vault we would recreate the original place.

Bob Wood got back to me and said he'd got a crew together and that he wanted to meet with Colin to discuss the job and the money and so on. As I predicted, the meeting didn't go so well. Bob Wood was to ties, suits and offices what Mahatma Gandhi was to drive-through burger joints. I think that Bob had an innate suspicion of anyone actually wearing a tie or a shirt and Colin wasn't easy with anyone wearing shorts and wellies without socks in January who had his large hairy dog sit in on the meeting. But nonetheless, they made a deal. And I began to wonder if Colin was not actually a born again hippy.

We decided to keep the warehouse on as we had loads of bulky materials to collect and nowhere to store them. For example, we had to take delivery in the coming months of a huge load of reeds for the thatched roofs. It wasn't so much that we couldn't build a giant haystack of it in the York basement, but we were told by the thatcher that the reeds had to be spread out on the floor and allowed to dry out before they could be used.

We also needed the studio for months after the move to serve as Jonathan's base where he planned the challenging job of building the full-scale boat that he was so assiduously and cleverly drawing up. I planned to move over to York; I wanted to be in on the build from start to finish.

Before we moved we had another specialist to find – the lighting director. We found yet another genius, Durham Marenghi, who in the decades since he lit Jorvik has literally and metaphorically illuminated the world in the most extraordinary ways. For example, in 2002 Durham designed the lighting for Her Majesty the Queen's Golden Jubilee Light and Fireworks Extravaganza performed at Buckingham Palace. He undertook the lighting design for the exterior of the London 2012 Olympic Stadium and in 2013 he was awarded Lighting Designer of the Year at the TPi Awards.

But back in the eighties like so many of us on the team, he too was at the early stage of his career and was as glad to get the job with us as we were to have him.

Durham's first job was to map out the basic lighting grid for the main exhibition areas. He estimated how many lamps we required as well as specifications for the control panel and its location. This had to be done at the planning stage so we could go on and buy the basic gear, get the fittings and have the power supply installed.

Lighting such as ours required dimming controls which were adjustable, allowing the designer and director to modify by brightening or dimming each light or a series of connected lights in turn. This not only affects what is visible, but also changes and sets the mood. This was as necessary for us as it was in a theatre production.

With controlled lighting we see what the director wants us to see. Shadows and areas of darkness can add just as much to the mood as light. Such would be the case at Jorvik; where although we intended to simulate late afternoon daylight, I wanted to use darkness and shadows to mask areas I didn't want visitors to see and to suggest a greater space overall.

We moved into the basement on schedule and Bob and his crew began laying out the basic areas, which would have elevated areas of earth and muck. Substructures had to be built and all according to the archaeological plan. This was going to take a couple of weeks.

Whilst Jonathan worked on the boat, Dave and Derek worked on the timbers, Carolyn sourced artefacts for reproduction and dealt with the people who were making them and Phoebe kept overall control of the schedules and budget. Colin stayed close to the clients and financial management and development of the finished cars.

My next task was to start considering the narrative script, the commentary that would be heard in the cars. That had to be done in conjunction with the laying of the copper-strip before the top slab of concrete sealed it in place forever.

Still making it up as we went along, I thought the best way of doing that would be to jump on that now-essential newspaper office handcart again. So we had it brought over from Wakefield to York. Then with me sat on it in the basement and the layout and the visualisation of the finished thing so real in my mind, Carolyn (I think it was she) pushed the handcart slowly over the rough concrete around the site following the path the cars would take. Making the right line for the copper strip to follow was crucial. So as we went along I kept asking for 'a bit to the left' and 'a bit to the right,' whilst drawing a line on the concrete with a piece of chalk bound with electrical tape to the end of a stick.

In many ways this unsung event was incredibly important because the path of the cars would, I believed, be the key to the success of the whole design. Once laid over in concrete, it would not be an easy thing to change. That chalk-line, once I felt we got it right, was not to be touched until Peter fixed the copper strip in place.

With the route laid out it was time to follow the track and do timings for the script. Sat once again on the handcart with Derek pushing and steering this time, I drafted an outline script to get a rough idea of how many words and what to say at a particular point during the ride.

This was so much like planning animation – a period of time, sequences of images, a length of track and the speed of the car. Using a stopwatch I recorded where we were on the circuit; doing it several times over I was able to average the timing of the trip out. I reckoned by doing this the ride would last somewhere in the region of fifteen minutes (in fact in the end it was fourteen).

The great thing about this technique was that within a second or two we could synchronise what was in view with what was being said. The storyboard approach and rough narrative would form the basis of the final script which

Peter Addyman and I worked on together with further input from a very famous archaeologist, scholar and television personality; more of him shortly.

Because in this, my story, a strange detour on my way to Jorvik was to occur. The telephone rang at home; it was the Kenny Everett mob again. They were planning a live action spoof horror film for the cinema, and they wanted me to art direct it and oversee the special effects.

I hardly dared ask if I could take three weeks off, but I was very tempted. After all none of us knew if we had a future in exhibitions and museums beyond Jorvik. After 'umming' and 'ahhing' a bit, Colin agreed, but he wasn't pleased. However, I was confident that work was on schedule and the team was performing fine so I took the chance to art direct Kenny's spoof horror movie, *Blood Bath at the House of Death.*

Don't bother looking it up, it was crap and the experience was like having a full-on nervous breakdown and suicidal toothache all at once. But I did get to blow up Vincent Price and incinerate Kenny amongst many other weird and crazy things.

Three weeks later I was happily back to a different reality with a man also known to millions who possessed another one of the most famous voices in Britain. To boot, he was Britain's most celebrated Viking, Magnus Magnusson. He was known as a scholar as well as a Viking of genuine descent and had been a champion of Jorvik since its inception. He welcomed the chance to do the commentary. It was wonderful; we couldn't have had a better choice for narrator.

For those that don't know, for years Magnus was the host of a very popular and long-running television series called *Mastermind,* one of the great hits of BBC television (and as I write, it still is, only now with John Humphries asking the questions). Magnus himself, a true scholar, archaeologist, historian and author in his own right, was also a dyed-in-the-wool populist.

I remember meeting him in his Edinburgh hotel. Phoebe was with me. We met Magnus to discuss the script for which he provided additional ideas and ways to make it work better as a commentary. The version used in the end was co-written with Dr Addyman. Later we accompanied him to his room where late into the night we did serious damage to a bottle of 12-year-old single malt.

Unfortunately the details of the evening are somewhat blurred; no, actually they've gone completely. Anyway he was a lovely chap and very accommodating and easy to work with, and a great credit to the project.

Drafting the first version of the narrative script was no big problem for me. It had been running through my head for months.

However, the *sound* of the multiple voices of the population of our little piece of Jorvik was more of a challenge. As the production process itself for the soundscape would take some time, I had to develop the 'screenplay', what the 'characters' were doing and saying in the reconstructions with advice from the archaeologists. The process had been going through my mind since I began positioning the figures which happened first on the plan. I then had an idea of who these people were and their ages. Much of the selection of figures and what they were doing related directly to the archaeological finds and where they were located. They knew a loom had been used and where because a spindle whorl had been found. They knew where a hearth was with food deposits around it. A lathe had stood outside one of the houses, known because of the wood shavings, which were trampled into the mud. And it was possible to locate where a stall selling jewellery stood because bits of jewellery fell to the ground.

Once I got the characters related to these finds, it wasn't difficult to imagine what they might have been saying. But to add to the drama, bearing in mind that it repeated every few minutes, I wanted some very expressive voices to break it up and make it seem more natural. A big part of this was that people were obviously living on top of one another. The collage of human voices added to the sense of density of the population. So, in the end, in the house the old man shouted after his granddaughter, 'Hilda, Hilda, Hilda!' And the little girl at the side of the house chasing after a boy shouted out to him, too. The older girl at the loom was overseeing the two little children who were laughing as she was telling them stories. Of course, while the finds could tell us what they were doing, they could not tell us what they were actually saying, whether they were laughing, shouting or whether they were upset; that was a matter for dramatisation and storytelling.

From this I then had to produce a script of specific dialogue with direction for emphasis in English, then get it translated into the nearest equivalent to 10th century Viking and recorded. How and where we would find the people to do this was a daunting question.

At least I knew who our characters were; several of them were already standing expectantly in a shed in Barnsley. Graham was hard at work producing them based on sketches I gave him. The sketches showed expression, age, sex, and physical position and how the characters were interacting with things (e.g., a wood lathe outside between the houses) and people (e.g., the three adults around the fire were all talking together as were the three children at the loom in the adjacent room). So it was not just a matter of sketching dummies in costume, but realising them related to character and interaction. With information on dress and objects, we created for example; the woman sat by the hearth in the house using the frying pan that after the ride could be seen in the museum. To me the figures were real people with personalities and their own voices.

In the end of the original production, there were all told 29 members of the cast of characters, human and animal. This is my initial list and how they played out:

— Young man at a market stall haggling with a large middle-aged woman over the price of a new horn comb.

— Largish lady, standing, giving the young man stallholder a hard time over the price of a horn comb (mixed dialogue between characters).

— Stallholder at a jewellery stall doing his best to persuade man to buy his wife a brooch.

— Husband of wife 'umming' and 'ahhing' over brooch and price.

— Woman who really wants brooch (mixed dialogue between characters).

— Man on top of roof mending thatch (note; I had him modelled after Colin).

— Man working lathe between houses. No speech.

— Girl running out of house shouting across the alley to her naughty brother.

— Boy other side of alley shouting back (mixed dialogue with sister).

— Baby crying in house (no figure can be seen, only heard).

— Inside house, first chamber / older woman mixing dough by fireside speaking to younger woman.

— Grandfather (angry) shouting for the girl that he wants more soup. She serves him.

— Younger woman (note: both women ignore grouchy old granddad). (Mixed dialogue with older woman.)

— Second chamber/girl late teens sits at loom with spindle. She spins wool and tells story to two younger siblings who sit at her feet (mixed dialogue happy and with laughter).

— Young boy aged about 8.

— Young girl about 6.

— Outside house/ man on toilet. No dialogue. No sound effects.

— Piglets and pig in sty.

— Chickens.

— Single dog lifting leg against side of warehouse.

— Two dogs fighting over bone growling.

— Three large geese, attack mode.

— Old woman carrying large bucket of water from well, surrounded by geese.

— Man unloading ship at wharf on deck.

— Second man unloading on deck.

— Third man unloading (mixed dialogue between all three, coarse and with laughter and cursing).

— Young man in conversation with another young man and one older man sit on levee. Slightly drunk.

— Young man as above.

— Older man as above (mixed dialogue).

Details of what the characters were wearing, their clothing and tools they were using etc. had been worked by the archaeologists. It was even possible to tell what the colours would have been like as enough of the dye along with pieces of fabric had also survived. The people of Jorvik wore not dun but bright colours, surprising to me. Up to that point, I generally thought of a commoner's life as being lived out in shades of brown and tan.

Not so in Jorvik. There was evidence for rich reds, greens, purples and browns mainly produced by vegetable dyes. And the fabrics were not all plain; many were patterned with plaid designs, which would have been produced on handlooms, again for which there was evidence. So when Graham turned up with his first figure, the goose lady with the bucket, she was suitably dressed in rich colours.

To go with Graham's trial figure we asked Dave to come up with a single goose to go with her. The old lady and the stuffed goose worked a treat together. I sketched them in the stop-frame mode so there was this great sense of action and importantly, the *real* goose and the fiberglass figure looked good and natural together. Colin, as everybody else, was delighted with the effect and the sense of animation.

Carried down in twos and threes, the inhabitants of Jorvik came to join us in the almost vacant basement at York where we were in the early stages of setting up prior to the construction beginning in earnest. While the place was pretty much vacant, I wanted to see them standing in the space to get a sense of scale.

Around now, shortly after we made our first move onto the exhibit site we began our curious relationship with the builders who were hard at work above ground building the shops and offices of the Coppergate complex.

At first they may have been surprised to see a burly bloke who looked just like one of them unloading a life size Viking woman from the back of his bright green 2CV Citroen and carrying her down into the bowels of the building past concrete mixers and piles of building materials. Following him was a little wiry bloke with a mane of black hair carrying a large and aggressive looking stuffed goose.

It was shortly after they and others of our motley crew started arriving on the site that a few of the builders from up top became curious enough to visit the basement to see what the hell was going on.

At first there was no point of reference and try as we might we couldn't quite explain what we were up to. But over time as the set developed, their respect for the skills of our team and their interest in what we were doing just kept on growing.

Graham's first figure was a great success and he got his contract. We transferred two of his first figures over to the warehouse where we placed them in the framed buildings, again so I could make a judgment on how they would work in the space. The mixed population of Jorvik was not that different to us, in stature anyway, if not in general health as evidence demonstrated.

Meanwhile Carolyn took on the complex job of working out, with the archaeologists' advice, just what the characters could have been saying. Though I had ideas about the characters' interactions and how I wanted the sound to be layered and overlapped, I thought it best to let the experts make suggestions about what they were actually talking about; it was unlikely they would be discussing the weekend's football match, or the rising cost of petrol.

Some on the team did wonder how much it really mattered what the people were saying in their strange alien sounding language. I believed it did. It was just another aspect of the reconstruction that we wanted to be as authentic as possible. I think it says a lot for the substance and quality of the research that we didn't have the people of Jorvik saying the Viking equivalent of 'rhubarb, rhubarb, rhubarb' on an endless sound loop. On the contrary, we gave it a lot of thought.

Once again, we were fortunate to find someone, just the right person, in fact a world authority on Viking language to help us with our quest for accuracy. Christine Fell was one of the world's leading experts on ancient Norse languages and she lived only about 25 miles away from Coppergate in North Yorkshire.

She agreed to help us with the translation of our script and to help us make more sense of it. Bringing this important aspect of the production off successfully fell into Carolyn's capable lap. She jumped to the job with her usual enthusiasm and came into her own and did a wonderful job.

Once Christine was on board and we had the dialogue mapped out, she translated it into Old Norse. Then the question was who could act this out, who could do the voices?

At first, Carolyn and Christine tried local actors, adults and children and the recording was made in the roof space of an ancient pub, The Star at Harome near Helmsley because they considered it had the right audio characteristics – low beams and thatch. But it was a tall order for amateur actors to speak expressively in an alien language in the roof space of a pub. The result sounded wooden, inanimate and fake, not at all natural. It didn't sound right no matter how much coaching the actors got. So who would speak Viking speech naturally? Where on earth could we find 10th century Vikings and Saxons?

Christine suggested that the best place for us to find the modern-day spoken equivalent was Iceland where the closest language to Old Norse is still spoken. That was the solution, to go to Iceland with our multi-part script and get a group of people together to act it out as naturally as possible. Carolyn made this her top priority project and got on with the arrangements.

Meanwhile, Bob Wood and his talented team of artisans arrived on site and started mapping out the construction, based on Jonathan's drawings and my art direction. It was now early spring of 1983 and time to order building materials.

The shopping list went something like this: concrete blocks, construction grade timber beams and framing, silver birches six to nine inch in diameter, silver birch saplings for wattle, horsehair, clay for daub, wheat straw and reeds. Not the kind of list you can drop into your standard builders' merchant for. However from our hyper-efficient research department (Carolyn and Phoebe) we learned that we could locate everything we needed. They also found the best, and *only* as it turned out, full-time thatcher in Yorkshire.

The reeds he would use arrived in great truckloads to the warehouse where they were spread out and allowed to dry. They had to be of two types, both identified by the environmental archaeologists. The first was wheat straw, which would have soon become water logged and rotten and therefore didn't make very good thatch but would have been easy for the inhabitants to get hold of. The other was a type of reed that would have grown on the edges of the rivers and surrounding swamps. It was more water resistant and would have made good thatch. But as it wasn't growing in a field was probably more difficult to acquire.

Delivery of truckloads of reeds to the industrial estate resulted in more curious looks from the ladies across the road, and further fuelling of what we were up to behind the blinds. I'd just arrived as the reeds had been delivered. It was around lunchtime and some of the girls from across the road were on their way to the local chip shop.

'Eyupp, 007!' It was the same lady who harangued me before. 'What's that lot for then, all that green stuff. What you doing in there?'

'We're hoping to start a new trend.'

'What kind of trend?' she asked.

'Ah, fashion,' I said.

'Oooh. What exactly?'

'Yorkshire grass skirts,' I said with a straight face.

'For men?'

'Yeah, course.'

'You're pulling my wotsits again aren't you,' she said, half believing me.

'No, honest, it's going to be a big hit this summer.'

'Will that tall handsome one with the motorbike be wearing one?'

'No,' I said. 'Too draughty on a motorbike. But the blonde one with the flash car, he will be.'

'Has he got nice legs?'

'You ladies will have to be the judge of that,' I said.

A week or so later I went with Colin to check on the reeds, which had been spread out across the floor of the warehouse. When we pulled up outside we noticed condensation running down the windows. Once inside we were met by a very strange swampy jungle smell, and it was a lot warmer than it had been.

We didn't think for a moment that two tons of damp reeds might act just like a pile of manure in a farmer's field. It was like a scene from the African Queen; great clouds of steam were rising up, and it was as hot and damp as a sauna.

You know how piled-up damp vegetation can start to steam and eventually set itself on fire if the internal temperature reaches a certain point. Well, as we didn't spread it thin enough, we found ourselves stood in the middle of a possible spontaneous combustion event. We almost burnt the building down.

Colin and I being quick off the mark realised that we had to turn the reeds so they could get ventilated. We found some useable tools for the job (a chair and coat stand) and started to turn them, which was when we discovered that we weren't alone. As soon as we began to move the stuff around we were met by hundreds of sets of tiny eyeballs. Little frogs had unwittingly taken a free ride and were now trying to colonise and mate in our warehouse. It was all very eco-friendly; we could probably have won an award.

They were impossible to catch as they jumped out of the reeds as we turned them, and they were just babies. So we just had to let them live in the reeds until they eventually perished. Poor frogs, what a rotten throw of the universal dice for them; one day you're swimming happily in the reed beds with your pals having escaped the predatory intentions of the local pike, then you find yourself starving to death in a West Riding warehouse next to a cake factory. No justice really.

Eventually the reeds and bales of wheat straw were delivered to the building site. I watched the line of willing hands off-load the reeds and carry them down the dirt ramp to the basement. The scene reminded me of jungle ants carrying bits of leaves and bark. We were the human bugs in the basement and now received not a second glance or comment from the builders.

When one thinks about it, there was a certain irony in that unfinished building. In the basement we were attempting to reconstruct the buildings of the 10th century from wattle, daub and straw, whilst above a high-tech building was rising up with all the accoutrements of the late 20th century.

In the basement, the buildings we were reconstructing came from two time periods; the houses and stores built in pits were the older ones. The above ground houses and wharf-side small warehouses had come later.

Some of the buildings were planked with broad heavy wooden planks, whilst others were timber-framed using silver birch poles and wattle and daub, this filled in between the main timbers creating the walls.

A couple of the members of Bob Wood's team were set builders who worked in theatre and television. It would have been really easy with their experience to fake the construction of the buildings, as long as they appeared like the archaeologists envisioned them based on the evidence from the dig. Who would know or care apart from the archaeologists? But I thought it was worth the effort to build, as the Vikings must have. I believed that not only would we learn through the process, but also somehow, they would be more real and authentic. And besides, it's not what we agreed to do.

Having said that, the archaeologists couldn't advise us accurately on all the details of the construction. Sometimes that was up to question. For example, there was a serious debate concerning the roofs. No identifiable roofing timbers had been found and there were no building plans from those far-off days. So there was no blueprint above a certain height. Our clients were rightly very sensitive about us making something up, not that we would have done anyway.

It was known that the original builders had used the reeds so it made sense that reed thatch in order to provide protection from the weather had to be laid down on the roof within certain angles of pitch in order for rain to run off efficiently. That made sense.

It's a testament to the archaeologists that in a speculative case like this, they brought in the very best experts they could find. But in the end even the Danish professor they brought over specially to advise us wouldn't be tied down to a definitive answer. He could only describe later Viking building methods that had survived by tradition.

But to Bob Wood and the rest of us, it made common sense how the timber frame roofs would have been constructed, besides which our thatcher knew everything there was about roof pitch angles. In the end there was agreement that we should try our ideas out and then they would be evaluated. However, it was my idea and it was also agreed that we would share with the public the fact that there wasn't the evidence and that we built what we considered the most likely solution.

That was a learning experience for me, a really valuable one because I realised that by telling or admitting to the public that we just don't know everything from the evidence and *why* we don't know is just as valuable as making it look like we know it all. In my view this engages the audience in the question and possible solutions.

I'm not sure that this philosophy had been used before Jorvik. But to me, by saying even the experts don't know or can't agree, lets everyone in on the discussion.

Since the Jorvik Viking Centre, having worked on several historic and archaeological projects, I've come to realise how little we do actually know about our human past. History, like the ocean, is only partly known let alone understood. That's why we keep looking. Admitting that we don't know everything became a positive factor in Heritage Interpretation ever since.

But here I am putting the thatch before the daub. We hadn't even built the buildings yet.

12 THE SMELLY OSCAR
NOMINATION
– THE GOLDEN STINKER

WE MADE THE TRANSITION TO the site without any real problems and now the fascinating business of reconstruction began, always under the watchful eyes of the archaeologists. I suspected some of them had a deep-seated fear that overnight we might build a set from the feature film *The Vikings* starring Kirk Douglas.

When I got back to York after the madness of filming *Blood Bath at the House of Death* I found not the concrete box that I left a few weeks earlier but the bones of a site of human occupation rising from the concrete, as though the buildings, which stood there a thousand years before, were re-emerging.

The main structures of the settlement were up. Their walls weren't built yet, just the frames, made from silver birch poles and shaped by authentic tools. It was immediately plain to see that the scale was right; like the stick village in the warehouse, it just felt right. But now we were coming up with a very serious problem, not the pitch of the roofs but what would happen if they caught fire.

Bob and his chaps were getting their heads round this possibility and the prospect that if that were to occur, it could actually hold up completion and opening or close us down before we even opened. The problem we faced was; how to effectively fireproof the thatch.

There are very tough Fire and Safety rules for public venues, not without good reason, and they're strictly enforced. We came under especially intense scrutiny because we were a new kind of venue. Making it worse for us was that the rules for an open travel-through exhibit like ours hadn't been written. This was a problem for the Fire Officers too, without whose certificate of approval we'd be a lost and rather foolish cause.

The City Fire Officers advised us that they would have to do a series of on-site tests, the toughest of them being the 'naked flame test' and the 'smoke test', trial by fire and smoke. For me it was a nightmare of anxiety. Would we pass?

Firstly this meant that a Fire Officer would walk along the edges of the thatch roofs with a cigarette lighter and a naked flame and try to set them on fire. Remember that the roofs of some of the lower buildings could literally be touched from the cars. We could all imagine some excited kid running his Zippo lighter under the thatch just to see what would happen.

Then there was the smoke ventilation test in which the place is intentionally filled with smoke setting off the ventilation system that then goes into hyper-drive to clear the smoke (which by now along with the lighting grids had been installed). How quickly this is achieved is crucial to the survival of the visitors and staff.

Smoke and panic, not fire, is the main killer. A person has to be able to breathe in order to escape and of course see where the escape route is; hence the need for illuminated exit signs at key locations. Unless the air-handling system could do its job in the required time, we wouldn't get the certificate.

These were the main tests: fire, smoke and provisions for safe exits with exit signs. Of these three provisions, it was fireproofing that gave us the biggest challenge.

Fortunately Bob's theatre experience provided the answer. Theatres also have stringent safety rules. He suggested we use the same chemicals used in theatres to fireproof things like curtains and fabrics. He thought they could also be used for organic materials. We held our collective breath as we checked with the manufacturers and discovered that indeed they could be.

The ventilation system was not installed by us but by a professional company who had already made assurance that the system would cope as it should. The provision of the exit signs, fire doors and routes to safety were a requirement of the building code and so were covered in the architectural design.

The practical problem in fireproofing the thatch was how to get the chemicals through and all over each reed, not just the top surfaces, which would happen if we just sprayed the chemicals on. The answer was a soaking bath into which the reeds were immersed.

Bob built wooden frames on the concrete floor and then lined them with industrial black plastic, into which was poured the fire retardant chemical followed by the reeds and straw which we had to make sure lay in such a way that they got the full immersion treatment.

Meanwhile our ventilation engineers carried out their own smoke test by using smoke generated from smoke pots. It was fascinating to see how the air flowed and eddied in the smoke just like a liquid once the powerful ventilators were turned on. At full thrust they sounded just like jet engines.

But I became really upset the day I realised that our beautiful exhibition chambers were to be hung with illuminated emergency exit signs in the most visible locations. The Vikings didn't use bright red illuminated exit signs. I thought the signs were bound to spoil the overall effect. I consoled myself with the facts that neither had they lighting systems, concrete basements or robot vehicles passing in and out of their houses.

The daunting prospect was that the Fire Officers would return only when the whole exhibition was complete to carry out their tests. We wouldn't know until the very end if we would get a certificate allowing the exhibit to open as scheduled.

The technical and chassis design for the Time Cars were now completed. Colin received the specification and the price for their production and gave the go ahead. Altogether the vehicles (there were around thirty of them, but I honestly don't remember the exact number) had a price tag of half a million pounds which of course was a huge investment.

Meanwhile, Peter Millward in his quiet and deliberate way was looking for a solution to the potential problem of the cars inflicting injuries if someone was trapped between two of them. He came up with an ingenious safety device. He fitted fat, very strong bumper-like devices resembling black inner tubes to the front and back of the vehicles. The new feature made them look like dodgem cars in an amusement park, but they weren't intended to act simply like bumpers. The tubes were inflated with air and kept at a certain pressure. If the car made even the slightest contact with an object or a person no matter how small or large, the instantaneous change in the pressure in the tube triggered an electronic relay stopping the vehicle immediately in its tracks. This appeared to be a foolproof system and it was added to the overall design specification.

Whilst this was going on, time was inexorably moving forward. It was now the summer of 1983. Whatever the weather outside, it was always the same down in the basement. Not many of us working on the job got summer tans. Instead we looked like we'd been doing time. We all got the Jorvik pallor.

Peter would be laying the copper strip soon and it would be time to lay the top level of concrete. I thought it made sense, as once it was poured there would be no turning back, to just go round on the hand-cart once again and double check. Derek who could now follow the course with his eyes closed, pushed the cart.

We were setting off down the course of the Time Tunnel, which was yet to be completed, when the phrase *back in time* that had been jingling around in the back of my mind, set off an epiphany moment.

'Derek,' I said, 'stop the cart! I missed something really important.'

'Oh no,' he said coming to a halt.

'It's okay,' I said, 'it's something good. It's the cars; they've first got to go *back* in time, *not* forwards.' His eyes widened.

'Until they arrive in Jorvik after the leather worker's shop, then they've got to turn round and go forward. See what I mean? 'Back' in time! It's beautiful.'

'Let's try it out then,' he said eagerly while pulling the handcart back to where the starting platform would be, my heels jiggling on the rough concrete.

'Alright, same speed but backwards.'

Derek pulled; I made up some commentary.

'It's good man, it's working!' he exclaimed.

'Look, can you imagine the power of this simple idea? Every one of the figures from the past in the tunnel is now walking past us to the future and no one on board knows where they're going. It's brilliant! Besides anything else, it's a great gag. People will love it.'

In my idea the cars needed to come out of the leather worker's still in reverse for the first reveal of the reconstruction, then come to a halt in the market area before setting off, this time going forwards.

But how would the cars run backwards with the pulse sniffer at the front end? I reassured myself that Peter could sort that out; it was too good an idea to pass up. Trouble was the cars were all but finished, and we were soon to see the first completed prototype. Would it be too late?

As luck would have it Peter was bringing the prototype up to show us in a couple of days and test it on the copper strip which he was going to tack down on top of my chalk line. Apart from Derek, who I vowed to silence, I didn't say anything to anyone till the day we were all stood around the car on the site.

We were standing in the reconstruction vault. Our clients were there, Peter Millward of course, Colin, and Phoebe, Carolyn and Jonathan all admiring out first Time Car. Peter was about to tack down the track, but not permanently in case there had to be changes. Just as well.

I piped up. 'I have something really important to say.'

Everyone turned and I got one of those 'Oh, God' looks again from Colin. I took a deep breath and carried on.

'I just realised a couple of days ago as I was checking the track line that at first, for the trip down the tunnel and to about here, the cars will have to go backwards.'

Suddenly I felt as popular as wind passed in a diving bell. Colin was taken aback; but Peter Millward showed no emotion whatsoever.

'Bloody hell, John,' said Colin genuinely miffed. 'We just got it to go forward. What the hell are you talking about?'

'Well,' I said, 'I'm genuinely not saying this to cause problems for the sake of it, but it's *got* to travel backwards from the starting platform until it gets to here.'

As it happened we were standing with the car in just the right place only pointing the wrong way.

'When it comes out of the leather worker's workshop it continues backwards.' I demonstrated by walking backwards. 'Then it stops, and then starts to move off forward and to the left.'

Everyone looked peeved. But I knew it was going to be the pivotal idea that would make the whole thing work.

'See, it's one of the most important ideas of the lot, *'travelling back in time'* literally! It will delight people and it means we can make so much more of the tunnel. It will be more effective as the passengers won't be able to look backwards, they won't know where they're going. It's pure theatre. It will add tremendously to the impact of the ride.'

I paused to let that sink in then continued.

'But it also means that after they've got off at the end, the cars will have to reverse so they can arrive at the starting platform going backwards again.'

Colin looked daggers at me but I stuck to my guns. I was the Project Designer. And more importantly I knew it was right. The view from the car was everything and I knew that Colin knew that I was right. He was just annoyed that it only just occurred to me and it was bound to cost a few extra bob.

'Can it be done Peter, or is it too late?' asked Colin.

'Yes, it can be done. It just means a bit more time and modification,' is all Peter said with a nod, bless his little helicopters.

And that's how the Time Cars came to travel famously *'back in time.'*

It might not sound like much now, even corny in a way. But that was one of the best ideas I ever had. It was so simple yet so perfect. Its effect was to produce extra dramatic impact in our staging as well as being a wonderful surprise and play on words.

Jumping forward a little, the effect on passengers was fantastic. They pulled out of the leather worker's shop still travelling backwards when they saw the whole set revealed for the first time on their left. It was indeed a pivotal point in the commentary marking the exact point when they arrived 1,000 years back in time in Jorvik.

Peter managed to get the cars to travel backwards and forwards (I think he could have managed sideways too if we'd asked). It was immediately evident that it made sense once we all got a chance to ride in the prototype. It was also going to help the impact of the commentary no end. (Incidentally, the phrase 'back in time' which would be heard by passengers at the beginning of the journey was copied by several Jorvik clones in the years that followed our opening.)

I was running unwritten pieces of script through my head for weeks. Every time I walked around, I could hear the kind of words we might use in the narrative. There was a rhythm to it and cadence where the key dramatic locations would be.

It wasn't just about synchronising the commentary to a particular location; it was about the dramatic effect of the story that Magnus would be telling. We were in effect turning the pages of an illustrated book as we moved from one scene to another.

I also realised just in time that this idea affected the design of the figures in the tunnel. Their poses should infer that they (with a few exceptions) were walking *towards* the future, in the opposite direction to the direction of the car. This would emphasise the idea that the cars were travelling backwards though history. So I called the Freeborns who thankfully had already got started on a standing figure rather than a walking one (a figure of a paper-boy selling newspapers on the corner of the street) and explained I had to revisit my sketches. I needed the figures to dynamically emphasise forward movement. This did not faze them at all.

Funnily enough, this was the kind of idea I was trying to get across in that early awkward meeting with the archaeologists. But now I think they were catching on fast and were getting terribly, if generally quietly, excited by what they saw developing.

One of the problems that any designer has in the early stages of a project is explaining and describing his or her vision, and then carrying it around until it takes form. In all the exhibition projects I undertook in subsequent years, there was always this period, about a quarter to a half a way into the scheme, when the client begins to lose confidence. There's nothing to see yet and they're still going on your promise, your vision.

That's what project designers are really paid for. Architects work with tangible products and materials. They might talk about ambience and mood, about character and feel of the places they are planning, but in the end they're designing solid physical things that people to one extent or another are familiar with. They can illustrate the structure and the way it will look and function, especially now with 3-D modelling.

But project designers, especially interpretive designers of immersive experiential exhibits, deal with less tangible effects, the suspension of disbelief for example. An interpretive designer plays with the mix and the balance between the physical experience (interpreted by the intellect) and the reactive response (interpreted through emotions) that each individual is having relative to the place and the story. The idea sounds great when you first describe it to the client, but as time goes on, and the project still hasn't taken form, it's like clutching bubbles, very expensive bubbles often.

At Jorvik, it sounded like so much romantic twaddle when I described the idea of 'the stopped frame of motion,' 'stopped time' and 'going back in time'. If you're a practical person, how do you appreciate such an idea until you experience it? A mistake visionary designers make (like I did initially) is expecting that everyone else not only shares his or her vision, but can see it in their heads too.

Generally one of the hardest things to manage is to maintain your own confidence in the tangibility of your intangible ideas. In the end you're saying, 'Look, right now I can't show you everything or make you feel a certain way, just trust me. You can't see it, I can. That's what you're paying me for.' That's a tall order for a client who may be risking millions in your fuzzy-edged vision.

In my subsequent career I designed and built over twenty national and international exhibitions and museums. A personal asset that I developed during Jorvik was the mental ability to *see* the scheme in my head and in effect walk or ride around it as though in a virtual display. I could visualise the finished product very clearly. It was a terrific thing to be able to do and this ability gave me lots of confidence to carry my client along with me whilst there was nothing yet for them to see, apart from plans and sketches.

Phoebe had news. She was searching for a company that could make smells and to our collective surprise she found one, in Blackpool of all places.

We doubted that such a company existed until Bob told us about a bakery in a new shopping mall in Leeds that he helped build. It used a special device to spread the synthetic aroma of freshly made bread into the air so it wafted out into the mall to attract customers. That itself was a revelation.

She spoke to a Mr Frank Knight of Dale Air whose company was based in Lancashire and arranged for him to come across to Jorvik. He arrived in the basement a few days later. He must have had a nose for business and could smell an ongoing lucrative opportunity.

As I remember him he was a solid man of average height in a trench coat and a brown trilby and looked like my idea of a cold war spy. I was working down the other end of the basement and was called over. When I got up to him I was hit by a strong feminine and not unpleasant smell.

'Well, that's quite a greeting card,' I said referring to the wafting aroma as I shook his hand.

'Oh,' he said taken slightly aback. 'That'll be Gwyneth.'

At which point his lovely assistant, blushing, slight and blonde, stepped out from the shadows behind him (why she was hiding I didn't know) revealing that she was in front of one of our big ventilation fans. It was *her* perfume, not his, I smelled. I must say I was relieved.

Gwyneth, who turned out to be chronically shy, carried a very professional looking sample case with a special coded lock on the top. I imagined that in it were all the usual samples, just-baked-bread, new car showroom smell, that sort of thing.

As I took him on a tour of the site, which by now had most of the internal frames completed and much of the sub-structure for the ground, I attempted to describe the place as a series of smells and overlapping odours. I explained how the environmental archaeologists discovered that organic waste was just dumped inside and outside, besides the pigpens and the cesspits, and that the place must have stunk to high heaven. To fully reconstitute the place we needed smells as much as we needed sound and light. I remember his expressions as he took off his hat then replaced it. His face went from surprise to bewilderment.

'Not nice smells?' he said.

'No, not overall,' I said blowing my nose.

'Normally see, we make good pleasant aromas to mask bad ones, or to wake up people's appetites. This is quite out of the ordinary, quite the opposite in point of fact. I can't remember being asked to create bad smells. Can you Gwyneth?' he asked his demure assistant.

'Oh no, I mean yes, Mr Knight,' she said with a little giggle and a nod. 'Not bad smells, no never.'

'Quite a challenge, it'll be a first for the industry,' he said. 'I'll come back to you on whether we can do it or not. You see, natural bad smells themselves are mainly organic; bacteria in the air, you know what I mean. And bacteria are unstable, unreliable. However, there are chemicals and gases that can be used, but they too are not easy to control either. It'll be a challenge Mr Sunderland, never been done before I'll bet. But, let's be positive. Let's make a list of the kind of aromas more specifically that you're after.'

So Gwyneth got out her notebook and wrote things down in shorthand as we did another walk.

'Well, this is where the leather worker's shop was,' I said.

'The smell of leather, quite raw and earthy, tanning I would think,' he said.

'And out here,' I said as I stepped into the main set from the leather shop doorway following the path of the car. 'There was a market here. On the left there'll be piles of baskets, apples and pears. And here, there's fish on sale.'

'A market was it?' he asked. 'How do they know?'

'Because of seeds and bones, things like that found in the ground.'

'Well, I never,' he said.

'Mr Knight,' I asked, 'would you like to take off your coat and hat?' I thought he must be very warm.

'Oh, no,' he said straight faced, 'you never know when it's going to rain.' I looked up at the concrete ceiling but said nothing.

'What kind of fish?' asked Gwyneth.

'Pickled herrings in barrels, one of which is open,' I said drawing the barrel with my finger in the air.

'My father loves pickled herrings, my mother can't stand the slimy things,' she said.

'Thank you Gwyneth, just take notes please,' said her boss.

'Yes, Mr Knight. Sorry,' she said blushing the pink of cherry blossom.

'Then generally,' I said, 'we want the place to have a background smell of rotting food, horse dung, fish, bad eggs, dog dirt, human excrement, sweat. Imagine,' I said, 'everything was just dumped outside and trod down into the mud.'

'Got the picture,' said Mr Knight. 'Quite a challenge, exciting really; nobody asks for bad smells; it'll be a first,' he said taking a folded hanky out of his pocket and wiping his nose.

'You might make a Smelly Oscar nomination. The Golden Stinker,' I said.

'Oooh,' giggled Gwyneth. 'That would be good, wouldn't it Mr Knight.'

We were now where the man turning wood on a lathe would stand. 'Here, wood shavings that fell from the lathe,' I explained.

'What kind of wood?' he asked.

'Oh, you've got me there. I'll find out,' I said, pulling my own notebook out of my back pocket.

'Could it have been knotty pine?' asked Gwyneth. I saw Mr Knight give her a sideways glance. She added, 'We've got gallons of that back at the factory. Sorry,' she said in a tiny voice as his look shut her up.

'Now,' I continued, 'we go inside the house here on the left.' We stepped inside the open framework of the largest house. 'This is the house with people inside where the car would pass through. Down there is where a hearth was found and lots of food and grain all round. As soon as you come in here I think the overwhelming smell should be cooking, a fatty bacon-like smell mixed in with the straw and the rushes and the sweaty smell of people, and smoke. There was no chimney it just went up through the roof. And chickens. Any chance of a goat?'

Gwyneth's pencil flicked goat in shorthand onto the list.

'See, normally,' paused Mr Knight giving his olfactory instrument a second overhaul, 'it's a challenge all right. It's not what we are geared up for you see; nice *pleasant* smells are what we normally do. But people like the smell of bacon.' I could see him thinking. 'Goat you say? We might become the laughing stock of the industry.' I thought I might be losing them.

'Well,' I asked, 'aren't bad smells easier to make?' thinking back to the gym changing room at school and our dog, well, and me to be honest.

'You'd think so, wouldn't you?' replied Mr Knight. 'But as I said, it's how to manufacture them and control them.'

'Yes,' said Gwyneth, 'I mean, no.' she said shaking her head.

'You're sure you wouldn't like to do a nice bouquet of multi-grain bread to go with the bacon? Very pleasant, you could sell Viking bread in the shop,' he offered.

'Tempting,' I said. 'There's a woman mixing dough who will be sat there by the fire.' I unrolled a drawing. 'But no, I don't think so. There's all these other smells, all mixed in,' I said. I didn't want to end up with shopping mall aromas. I could see the way his mind was working, fresh pine, green apples and hot dough. Nice little stall down by the river.

'Well, if it's too much of a challenge then,' I said.

'We'll see what we can do,' he said assertively.

We stepped out of the side door of the house.

'Here.' I walked over and bent down to sit on an imaginary toilet seat plank. 'There was a cesspit here, a toilet.'

'I know what a cesspit is,' said Mr Knight

' I don't,' admitted Gwyneth. He didn't even bother looking at her.

'And there's a man sat using it,' I said. 'It should smell accordingly.'

'Good Lord, I got it,' said Gwyneth. 'How about an air freshener, apple and citrus?'

'And over here?' asked Mr Knight indicating a square enclosure I'd drawn on the concrete.

'A litter of pigs in a wattle fenced sty with the feeding mother.'

'It's *really* smelly down here then, pooh,' imagined Gwyneth pausing as she made her notes to take a delicate little lace edged hanky from her sleeve.

'Then running along the back wall is the river bank and beyond.'

'The river?' Mr Knight interjected. 'You want a *river* as well? Was it tidal?'

'Ah, yes,' I said, 'Well, I'm not sure. I'll check.'

'Details, Mr Sunderland, are the founding alchemy of my product. They count.'

'There'll be a boat here,' I showed them, 'unloading sacks and barrels. And fish, dried cod and herrings and there'll be lots of tarred rope. So I think river water, tarry rope, and fishy smells. But most of all the muddy smell of the river and human effluent.'

'A challenge alright,' said Mr Knight rubbing his sweaty forehead under the brim of his hat and shaking his head at the same time.

'And that's about it,' I said.

'Hmm,' he said. 'And so, Mr Sunderland, how long will the exhibition be up for do you think, a few months?'

'Oh no, years and years hopefully,' I said as we slowly walked back between the house frames.

'Years eh, and will you be wanting the same smells to continue?' he asked. What I was asking for was beginning to smell like money, lots of money to him.

'Definitely,' I said, 'if things work out.'

He brightened up. 'You see this is an original! We'll have to make up things that don't exist in the world of aromatic environmental planning.'

'Back to the drawing board,' added Gwyneth seriously.

'We'll need a contract,' he said.

'Of course,' I said. 'First though we have to know that you can make the stuff and make it work in the exhibition on a day-to-day basis.' I could see he was already planning his retirement villa in Malaga, imagining a long-term enhanced income stream. He had the smell of dough right up his nose.

'Alright then,' he said.

'So, what's in the case?' I asked.

'Samples,' said Gwyneth proudly holding it up with two hands.

'Oh, interesting.' I said.

'Would you like to try one, or two? Gwyneth, please,' said Mr Knight.

Gwyneth opened the case on the floor. Inside were two lines of small white plastic bottles with screw tops. He picked one up and opened the top.

'Now you have to remember that this is a concentrate.'

I sniffed. 'Apples,' I said.

Gwyneth nodded and beamed. I beamed back. By gum she really was lovely.

'Bread,' I said after she wafted another bottle under my nose. 'The Merrion Centre shopping mall,' I said, surprising myself at the memory.

'Correct, impressive,' he said. 'All made by chemicals, synthetic, fooling the olfactory senses,' he said with a thin smile. 'The human mind fills in the rest, imagines things that aren't there. Smells remind us of places and events and people. Your granddad's pipe, mother's cooking, the lavender in your grandma's cupboards and drawers.'

'My gym pumps,' I said. But how did he know about my grandma's lavender?

He squared his hat on his head. 'We'll come back to you shortly. Give me a week or two to try things out. Then if we think we can do this, we'll arrange a time for a demonstration,' he said business-like.

'Great. Thanks for coming all this way,' I said. I was now in love with Gwyneth and she knew it. She smiled a smile that made me wish I had an unmarried twin brother so I could be with her always vicariously.

'It's been a pleasure. Gwyneth!' he said sternly pointing to the open case. 'We'll say goodbye then.'

'Anyway, the rain held off,' I said looking up.

'People from the west have second sight when it comes to rain,' were his last words.

13 METICULOUSLY MODELED MUCK AND WASTE

ON SITE THE DESIGNERS, THE builders, the special effects people, Carolyn, Phoebe, everyone were now bonded as one tribe with one object in mind. Like troglodytes on a mission, we were human ant artisans scurrying about out of sight under the building, creating a life-scale lower earth settlement, a middle-earth of the past and loving every precious minute of it.

Now that the frames of the buildings were in place and the top layer of the concrete floor had been poured we could begin fleshing out the reconstructions at both sides of the dividing wall. It was early autumn and days in the basement slid like sand through the neck of an hourglass we could not control. But at least we were more or less on schedule. It was time to put the walls and the roofs on the buildings.

There was only one daub and wattle building and it was a messy job to complete. The great thing was we used the actual materials and so from the outset it looked real. The other buildings had heavy hand-sawn plank walls attached to the upright beams of the internal wooden frame with wooden pegs.

We cast the planks according to Jonathan's clever plan, which was to take casts of a number of original planks and then assemble the reproductions in different combinations. We observed from the originals that each was slightly different in length, warp, grain and thickness. The originals were as precious as gold and had undergone a special process of conservation. Once removed from the site to the conservation laboratory they were immersed in a special fluid for a period of time during which their cellular structure had been replaced with a kind of wax. This stopped them from rotting away and held them in a kind of inertia. And it was from these now stable originals that our moulds were made.

Once attached to the wooden frames which were now fastened to the outside of the concrete block-built Time Car garage, we were able to work on each plank one by one with wire–brushes enhancing the individual grain effects.

Dave Astley revelled in this work; his talent for naturalistic observation came to the fore. Each plank ended up being a unique version of the original. By the time we attached all the planks, stained them the same dark colour as the ones from the dig and added effects of damp dirt and mould, you'd swear they were the real things.

Now we worked as though possessed. Bit by bit we built up the picture, starting with the outside of the buildings then raising the landscape of muck, mud and mess on top of the flat concrete floor with its now buried copper guide tape.

Meanwhile the crew was hard at work at the other side of the exhibit reconstructing the archaeological dig. On both fronts, as the autumn nights outside got darker and longer, we down below in our nether world were heading towards the final detail dressing as our subterranean days stretched out into the evenings.

Off-site hundreds and hundreds of objects were being produced to our specification by craftspeople all over the country, mostly individuals that were tracked down in the oddest places by Phoebe and Carolyn. When we received samples we marvelled at what had been produced like we were looking at treasure. The quality of the objects we received was incredible; jewellery and coins, horn goblets and fire dogs, trugs and textiles, barrels and combs and brooches, shoes and bags. There were also pots and pans and pottery, knives and axes, woodworking tools and baskets. The list went on and on.

On the site Bob's boys created a credible landscape. Though the car track had to be flat and in the archaeological exhibit 'cut' into the ground, I reckoned that the public wouldn't notice it, they'd see the greater landscape.

Though the layout was almost identical to the locations of the houses now beneath the concrete, consummate artistry came in bringing the scene together using only things that we were advised had existed. The skill lay in creating a convincing version of a reality that said real people had lived here.

I tried to think how things would have been arranged, how things would have fallen, where would things be stored, what kind of mess would Viking kids have made, the accidental, the spontaneous.

An attempt at mirroring a real-life situation we could only conjecture. Okay, so we couldn't place ourselves in the past. But what we shared with the original inhabitants was our humanity and I reckoned that if we could somehow capture that sense in the reconstruction then the public would be engaged at a deep and human level, connected to their own life experience.

The thatcher who Phoebe discovered, William Tegetmeier, came to work on site, every inch of him the epitome of a young man who worked with his hands in the open air under open skies.

He looked like a harvest field himself, with his gold blonde hair and straggly beard. By now the thatch had been treated with the fire proofing chemicals so he got on with the job, admitting as he did, that it was the most unusual commission he'd ever had.

He was happy to share the secrets of his trade with us, but as with everything we were doing, we had to attempt at least to put it in the context of the 10th century. As to the roofs, in the end we applied the common sense law. Make it serviceable and simple, and that's what our thatcher also did with the thatch.

Whilst he was up on the roofs of the houses we got down on our knees to meticulously model muck and domestic waste that environmental evidence had shown had been thrown out into the spaces between the houses to rot. Strangely enough dirt and rotting garbage was not easy to replicate. If only we could have just spread real organic stuff about and hope for the best. That would have worked for about a week though.

Speaking of which there was some real organic stuff already down there in the basement. The wattle started to come into leaf and the last of the frogs and the new insects that had arrived as unwitting passengers with the birch trees did their best to create their own micro-world, but that didn't last long either.

Bob's team wasn't composed of only carpenters and builders; they were also set painters and artists in their own right working day by precious day along side us and doing a wonderful job. We all mucked in. It was an enriching experience to be involved in the build process. For me, there's nothing like getting 'down and dirty', hands-on in the build process to allow me to see my ideas forming into the physical.

As the reconstructed settlement was taking on fuller shape and detail, there were more builders from the above ground world coming down to see what we were doing. I saw them stand at the entrance with mouths agape. Now they could see what we were about.

They asked questions about it. Some were totally fascinated and became regular visitors. We welcomed their interest. After all, here were prospective visitors coming with their girlfriends and families. I like to think they shared pride in what we were building on that site, not just us below, but them above as well.

Work was going on at an increasing pace in the other half of the exhibit where the Coppergate dig was being reconstructed. Members of the archaeological team joined our people in the hands-on details of reconstruction. Every inch of the site could be minutely replicated because of archaeological records and of course from first-hand experience of the archaeologists.

The dig reconstruction wasn't a technical exercise alone; I wanted the place to look as convincingly real as the 10th century reconstruction. So it wasn't just the features like hearths, cesspits and postholes. I wanted them to show us where the planks had been positioned that they walked on when conditions were too wet, what kinds of buckets and trowels and wheel-barrows they'd used and so on. We even incorporated two figures of archaeologists working on the site, one using a theodolite.

A lot of this stuff we were able to 'borrow' from YAT; buckets still with mud on, trowels with worn edges, boards with actual plans half finished and measuring frames with their grids of cross-strings. We filched everything we could for the cause, from theodolites, to tea towels, from worn Wellington boots to threadbare jackets and hats, tin mugs to scaffolding.

But for all these things, the stars of the show were the *real* timbers. It was an ambitious idea to replace some of the now conserved timbers in their original positions, just as they'd been discovered. Believe me that was a radical idea.

Of course, we could have replicated them. But the real objects (now conserved) spoke volumes. It was real evidence of occupation plain for all to see from a thousand years before, and it could be seen without the aid of a microscope.

Rusty ribbed steel walls had surrounded the dig and held back the damp earth. We replicated them. Scenically those rusting steel walls gave the impression that we were indeed in a deep hole. Over it we built a scaffold lattice roof to keep Mr Knight's rain off and then we suspended working lights from it.

Later to complete the illusion with sound, speakers were fixed up there and a sound track of actual modern York traffic and street noises played continuously. The scaffold and sheeted roof added a convincing touch whilst masking the actual concrete roof.

Employing the same detail to Craven's cellar that the archaeologists used as a crew room, we first talked with the people who used it, about what it had been like and dressed it accordingly with litter and mugs, ashtrays, newspapers and plans. For all the world when we finished, it looked as though a tea break had just ended minutes before. In fact, after the opening there was a real problem keeping the museum staff from tidying up the mess and washing out the stained coffee cups.

This level of reconstructive display was new to the museum world, as was the idea of immersing people in it. What we were doing was so unlike a traditional museum that Jorvik's staff was confused at first as to what was real and what was *simulated reality*.

Tidying up the place into their idea of what a museum should look like was a serious worry. A couple of years after opening I went back to see how the exhibit was faring and sure enough, new people on staff had tidied up. All the rubbish and the spontaneous look of lived-in effects had gone. It was an unforeseen problem made worse by the fact that we did not record each area in detail on film. I thought at the time that it only went to show that our view of history is much tidier than reality.

Whilst the reconstruction of the dig itself with its trenches and standing sections, fire pits and postholes and timbers in place was really superb, for me the one effect that worked the best in the simulation of the dig was the Portakabin. We had a real one donated to us by the Portakabin Company. To their surprise when we took delivery, we cut it in half and fixed it to the wall overlooking the set. It was positioned so it wasn't straight on, but at a slight angle. This improved the illusion and gave it more depth. We partially covered the windows with plans and newspapers, so it was hard to tell that it was only a couple of feet deep. It worked very well.

I learned how the simplest reproduced signs of human interaction in situ were essential to carry the illusion convincingly; things like footprints made with real boots, mud on the rungs of the ladders, a bottle of rancid milk in the window of the Portakabin and yellow construction helmets personalised with names, stickers and jokes, and a hundred other things created an enhanced sense of realism. I think my favourite small effects were a couple of tea towels hung out to dry on a string washing line next to a pair of heavy well-worn wellie socks.

By mid November 1983 virtually all the major construction work had been completed, including all the roofs. All the display lighting was in as were the lighting dimmers and Durham had made an initial balance of the lights which now illuminated the site through coloured gels. Next we had to start to dress all elements of the 'ridescape' in detail.

The figures, taxidermy and the hundreds of objects, for the market place, the leather worker's hut, the interior of the house, the ship and the warehouses had yet to be placed in their settings. However, whilst the place was well from finished, I noticed a subtle switch late one afternoon.

It was after six and I was the last in the basement. Everyone had been tired that day and as there was a threat of fog, they took off from work a little earlier.

I was on my way out. We were working on the lighting scheme and the effect on the set had been dramatic, adding depth, atmosphere and richness. The scene in front of me now consisted of all the finished buildings with the wharf in the distance, which now included a full scale Viking ship with furled sail.

I stood by the master electrical switch to turn off the lights for the night. The scene, which I had now come to know so well, was somehow different; it had taken on a new quality. It had become *real*. I don't mean a real model of a place, or a set, just completely and utterly real.

I stood there. A little shiver travelled up and down my spine. It was something to do with the fact that the whole place was based on and had been built on evidence. It was as though it had come to life again.

It was then, in that moment, that I really believed that Jorvik could be a sensation and successful beyond our wildest dreams.

For me personally, I was inside my own dream. Transfixed, I expected to see curls of smoke coming from the roofs and hear the voices of the inhabitants, but it was as quiet as a grave.

It was a wonderful moment, my own personal suspension of disbelief. I knew then that the archaeologists' concept had been exceptional and we had created something unique and *very* special. But in truth I had a lingering doubt; would a glimpse of this reality be as compelling to the public as the other violent Viking reality, the escapades of warriors? Would people really be interested in the ordinary everyday life of Jorvik folks?

Besides our team down in the bowels, above us in the recently occupied new building which accommodated the entrance and offices, a new management team was being trained. This team was under the control and direction of Anthony Gaynor. As a military man he continued to make a very effective Project Manager. In 1983 Anthony began to assemble the operations team for the ongoing operation of Jorvik once it was open.

Besides day-to-day management, there were the front of house staff, the promotions and marketing people, the bookings staff, office staff and the team who would manage and operate the all-important shop. And last but not least there was the technical and security staff and maintenance staff. They all made up a small army of people, and once underway, a lot of wages had to be paid.

In many ways the whole operations plan was breaking new ground, writing the rules as it went along. What made it different back then was its mix of commercialism, military discipline and efficiency.

The Jorvik Viking Centre was (and is) a private enterprise, which had to be run effectively and profitably as a business from the get go otherwise the whole thing would fail and fail quickly. Many eyes in the museum community were upon the venture, and many doubted it had a future.

One couldn't help but to get the impression that management boards of some nationally funded museums and others that were grant-aided seemed to think that society owed them a living. If Jorvik were successful financially, a spotlight would be turned onto to them to demonstrate whether they could do the same.

With Ian Skipper's dynamic business leadership, our reality was that no one owed Jorvik anything. We, the whole team, had to produce everything from scratch, and what we produced had to be worth visiting and worth the admission price. It was about now that we started thinking of the Jorvik Viking Centre as a 'Heritage Attraction.'

The critics of the commercial aspects of the project saw the word 'Attraction' and thought the worst. However, it was a simple fact of life for Jorvik – attract visitors or perish.

Behind it there was no wealthy foundation, no grants beyond the original one from the English Tourist Board, which had gone into the development capital fund. The banks and backers who were involved wanted their loans back with interest. The JVC was a business, owned by a not-for profit charitable organisation, yes, but a business nonetheless. And it had to be a day-to-day streamlined and efficient operation with a smile on its face.

So besides anything else that made Jorvik different it was that it stood alone, and so it was absolutely essential that the story from dig to ground-breaking museum reached the public.

One department that was already operating very effectively in 1983 was the PR and marketing department. They were essential in drumming up and maintaining public interest through all the media and not just at home, but abroad too. Their task became easier once the exhibit reached the point where there was something substantial to see, which it had at the end of 1983. It was then that they went into overdrive and set about stimulating interest in the press, television and radio.

A whole new bunch of curious visitors began turning up on a daily basis. Media interest and coverage was essential if we were going to get the numbers of paying visitors the project needed, so we all had to put up with the disruption that being 'on show' caused.

Luckily, Vikings along with dinosaurs and pirates have huge public appeal especially with children. The story of a rescue excavation that had almost run out of money and its subsequent development as a world-class and unique exhibition made good copy. That kind of story always had. But now that story could be illustrated with new images of what the Anglo-Saxon Viking world looked like. It wasn't that difficult to raise the interest.

Though as with the earlier press coverage, which followed the original launch, there was again considerable negative comment about the 'exploitation of the National Heritage for commercial gain'. There were snide references to our 'Disneyfication' of an archaeological treasure. Some of the more conservative critics of the project viewed the use of technology and unconventional means of presentation with disdain. They considered the Time Cars more as a thrill ride that one might experience in a theme park rather than what they were, an efficient transport system and literally a vehicle for interpretation.

One got the impression that our critics believed that to seek promotion and publicity, and worst still, actually aggressively going out to sell the project as an attraction, could only cheapen British Heritage and archaeology in particular.

Throughout the negative media there was a general suspicion that we were somehow dumbing-down the subject and sensationalising it at the same time. Of course, nothing could have been further from the truth. Dr Addyman was upfront and brilliant at answering the project's critics.

However, the truly fantastic positive coverage and resulting public interest in the project was due in a huge part to the genius of the marketing people. They and management recognised that Vikings made hot copy and anything to do with rescue archaeology when presented as it was (in this case as a race against the clock before the concrete was poured), it was sexy stuff and worth a fortune in free publicity. And anyone that could stir up interest and tell our story to the public was encouraged to do so.

At the time and in the background there was a national debate going on about whether or not museums should charge the public for entry. The JVC being privately owned could do what it liked and besides had no other course to follow other than to charge for entry as it had to be commercially independent. But there were those, I got the feeling, who were keen on seeing it *not* succeed as a private venture who would be only too pleased to gloat if it failed.

Colin and myself and our wonderful team were in reality just employees on the job. We could have had no further interest other than a sense of pride in what we were doing. We were under contract, one that would come to an end shortly after the opening of the Centre. But it didn't feel like that. We were caught up in the growing excitement and were desperate for Jorvik to be a success. Our hearts were in it and it showed in everyone's work.

This great energy of purpose ran through everything. Anthony, Peter and Ian from the top enthused everybody with a great sense of direction and purpose. We felt ourselves to be a family.

There was also the money to build Jorvik to consider. It would cost three and a half million pounds, chicken feed when you think of contemporary price tags for new museums. This money had not been as easy to raise, as it was to get publicity.

It took a great deal of time, acumen, faith and energy to raise the funds and in the end it came from a consortium of banks plus other sources. The English Tourist Board made the largest grant and Ian who backed the scheme with his entrepreneurial skills also put up his cash. His was a very substantial first in, last out loan. But it was more than his money. The banks viewed him as a successful businessman and entrepreneur and judged that if he believed in the project then they surely could. Ian Skipper's confidence became the keystone in the financial bridge to Jorvik.

Having said that, everyone knew that it was a huge gamble and no one could predict with confidence whether or not it would succeed. If it failed heads would roll, careers and reputations would be ruined and the project would lapse into bankruptcy and receivership with the loss of many jobs. Looking back now, I wonder just how many of the stellar careers and businesses that grew from Jorvik's success would have occurred. My own career, my entire professional freelance adventure, was to fruit from Viking roots, as were the careers and businesses of others, like Carolyn's and Colin's. Still at the end of the year, as we were about to step apprehensively into 1984 no one knew what was going to happen in the next few months.

In the winter of 1983 the operations team geared up for a soft opening in March following the fitting out of the exhibition in February. Soft openings are used to test public response. But before that acid test occurred, the doors were fully opened to the media at large.

So whilst we were doing our best to dress in the figures, complete the set-dressing in minute detail and install and test the 62-track sound system, we had to break off repeatedly to give one or more media representatives our undivided attention. And it wasn't just media hacks; there were VIPs, politicians, ministers of this and that, members of minor royalty from home and major royalty from overseas.

Though somedays the place glittered, it was a circus and for us, something of a pain. We creative types were to act as ambassadors for the project as much as anybody because we were down there. We were expected to walk the walk and talk the talk.

At first we didn't mind. Often when people came below to look at the developing exhibit, as Project Designer I had to address the visitors and act as guide. Carolyn, blessed with her archaeological experience, confidence, enthusiasm and charm, was a natural at the PR game and a great asset in that regard to the project.

We had to focus our attention on each visitor, think of who or what he or she represented and make him or her the centre of our attention for the time whilst they were there. If we were to receive positive press, it was essential that the media people understood the scholarly foundation of the project and why it had developed the way it had. Especially, as there was suspicion about our motives. The term I used to summarise our approach was 'populism with integrity'.

When it came to criticism, there were also surprises. I had one journalist that stopped me in my tracks. He represented one of the major quality national newspapers and he really gave me a jolt.

I took him on the usual tour and explained why things were the way they were. (By the time of his visit, late in the year, several of the figures had been installed.) As we walked around, I could see he was getting unsettled and irritated, and then he began an out and out tirade.

'I just don't get it,' he said going red in the face. 'I've made a special trip up here from London. I have to say I'm surprised and disappointed!'

I was taken aback as so many other visitors had loved what they saw. 'What about?' I asked.

'Where are the bloody Vikings?' he asked standing next to a figure.

'You're standing next to one,' I said.

'No, not *these*,' he exclaimed. '*Real* Vikings. Where's the blood and gore, the horned helmets, the axes, the rape and pillage. This is not what I expected. It's not what anyone will expect. It's a disaster waiting to happen!'

'It's about the Viking and Anglo-Saxon settlement of Jorvik,' I said in defense, 'about how people lived here in the 10th century as it's been revealed through archaeology. It's as much about the science of archaeology as it is about Vikings.' But he wasn't having any of it and stormed out in anger, loudly proclaiming over his shoulder,

'It's a waste of time and money, that's what it is,' he said going purple. 'Mark my words, it will be a complete lame duck.' I felt like presenting an axe in his skull as a memento of his visit. We were used to criticism and could handle it, but his view was just stupid and ignorant and, thank Thor, totally wrong.

I learned you couldn't please *all* the people not even *some* of the time. In the end surprisingly his write up wasn't as bad as expected, but I was relieved at not having shared with him the awful truth; Vikings *didn't* have horns on their helmets. I think he would have had a coronary.

The most effective and positive support we had in my view was from the twice-weekly children's BBC television series *Blue Peter*. It was a staple of British childhood, with a huge following of kids and adults. Immensely popular, year after year it reached millions who loved its teatime wholesomeness and sometimes downright quirky daftness.

Blue Peter was nothing less than a British institution. So you may imagine how thrilled we were when we heard the show's producer was interested in doing a feature on Jorvik.

I was lucky to be the one to show the television people round on that first visit and remember being in the daub and wattle house talking about the way people lived to one of their famous presenters. Funnily enough, the fact there were no battleaxes and definitely no sign of pillaging didn't seem to upset the reporter or millions of viewers. As I have always said, fact when well presented and brought to life, beats fiction nine times out of ten.

What we didn't realise was just how many people the programme actually reached. Neither did we realise how effective a promotional tool *Blue Peter* could be for us. It was like we spoke to the whole country. In the end they followed us to opening and did two more features, each priceless in giving us credibility and immensely valuable publicity. And yes, Colin, Carolyn and I all got a *Blue Peter* Badge each. You have to be British to know what that means.

However, I now have to reveal the awful truth that Goldie, the show's pet Golden Retriever who appeared on the show every week, peed on our goose. Sorry, but it's time that came out into the open.

Underneath the surface, what with the looming deadline and the million and one things that still had to be done and the incessant publicity visits, as 1983 became 1984, we were now in a state of organised chaos, desperately trying to get finished.

Major events successfully leapt out from the schedule; the figures from both Graham, Dave the Punk Stuffer and the Freeborns arrived on time. They were fixed in position and given a final painting. The detailed modelling and dressing of the sets with specially made props was completed, and despite the chaos, also on time.

Then (roll of drums) the first Time Cars were delivered, complete with their guidance systems and signal generator. And YES they did go backwards as well as forwards. The huge and complex tape-based show-control sound system was installed and was undergoing tests and sound balancing. The Show Control room, hidden out of sight, looked like a set from *The Man from Uncle*, the American television series of the 60s with its whirling tape wheels and flashing lights (I loved it). The control system had been developed for use in the Disney parks, for controlling hundreds of functions: sound, lighting, electronic effects and animatronics, and it was still tape-based at that time.

It's worth mentioning solid-state show control devices were not widely available yet. They were being developed and would be chip-based and about the size of your smart phone or smaller in a few years. But thirty years ago in 1984, unbeknownst to the public, ours was a behemoth of a machine concealed inside one of the reconstructed buildings. This wondrous thing with its starting and stopping tapes and flashing lights was the brain and the multiple voices of Jorvik; 62 tracks played from morning to night (cleverly timed so as not to sound overly repetitious to someone going round), and multi-layered, voices, animals, and atmospheric sounds, all of which had been expertly mixed by Trevor Wishart. Even the hearth in the house had its own sound track, crackling embers and the hiss of frying bacon. The day it was installed we had the big sound switch-on ceremony and weren't disappointed. It was simply mind-blowing. The extra dimension of environmental surround-sound, with the dogs barking and people shouting, cocks crowing and hens clucking, pigs squealing as geese honked brought the place to life just as we dreamed.

Meanwhile, as these crucial benchmarks took us closer to completion, word got out through the media (and of course *Blue Peter*) that we had pulled off something special. So people were even keener to visit for a sneak preview. There was only one thing missing in our reconstruction now, the smells. With just weeks to go to the soft opening, where were Mr Knight and the lovely and aromatic Gwyneth?

I worried that after the level of challenge we faced them with that they may have dissipated into the wind themselves. And frustratingly we couldn't reach them. Phoebe had actually started looking for other companies, but the ones she found were not interested. 'Sorry, we only do car showrooms,' they said.

The 'aromascape' we needed because we had already told the press that Jorvik was an exhibition in which you will smell as well as hear, see and touch. It was a really great sales gimmick; no one had done it before, well at least not with offensive smells. The media got the message out for us, *'Travelling Back in Time a Thousand Years to 'Viking Smellorama''* was how one tabloid put it.

Fortunately, Mr Knight was true to his word. He showed up with the lovely Gwyneth after a period of intense research and development with enough time to make the installation of his 'delivery units' into the locations that I'd drawn up onto the master pong plan.

A curious group of team members gathered to apprehensively sniff the various samples. Before any sniffing began we had the explanation again as to how it wasn't easy to simulate bad smells. And, of course, we had to suffer the jokes and the sniggers that went along with the idea. But Dale Air and Co. had done their alchemical best, and pulled off something putrid for Lancashire. I wished that I could have been a fly on the wall of their laboratory as they mixed and sampled (on reflection perhaps not; then again a fly might have loved it).

The smells that everyone wanted to try were the bad ones. And they were really unpleasant, nauseating actually in the concentrated form. But as far as I was concerned they weren't natural. Would you believe, they couldn't make a fishy smell? We had to settle for tarry rope. And no pig smells or cesspit, though what they synthesised was revolting.

None of our team complained though and everyone reacted accordingly and positively. There were lots of, 'Oh my God! That's terrible!' reactions which meant we'd probably get a positive response from the public. So with a few modifications Mr Knight was in business and shortly thereafter he received a very decent contract plus a long-term retainer, something not to be sniffed at.

But how do you deliver the smell, day after day and just where you want it? That had remained a trade secret until they had the job in the bag. And, of course, whatever it was, it was key.

This is how it was done; the chosen aromas would be delivered in plastic bottles, in concentrated form and kept somewhere very secure; the last thing you wanted was to spill the stuff. Ordinarily when the liquid was at an average room temperature only a minimal amount of aroma was released. To release a larger volume where we wanted it, in the house for example, the oil needed to be warmed and dispersed in that localised setting.

Mr Knight's device was as ingenious as it was simple and looked just like an upturned metal lampshade. At the bottom of the metal cone an enclosed heating filament was fixed below a container that held the aromatic concentrate. When the liquid was poured in, it warmed up, or heated up, depending on how much vapour was needed. This was a bit trial and error for us at first but not rocket science. The smell-pots (as we called them) had to be hidden but accessible and replenished on a regular basis. We were delighted at how effectively they worked.

In effect the smell-pot was a high-tech version of those pottery oil heaters that perfume a room with a tea-candle to warm up the oil. The Dale device was more sophisticated and the fire risk was negligible and acceptable. All the smell-pots were connected to a central circuit so that they could be linked to the master show control. We had instant and controllable pong.

Obviously we didn't want all the smells to mix too much. That worked out okay because the ventilation system extracted the warmer smellier air from above where it had originated. And that's how the original Jorvik got its smells, which were to become as famous as any other part of it.

The interesting thing about the smells was that (as he had told us earlier) while they were seldom close to the real thing, (cesspit, pigpen, herrings), the suggestion that you will smell them makes you think that you *are* smelling the real thing. It seems that you don't always smell what you *think* you are smelling.

Real or not, Mr Knight after his success at Jorvik became the go-to person in museum and display design if you wanted the smell of something earthy and unpleasant. In fact, Mr Knight's company created the themed aromas industry, where you went for a whiff of a soldier's armpit or the breath of a dinosaur. Mr Knight in his own right, to me at least, was the 'Godfather of Pong'.

As an anectdotal after-smell; for years I walked down the Coppergate open-air shopping mall built above the exhibition and could smell different parts of it below as the rising aromas were sucked up and out through air vents built into the pedestrian way. No one else knew they smelled 10th century pigpen outside the patisserie. But each time I picked up a whiff from down below I thought of Mr Knight in his hat and coat waiting for rain and the very fragrant and lovely Gwyneth.

14   HRH PRINCE CHARLES LOST
IN TIME

I DON'T THINK ANY OF us had much of a Christmas. I know my mind was eighteen feet underground. And I'm sure the others from the team were equally distracted. Christmas and New Year celebrations came and went. We returned to the basement with just weeks left to the finish.

As we got closer to opening, visits by the great, the good and the downright nosey (besides the media) increased. As I said, the constant interruptions were getting on our nerves and screwing with our complex multi-tasking schedule. But what could we do but do them? By now, every single day we got a list of VIP visitors; a Government Minister here, Chairman of the English Tourist Board there, Lord This and Lord and Lady That, the MP for here there and everywhere and Lady Muck thrown in as well. It took so much time it got way beyond a joke. In fact, I eventually complained hard to Anthony and Ian that we wouldn't be able to complete our job if we were constantly being interrupted. Ian took this seriously and putting his foot down called a three-day halt to visits so that we could catch up with our work.

However, undoubtedly *the* most significant and elevated of all visits and visitors was the second by HRH Prince Charles. It was a follow-up, which apparently he'd been looking forward to since he first came to York to launch the project three years earlier.

For all intents and purposes the project was pretty much completed by the time of his visit. We were into the stage where we were running and testing all the technical systems. I was doing the very last placements of props and set dressing.

He wanted to come and see how everything turned out and to have a chat with the folks that built it. Most often, I know from experience, cynical though it sounds, the designers and builders are shunted off into the shadows so the big wigs and politicians can take the credit. To be fair, this wasn't and never had been the case with Jorvik.

The worst instance of being made suddenly invisible in this way happened to a friend and colleague of mine with whom I later worked. I won't mention his name, but he was employed as Head of Design at a very important national institution in central London.

It was the opening day of a brand new international exhibition which this colleague of mine had sweated blood over. The King, Queen and Prime Minister of the country whose exhibition it was were coming from Africa to see the show and open it to the public. And British Royals were there too to welcome them. You might say it was a 'flash do'.

My friend got out his best suit and shone his shoes ready to get a royal pat on the head for the lovely job he and his team had done. Then as the Royal entourage climbed the stairs, just seconds away before the line up the Director of the place asked him if he wouldn't mind removing himself and worse, step into an adjacent room. There was no time to talk about it; the nearest room was a cleaner's closet.

Apart from throwing a tantrum there was nothing my friend could do but comply. He had two daughters in college and a mortgage to pay off. This incident came to be known in the business as 'the Broom Cupboard syndrome'.

In contrast we all got a fair share of the glory at Jorvik.

The special policemen who check out places before such high level visits are generally looking for bombs and assassins. HRH's personnel came to do their customary sweep a couple of days before his visit. We watched via the security cameras as they searched under thatched roofs and piles of fibreglass herrings, shone their torches into imitation cesspits and under piles of firewood, peered in buckets and sacks, and sniffed and Geiger countered beneath the man on the toilet. Must have been a first for them too, yet their stoic faces gave nothing away.

The day of the visit arrived. It was strange to see one's working colleagues in shirts and ties. We didn't recognise each other. The Prince and his party of notables arrived at the starting platform. We hadn't installed the sound systems in the car yet, so Peter Addyman accompanied HRH as he stepped into a car to act as his guide and tell him the story as they went round.

Then a bit like launching a ship, they set off backwards followed by a posse of detectives and personal assistants who thought it all great fun, but of course couldn't show it. Gosh, it was funny. We all had to keep straight faces even though we wanted to wave goodbye.

Then we left the starting platform and went over to the end of the ride. There the 'meet and greet party' were all lined up waiting for the Royal intrepid time travellers to arrive. There were other senior archaeologists from YAT, Ian Skipper, high-level representatives from the English Tourist Board and others present that I had never seen before.

Anthony Gaynor was to do the introductions; Colin, myself, and senior Jorvik Viking Centre management people were all lined up neatly and told what to say and do and waited, a little nervously. Whilst over our heads in Coppergate Square a large crowd with Union Jack flags in hand had gathered under blue early spring skies to welcome the Prince back to the present. Of course, the cars had been fully tested and screened for high explosives and atom bombs and they were running perfectly.

The Prince's car with Dr Addyman and HRH in the front seat with Her Majesty's Lord Lieutenant for Yorkshire, Lord Normanby, riding shotgun had actually been the second car to set off (at the rapid rate of four inches a second). Believe it or not, a car full of detectives went first just in case one of the Viking figures came to life to curtail the Royal line with a double-edged axe.

Before the visit, we were coached by equerries how to act when the Royal personage addressed one and how to respond. We were instructed not to speak first and only to offer one's hand after HRH offered his, and not to attempt to engage in a meaningful or anecdotal conversation, and basically agree with whatever he said. It must be really boring being a Royal.

So there we all were in line, Ian, Anthony and Colin and me, and others nervously waiting and looking at our watches. The ride lasted fourteen minutes; time was knocking on.

I slipped down the back of the line and whispered in Ian's ear, and said, 'Thanks Ian. It's your day. If it hadn't been for you, none of this would have happened.'

Graciously he replied, 'No John, today is *your* day.'

That meant so much to me, but in reality it was a thank you to all our team.

From the landing platform you couldn't see too far down the last track, only into the archaeologists' tearoom. Time passed, it was taking forever. Thirteen minutes went by, then fourteen. Where was the future King of England? Would there be a ransom note from Denmark?

We started looking at each other in the line-up and muttered, 'Where the hell are they?' Fifteen minutes came and went and there was still no sign. And then it dawned; we actually managed to lose a Prince down a wormhole in Time! How would we explain where he had gone? But let's face it; it would be worth it for the publicity. I could see the headlines: 'Prince Lost in Time, Kidnapped by Vikings' and 'Dr Who Sent Back In Time to Jorvik to Rescue Heir to Throne'.

It would be the ultimate press and media promotion. People would flock in millions to see if he would miraculously reappear as they went round. I'd end up in the Tower along with the others of course, but what the hell. It would have been almost worth it for the promotion. But seriously, on a more down to earth level we just didn't know what had happened and we couldn't go and find out; we just had to stand there or be shot.

In my subsequent experiences, something most always screwed up on the really big visit day, and it was nearly always technical. The reason is that all the gremlins weren't chased out of the system yet; they hung around hiding in corners and crevices in the control rooms just waiting to tilt a handle or burn out a fuse.

Sixteen-and-a-half minutes and still no sign. Nervous whispered chat broke out on the line-up; something or someone had definitely screwed up big time.

We all stood there like idiots not knowing quite what to do. After a couple more minutes a search party was sent out on foot into the mists of time to locate the future king and deliver him safely back to the 20th century.

The Royal party was discovered taking a leisurely stroll through the archaeo-logical dig. They were stranded in time. For about ten minutes they sat in their cars amongst the pig droppings and the rotten smells, wondering what to do, waiting for the cars, which had inexplicably come to a complete halt, to start moving again. Then Peter, bright red with embarrassment, suggested they walk back and led them back to the future. What had actually happened was an awesome piece of gremlinship.

Unknown to us in the bowels of the building, above in the outside world thun-derclouds had rolled out across the bright spring sky. People unfurled umbrellas. Ominous rumblings in the distance heralded a storm coming. The storm had caused a small fluctuation in atmospheric pressure and caused the cars to stop in their tracks. Why? Because those pressurised bumpers front and back that Peter had so cleverly designed were so sensitively set up that even a minute change in pressure caused a car to stop immediately. Who knew? We didn't, even as HRH approached the landing platform. In fact it took some serious deduction after the visit to work out what caused the cars to stop. Imagine how exciting it must have been for the detectives and bodyguards.

It didn't matter of course. Royals do enough visits to know about show gremlins. I think HRH thought it was great fun being lost in time. He probably thought he'd get to meet some real Viking people and have a chat over a horn or two of ale.

Thankfully, he was all smiles when he got back to the landing platform where we, much relieved, still stood waiting in line.

Anthony took over and introduced everyone.

Ian was the first Jorvik person quite rightly, then Colin who did a little bow and then it was my turn. By now I was convinced that I would open my mouth in reply to HRH and say something like 'qwerdioomiflop asterficajicle' as my nerves suddenly swamped my brain.

'So,' he said, 'You're the ideas man are you?' Up close I realised he was about my age.

'Yes sir, I am,' I replied.

'I really enjoyed it, thank you,' he said smiling. 'I especially liked the smell of the fish, herrings are they?'

Luckily Anthony knew that I was going to go into a really interesting piece about the smells and how difficult it is to reproduce the smell of fish, particularly herring, and that in fact what the royal nose had detected was the smell of *tarry rope*. So as I opened my mouth a second time Anthony moved the Prince on. HRH looked back at me though for a glancing moment and said, 'Good show.'

It was getting to the point when with a mounting sense of excitement we could all dare to believe we had indeed pulled off a good, possibly even, a great show.

With now just a few weeks to go we started in on the very *final* dressing. All the objects and props were in place so we could apply the last layer of dirt and dust and signs of use. The archaeological team brought the last conserved timbers from their labs and installed them on the site. They watched us carefully and respectfully, as everything had to be just right.

There was one sound effect we hadn't yet turned on; the street sounds around the dig site. It was basically the same idea as the baby crying in the Viking house. I reckoned that subconsciously the street noises would complete the illusion.

Early 80s York had a terrible amount of traffic within the city walls and was very noisy with the trucks and buses thundering by. When we turned on the street noise you could hear it from speakers from above and over the metal sidings. Once it was playing in the background, you would have sworn that a busy city was up there. It was one of my favorite effects, yet if any of our visitors ever noticed it, I would have been surprised; it was so subtle. That didn't matter, for like so many of our other environmental effects it added to the all important suspension of disbelief.

After the Royal visit those last weeks of completion were just a blur. I don't even have any notes in my journals of the time; we were so busy bringing all the remaining strands of the exhibition together. But little by little, completion came closer and closer and we were running out of things to do, as the strands came together to form a single rope. Then it was done and the last task on the master schedule was crossed off and given a big tick.

From being a team of odd-bods with no previous experience of taking on such a job, it was evident we had pulled it off. Yet even at this time we had no way of knowing if all of the effort had been worthwhile. However, whilst the exhibit was complete there was no time to relax as we still had four major hurdles to clear.

The first was the day that the Fire Officer came down to test the combustibility of the exhibit. Of course, not leaving it to chance we conducted our own tests. Still we had our fingers crossed as the Fire Officer, complete with extinguishers to hand, walked slowly along the edges of the roofs with a lit cigarette lighter holding the flame to the thatch. If it started to burn at even one spot they would refuse us our Fire and Safety certificate. We wouldn't open on time and would have to wait until we were granted another inspection. That could take weeks or months.

We held our breath as he lifted the thatch to see if it would light beneath. My heart felt like it was going to explode and Colin's face was ashen. We should have not worried; Bob and the boys had done their job very well; the thatch didn't even smoulder. We got the all-important certificate.

The second big hurdle was the day the Time Cars were equipped with their commentary tracks. The narration was co-written by Peter, Magnus and myself. Magnus made a wonderful job of recording the narrative. It added so much to the whole thing. As he told the story and referred to what was seen, the exhibition unfolded like the film I always imagined.

The commentary began as the cars slipped away from the starting platform with the famous phrase in the deep warm voice of Magnus the Viking, 'We're deep below the streets of York travelling back a thousand years in time....' It was as though Magnus was in the car sitting next to you, telling just you the story.

Although the first commentary we opened with was recorded in English, once Jorvik opened it wasn't long before it was available in a choice of languages. Though I always thought that Magnus' English commentary was the most perfect.

There was another point in the commentary where the whole thing really came together. It was as the cars still travelling backwards left the leather worker's shop and visitors saw the whole of the settlement reaching out before them for the first time. At this moment, Magnus, with his great sense of timing and delivery says, 'This is Jorvik.' That always made me shiver.

The third big hurdle was the sign-off by the client. That's when your client agrees to take delivery of the completed job. In our case it had to happen on time, about a month before the Official Opening scheduled for the 14th of April. We got it and YAT were very pleased. Colin, who risked as much as anyone, breathed a huge sigh of relief.

But although we got the sign-off, the fourth and last hurdle was perhaps the toughest: the Soft Opening. Why is it called a soft opening? I don't know, for a soft opening is one of the hardest things to do. It is the acid test of the visitor experience and response.

The Viking Centre had to be tested and proved through four weeks of operation. We may have come to our completion, but now it had to be tested by *real* people, visitors who were specially invited, school kids and tea ladies, retirees from clubs and nurses, policemen and bus drivers and so on. During this period you watch, learn, monitor and train. And my God was it nerve racking.

The new operations staff; the under-managers in their blazers, those on the tills at the entrance and in the shop, the ladies who acted as guides and hosts, the technical staff and the cleaners, they all had to be trained in a live situation before we could go public. Those first parties got the initial taste of what we created. They each were asked at the end of their experience what they thought about it and how, if they felt necessary, it could be improved. It was a testing time for our clients and us, seeing how people reacted.

It was during this birthing time that I learned the value of the expression, 'Do not design for the *wedding*, design for the *marriage*.' Really successful museum design is defined beyond its level of popularity or even financial success. It's a good design when it operates smoothly and stays fresh day after day, year after year, decade after decade. That's what designing for the marriage is about.

Well, our first guests were generally positive about their experience but weren't jumping up and down with glee. To be honest it was a bit of an anti-climax and hard for us to judge. Later we realised the somewhat flat reaction from invited guests was caused by them being totally overwhelmed, as they'd never seen or experienced anything like it. It was difficult for them to make a value judgment. Still it was a disquieting time. Maybe after all we weren't going to be a success?

An interesting fact about an invited audience is that they're *invited*, they aren't in fact *real* visitors, people who in a few days time we hoped and prayed would be actually parting with cash to come in and see the show. Paying for something gives more value to something than what you get for free. Paying visitors have a more critical eye for what they paid for. And Yorkshire folk are famously 'tight' when it comes to forking out. In point of fact there was a murmuring rumour going on around the streets that York people should in fact be able to get in for free.

There was a silver lining to the soft opening. The media, without exception, loved it right across the board, and our hopes were lifted again. However, no matter how positive the press had been as the last days turned over, there was a growing and palpable sense of nervousness and apprehension. Nerves were frayed. We were also tired out.

As planned the soft opening helped us tweak the technical aspect of the overall show and its daily management and operation and there were no major glitches. The operations team turned the theory of their training into practice.

However, something unforeseen showed up during the soft opening that involved the car rescue boys. It was their job to stay out of sight in the garage and monotonously watch a number of video screens. Cameras hidden away in the shadows covered the whole of the track and relayed images back to the control station. Every now and then there would be a problem with a car, especially in the early days. The rescue team then had to dash out of hiding and take care of the situation.

We expected some mechanical glitches every now and then. When this happened the rescue team darted out and went 'live', much to the surprise of passengers, who were guided to step out of the vehicle by one of them, whilst the rescue team pulled out the car from circulation before re-installing them in another, then disappear like will 'o the wisps. They learned how to do this as unobtrusively as possible, not an easy task if there was a party of senior WI ladies in the malfunctioning car. It could be a bit of a shock. Some visitors even thought they were under attack from errant Vikings.

One positive sign that we would have an audience was in advance booking sales. A week to go and the office that handled them was in full swing and the machine that printed the details out never stopped rattling off names, dates and details.

I hated that machine because it made a terrible noise, just like a machine gun. It kept rattling away as the diary for the coming year, not only the coming few weeks, began to fill up with advance party bookings. But besides them, would any one else show up? Those advance bookings didn't ensure that the Centre would have the major numbers it needed.

A nervous laugh, an affliction of apprehension if not outright fear, was breaking out all over. Everyone on the staff including us (our contract called for us to be around for several weeks after being signed off) was laughing but not really if you see what I mean.

Coinciding with the opening on April 14th was the parallel completion of the new shopping centre in which Jorvik was situated. 'Coppergate' was the name taken from the ancient street that ran across the top of the development. From there you could walk down a paved pedestrianised way between new shops for about 100 metres before entering a large open square with a beautiful mature tree in the middle.

This was Coppergate Square, enclosed by new shops and a large department store. A medieval desanctified church that housed an exhibition of the history of York also backed onto the square, a fitting complement to the shortly-to-be-opened Jorvik Viking Centre, the front of which now sported a sign with its striking black and white logo.

Standing in the new Square, unless you knew the more recent history of the site, you would have no idea that not so long before there was a huge pit beneath you where in that damp and muddy hole teams of archaeologists worked virtually around the clock for years to rescue the precious remains of Viking York before money and time ran out and the builders moved in.

The entrance to Jorvik is on the Square, as is the Museum Shop, which is at ground level today (when originally it was at the lower level). The shop and the whole retail sales side of the enterprise was brilliantly thought out and put together.

The shop itself wasn't large, but from the start it was packed with the most interesting things, mostly and ingeniously themed to Vikings. There were items related to archaeology and history, from pencils and plastic swords bought for pocket money, to expensive solid gold reproduction jewellery. Once open and for a long time after, the Jorvik Shop was to become one of the most successful and profitable retail spaces in England, more profitable per square metre-wise than Marks and Spencer on Oxford Street, for a time anyway, even though it didn't sell Viking underwear.

But that business was to come. First we needed visitors and customers.

With the last few days passing by, curious faces peered in through the windows at street level and watched as television news crews from all over the world arrived for a trip round and an interview or two to be broadcast on opening day. Meanwhile all over Jorvik we fussed over last minute details, whilst trying to hide our nerves.

The fateful day arrived, April 14, 1984.

We the core team, Ian and his wife, clients, management and designers, Colin, Phoebe and I sat around a small conference table in the first floor room. It was 9:40 am. All of a sudden after years of intense work by everyone, it was time to open to the public.

The atmosphere was tense to say the least. Ian smoked and cleaned ashtrays; Colin just smoked. I nervously joked with Phoebe. For some reason Carolyn hadn't been included in the group; she should have been.

We all glanced at the minute hand of the clock on the bare wall as it ticked its way to our first real opening. Believe it or not in that last hour not one of us in that room dared to look outside to see if anyone had shown up in the square below, and the windows remained closed. Just a small queue would have been okay, or even the first two people, anyone.

What if the newspaper reporter that wanted blood and guts had been right? What if we'd taken the excitement out of the story? What if nobody cared; after all there was no battle going on downstairs, no blood curdling screams, no wenches being dragged by their hair to the dragon ships, or monks being cut to ribbons as their monasteries were stripped of relics and treasures. None of that not even a blood blister. Just a bunch of shabby huts, a few dummies and stuffed animals and some old bits of wood and pottery, nothing much really to get excited about.

I sat there wearing a jacket and tie for the second time in my adult professional life. It felt weird; well, the whole situation was weird.

Then it was ten.

I watched Ian and Peter apprehensively approach the windows. When they got there and looked down they stood stock still and silent with their backs to us. 'Oh God,' I thought. 'It's bad.' I hadn't been able to move and neither had Colin.

Phoebe couldn't control herself now and went to the window next. When she looked out she put her hand to her mouth.

'Oh my God,' she cried out. 'Oh my GOD!'

'Bloody hell, boys!' Ian exclaimed.

Peter in his usual controlled voice said to us, 'I think you should all come and take a look at this.'

We got up from the table and crowded together at the windows and stared in disbelief into the square below.

'Oh, wow!' I said laughing.

'Look at that!' cheered Colin.

'I don't believe it!' shrieked Phoebe.

Below, snaking from the entrance where the doors had recently opened, right around the big open square with the old tree in the centre sporting its new spring leaves, round and back up on the other side of the square and coming back opposite the entrance and then further up all the way and out of sight, in fact as we were to find when we ran downstairs to look, up to and along Coppergate Street, was the longest queue any of us had ever seen, or dreamed could have happened. Thousands and thousands of people had turned up.

It was to be the same the next day and the next, day after day; long queues formed every morning before ten, in the rain, under the hot sun as summer arrived, as leaves fell from the tree in the square in the autumn, all the way on to the frosts and fog and snow of winter 1984. And then into the New Year into '85 and '86, the never-ending queue became as famous as Jorvik itself. People voted their support with their feet for our fresh, fun, and accessible way of presenting history.

Close on a million came in that first year, shuffling slowly, patiently, sometimes waiting up to four hours to reach the entrance and begin their journey back in time. By the year 2000 when the original exhibit was re-furbished after 16 years of service, that number of visitors had risen to 13 million.

Jorvik began life as an extraordinary and daring idea and once opened became a phenomenon, a legend, as generations who first visited with their parents and grew to maturity and then took their own kids along to ride in the Time Cars to visit the past.

It became a great success in another way unseen in the spring of 1984. Jorvik and our populist approach to presentation resulted in the birth of an industry, which came to be known as the 'Heritage Industry', of which York became and still remains the centre, employing hundreds if not thousands of artisans and designers over the last four decades on projects created for sites around the world.

What I don't think any of us who were closely involved expected was the impact Jorvik was to have on our own lives and careers. The sheer excitement of putting the exhibition together and then seeing it have such a successful birth was a life changer.

The core team hung on for a few more weeks after opening. It was during that time I suggested another idea to Colin and Phoebe one afternoon when we were driving back to Wakefield from York, still in the afterglow with stars in our eyes. Colin should have learnt not to listen to my crazy ideas, considering what happened to him the last time.

I was sat in the back of Colin's car. We were still as high as kites with what had happened and the way that Jorvik had been received.

I leant forward and said to them both, 'I don't think I can go back to normal life after this.'

'What's normal life to you?' asked Colin.

'You know what I mean,' I said.

'I know what you mean,' said Phoebe. 'Bookkeeping is going to seem very dull after this.'

There was a pause.

'I've got an idea,' I said.

'Oh God,' said Colin. 'Here we go.'

'Okay, so we now know that nobody does this sort of thing; we had to put it together ourselves.'

'True,' said Colin.

'So, why don't we keep doing it and, I know, we'll call it Heritage Projects Ltd.'

'I like that,' said Phoebe.

'Why don't we talk to Peter, Anthony and Ian? Maybe they feel the same. I think we could work together, don't you?'

'Why not indeed?' said Colin.

'Why don't you give Anthony a call tomorrow?' I asked, seeing the possibilities opening up.

'Isn't this where we came in?' said Colin.

'Yeah, it was,' I said settling back into the seat. A warm glow filled me physically and mentally and I sighed a deep sigh.

'Flippin''eck,' I said to myself in my head. 'We did it!'

As I smiled to myself, Colin and Phoebe talked happy talk up front. Then I had another thought. Where it came from I don't know, but it said quite clearly, 'You're on your way now, boy. You're on your way.'

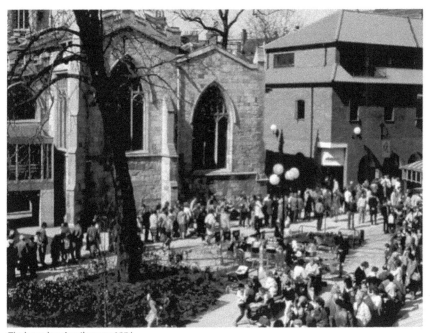

The legendary Jorvik queue 1984

Thank you for reading *On My Way to Jorvik*. I hope you enjoyed it. If you did…

1.) Join my mailing list at www.johnsunderland.co.uk/contact
2.) Come like my Facebook page www.facebook.com/johnsunderlandwrites
3.) Visit my website www.johnsunderland.co.uk
4.) Help other people find this book by writing a review. If you've enjoyed this book I would be very grateful if you could spend just five minutes leaving a review (it can be as short as you like) on the book's Amazon page or your favourite reading site.

If you enjoyed this book, you'll love the FREE bonus stories from my next book which you can get here: https://johnsunderland.co.uk

ABOUT THE AUTHOR

JOHN SUNDERLAND BEGAN HIS EARLY career as a freelance designer, filmmaker and animator. Following the opening of Jorvik in 1984, John, along with other key members of the original JVC team, founded Heritage Projects, York, of which he was the Creative Director. In 1988 he went freelance once again. In total, he designed and saw built 24 commercially successful and award-winning international museums and cultural heritage centres many of which were still in operation at the time of original writing. Below is a list of his major international design and build projects completed between1981 to 2008.

During that period he completed over 150 consultancy projects, several of which later became developments in their own right. He also undertook commissions for television and feature film work as well as scripts for text and film. He produced, directed and wrote the scripts and dramatizations for the films and videos for his exhibitions.

John met his wife Kathy in 2003 in Provincetown, Cape Cod in Massachusetts, USA. In 2004 he became involved with her businesses, Life Café in New York City (featured in the Pulitzer Prize winning Broadway musical RENT) and Bushwick, Brooklyn. They married in 2006. In 2012 they left New York City and now live in the foothills of the Sierra Bernia on the Costa Blanca of Spain with their dog Pascual.

John's eclectic career transported him to North America, India, Israel, the Nevada desert, Ireland, Scotland, the Isle of Man, Wales, England and Belgium. He collaborated with hundreds of extraordinary talented people and was introduced to a multitude of worlds long dead and living that revealed real and legendary stories. His professional experiences became fodder for his perpetual personal creative work.

John hasn't finished creating. He's written a collection of short stories, a book of poems and is working on fictional titles, several directly inspired by his project development experiences. In between the words he illustrates children's and young adult books, paints, carves walking sticks and adds to his collection of journals.

Explore the many goings-on in John's out-of-the-box mind. View his various creations and stay up-to-date with his motley musings by visiting him at www. johnsunderland.co.uk. John can be contacted at: info@johnsunderland.co.uk.

List of Museum and Cultural Heritage Attraction Projects by John Sunderland:

The Jorvik Viking Centre, YAT, York, England
(Original version, open 1984-2000, Project Designer)
The Dynamic Earth, Scottish and Newcastle Breweries, Edinburgh, Scotland
(1987, preceding as *The Younger Universe* Original Concept Development
and Initial Visualisation)
The Canterbury Tales Heritage Projects, Canterbury, England
(Opened 1988, Project Designer)
The Oxford Story, University of Oxford and Heritage Projects, Oxford, England
(Opened 1988, Project Designer)
The Whisky Heritage Centre, Edinburgh, Scotland
(Opened 1988, Project Designer)
The Spirit of London, Madame Tussauds Ltd. London, England
(Opened 1990, Concept Designer)
The White Cliffs Experience, Dover District Council, Dover, England
(Opened 1991, Project Designer)
The Eurotunnel Visitor Centre, Eurotunnel, Folkestone, England
(Opened 1993, Project Designer)
The Mannanan Centre, Peel, the Isle of Man, The Museum of Man
(1991, Concept/Detailed Concept Designer)
The Mappa Mundi Exhibition, Hereford Cathedral, England
(1991, Project Producer and Designer)
The Weymouth Time-Walk, Weymouth, England
(Opened 1992, Project Designer)
Celtica, Machynlleth, North Wales
(Opened 1996, Project Designer)
Quest For a Pirate, Cape Cod, USA and world travelling
(Opened in Edinburgh 1996. Project Designer and Filmmaker)
Blue Planet Aquarium, Cheshire, England
(1996, Concept Designer)
Ename, Archaeological Site Interpretation, Oudenarde, Regional
Government of Flanders
(Opened 1997, Project Originator and Designer)

Ename Museum, As above

(Opened 1998, Project Designer)

ENAME CENTRE FOR HERITAGE INTERPRETATION, as above

(Opened 2004, Project Design consultant for exhibit content)

TIMEFRAMES. Invention of world's first on-site virtual and augmented reality synchronous interpretation of archaeological locations. 1997

WHALERS WHARF, Provincetown Town Council, Provincetown, Cape Cod, USA

(1998-2001, Building design concept, Design and Build Theatre and Exhibition Space, Produced and directed film *Great Fire of Provincetown*)

The RHEGED DISCOVERY CENTRE, Penrith, England, Private Client

(2000, Interpretive Project Designer and Filmmaker)

The NATIONAL MOUNTAINEERING EXHIBITION, British Mountaineering Association, Penrith, England

(Opened 2001, Project Designer)

NEW PROVINCETOWN LIBRARY, Provincetown Council, Cape Cod, USA

(2004, Logo Design, Designer)

FELLS POINT VISITOR CENTER, Cultural Sites Research and Management, Baltimore, USA

(2006, Writer and Project Designer)

LOGANDALE TRAILS CONSERVATION PROJECT, Bureau of Land Management, Nevada USA

(2006, writer, illustrator, designer)

YORK MINSTER VISITOR INTERPRETIVE SCHEME, York Minster, England

(2008, Interpretive Designer and Concept Origination for the South Transept Exterior Plaza)

GLASTONBURY MUSIC AND ARTS FESTIVAL, PERMANENT EXHIBITION FOR GLASTONBURY ABBEY, The Festival Owner.

(2009, Concept design consultancy)

Coppergate excavation © York Archaelogical Trust

ORIGINAL 2014 FOREWORD

BELOW IS THE ORIGINAL FOREWORD written by Dr. Peter Addyman, Director of York Archaeological Trust, for the first edition of *On My Way to Jorvik* published in 2014.

IN 1976 THE YORK ARCHAEOLOGICAL Trust began excavating in Coppergate, an ancient street in the heart of the city of York, on the site of recently demolished properties. A new shopping complex was to be built there but the Trust knew that deep and well-preserved archaeological deposits of the Viking age existed which would be damaged by the new development. They were not disappointed. Within weeks the trial excavation started to reveal timber buildings, amazingly complete and undecayed, belonging to the 10th century – York's Viking age. The wet ground conditions had preserved them – and around them lay an extraordinary range of objects, even organic material such as textiles, leatherwork and plant remains, and all the junk and rubbish of everyday life 1,000 years ago.

This was a truly exceptional opportunity, calling for exceptional measures. The Trust enlisted an immensely effective fund raising team to produce the vast sum of money needed for a proper excavation. Its royal and presidential patrons were The Prince of Wales, Queen Margrethe II of Denmark, King Carl XVI Gustaf of Sweden, Crown Prince Harald of Norway and Kristjan Eldjarn, President of Iceland. The campaign was chaired by Magnus Magnusson, then at the height of his fame as BBC TV's much-loved Mastermind quizmaster.

The result was York's longest running, largest, and arguably its most productive archaeological excavation ever – and the recovery of an extraordinary story of life in the commercial heart of a Viking city. As find after amazing find came out of the ground the discoveries generated an international media frenzy. Who could resist a story about a well-preserved Viking sock – with a hole in its toe? The news of its discovery went round the world. Someone in Australia even wrote an ode about it. Could Scandinavians resist stories about the remarkable things achieved by their ancestors in their capital city of Jorvik in their colonial age? The Nordic media knew they couldn't and were regular visitors to Coppergate for years.

And the millions of tourists who annually visit York – to stay awhile amid its ancient charms – found a new ancient attraction in the city while the dig was in progress. They could pay to tour the excavations. Probably a million people did so over five and a half years, seeing history being unearthed before their eyes, and hearing a commentary on what was happening as they watched from elevated walkways. The Viking Dig became York's most popular new tourist attraction. But it had to come to an end. A new city centre shopping complex was to be built. The Vikings would have to go.

Archaeologists are used to their discoveries being recorded then swept away for modern development. It happens everywhere all the time. These remarkable finds, however, struck at least one person as being too exceptional to sweep away. Ian Skipper, an outstandingly successful Lancashire entrepreneur, had heard about the excavation – and had joined the fund raising team. As the work progressed he kept telling the archaeologists that the site had to be kept. They kept telling him it couldn't be. Would the Trust ever be let on another development site again if it were? Skipper's business success had been achieved by positive thinking and by thinking outside the box so quite soon the archaeological team was being badgered to think how could this extraordinary Viking neighbourhood be preserved.

One thing was certain. The well-preserved timber shops, workshops and warehouses, all completely waterlogged, would have to go to a wet-wood treatment laboratory for years before they could safely be displayed. Why not after that just display them in some museum elsewhere? Both Skipper and I felt that they would have much more impact if they were displayed exactly where they were found. How could we do that if the Coppergate Shopping Centre was to be built? Well – we'd dug a huge enough hole. Maybe we could build a basement in it, below the shopping centre, and re-position the buildings where they were found. Skipper assembled a team of architects, surveyors and consultants to create such a scheme – which was eventually sent to the York City Council, owners and potential developers of the site, to be considered alongside submissions from other tenderers for the development.

There was a hiatus. The City authorities suddenly realised that a much better scheme could be developed if they enlarged the site. Back to the drawing board we all went, and into a new competition. The York Archaeological Trust's new scheme did not win – but we were shattered to find our original proposal had been incorporated in the rival scheme, which did win. When we asked the jovial Town Clerk Roy Howell whether we shouldn't sue for plagiarism he cheerfully said, 'If you do, you won't get your Jorvik. If you accept the situation you'll get what you originally wanted'. His logic was unassailable, and the Trust began to work with Wimpey Construction, the successful bidder, to create an underground Viking world.

How do you explain to ordinary people who know precious little about archaeology what the Viking town of Jorvik was like, even if you do have the best preserved Viking age houses anywhere? These look to the untutored eye like so many blackened old timbers. Houses? Really? Are you sure? Wicker fences? No, they are just bits of hurdle…! And so on. After much thought we felt that first we must show visitors our interpretation of what we had found – and then they might have a hope of recognising the 'evidence' when they saw it. Let's rebuild a neighbourhood of Jorvik, based on the mass of evidence we found – and take people through that. Then let's take people through the real ancient remains. Then they'll be able to understand them.

So that was what we decided to do. The next problem was how to do it. Where do you find people who can design, make and install a Viking town neighbourhood, then install a mass of precious Viking timbers and finds? Certainly in 1980 the answer seemed to be nowhere. Museum designers at that time were operating in a completely different mind frame. And that is where the story told in this book comes in. Skipper, myself and our project director Anthony Gaynor began a quest to find someone who could do it, someone who did not have precon-ceived notions about how you create a museum display, someone with brilliant design skills, and someone who could share our vision. We didn't quite know what we were looking for but we thought we would recognise it when we saw it.

This remarkable book takes you in a compelling, heart-churning and highly entertaining way through the complex series of influences and experiences that produced the person who could re-build Jorvik and who could give us trium-phantly what we were looking for. It goes on to take us – very precisely, for John Sunderland, our designer, always kept notes on his day-by-day activities – through the processes that the creative mind goes through to come up with a compelling and successful result. We see the Jorvik Viking Centre developing, we share the problems, find the solutions, see the talented team of constructors form up, feel the anxieties and share the growing tensions as time begins to run out, technical problems suddenly appear and solutions are rapidly found. Towards the end, too, we share the growing feeling of triumph as it becomes clear the Jorvik Viking Centre is going to work, the tension when, because of an unexpected technical error, a royal patron gets lost in time, and the team's amazement and euphoria when Jorvik proves an immediate and sensational success.

John Sunderland's story is important on two fronts. It gives an unusual and precious insight into how great designers come about and great designs are created. It also is an important and revealing blow-by-blow account of how one of the 20th century's most influential and innovative presentations of complicated heritage material came about. The Jorvik that John Sunderland created has now very largely been swept away. Its technology was a technology of the 1980s – obsolete twenty years later, worn out by intensive use and bound to be replaced by something quite different. By that time, however, it had introduced the Vikings to over 12 million people from round the globe and to generations of British schoolchildren. By then, too, a new heritage industry had emerged in Britain – stimulated by Sunderland's Jorvik – that offered new story-telling techniques and had produced a new genera-tion of creative interpreters. New minds found new ways to convey Jorvik's messages. After many years of archaeological research on the Coppergate discoveries even the messages themselves had sometimes to be changed and modified. So Sunderland's Jorvik has gone - but what a boon that we now have his account of it.

Peter Addyman, CBE, FSA
Director of York Archaeological Trust 1972-2002

ACKNOWLEDGEMENTS

When I began writing this book I dredged through the first few volumes of my 129 journals (to date), which I started writing in 1981 to keep track of things when thinking about and planning Jorvik. (My journal writing became a habit and I've kept them up ever since.) In them I searched for any relevant particulars useful to this account. The words and my old design sketches were extremely helpful in keeping many facts straight. Coming across the drawings again was like meeting old friends. At the least my journals were helpful catalysts for my memory, which has been the main source for my story.

Still, I must point out that because I didn't record what was said in detail, all dialogue within this book is based on personal recollection, and therefore is not verbatim and may not be literally true. Because I could not recall all dialogue with precision, I used poetic license throughout (okay, there were a couple of times when I just could not resist the good-humoured pun). What I present as dialogue is in the spirit of the conversation as I recalled it. It goes without saying that whilst I have been faithful to my memory and in a spirit of good faith towards the people who appear in this story, my subjects may remember things differently.

Also, I should say that I have changed the names of some people where I thought it sensitive and necessary, whilst others appear as themselves.

Although I have been writing all my life, scripts and texts and so on, I have never squared the circle of words with an actual book. And here it is done. However, the last stages of completion I admit have been like pulling out one's own teeth with red-hot serving spoons. 'What happened to retirement?' has been a question frequently asked of my wife over the last months, as she and I discovered that it's one thing to go to Lalaland and lollygag in one's memories and imagination and eventually bring home a completed manuscript (even if took nine years to find the way back), it is quite another to tidy it up, correct and amend, edit and proof. Who knew?

Still, I wrote it because I felt that there ought to be a record, albeit from a personal perspective, of a very special experience shared by a rare collective of people. Let's face it; we're none of us getting any younger.

Cases in point are the loss in the last couple of years of two essentially important people in this story, sadly and irrecoverably missed. Dr Richard Hall was the Director of the Coppergate dig and perhaps thereafter the foremost expert on the Vikings. And Mr Ian Skipper, unique, enigmatic, the mentor in so many ways of the original Jorvik Viking Centre. I think I can hear him chuckling somewhere in the ether as he clicks his gold lighter and lights up another cigarette, remembering just what he started.

Whilst I acknowledge the great and wide field of all those who were involved in large or small ways, client or contractor, in the creation of the Centre and of course in its continued and evolving operation, my list of named persons is limited to those who had a direct and influential input in this book. I thank them all from the bottom of my heart.

I would like to thank my American editor, Jill Dearman who I initially employed years ago to wade through my first draft, close on 1,500 pages. She told me encouragingly that I could tell a story, just not everybody's. And so began the business of killing my darlings (don't dwell on this, but somewhere there's a landfill full of them) and editing, reducing and focusing on the path to Jorvik.

I have special thanks to extend to ex-director of York Archaeological Trust, Peter Addyman. He who of all possible judges and critics of this, my account of Jorvik, I feared would be the harshest. But to the contrary, he has given me the greatest support in the final stages in bringing this work to fruition. And, the icing on my cake, he has contributed a most wonderful Foreword that provides the reader with such an enlightening pre-amble to the creation of the Jorvik Viking Centre. Thanks, once again, Peter.

I want to thank all those courageous souls who, in the knowledge that this was my first attempt at completing a book, agreed to read, review and comment on my drafts. To hand over to a friend or respected colleague a fat manuscript crawling with typos and grammatical nasties for their objective comment means asking a great deal of a person especially if by the end of page 10 (with 370 more to go) they know the thing is rubbish, or I think worse, not complete rubbish but patchy like mold on cheese. I thank you all my draft readers, dear hit-upon pals. You have been so gracious and kind:

Colin Pyrah, OBE. No one knew this story better; he's in it more than I am and it's my memoir. He's been tireless in support. Honestly, one day I hope to grow up like him. Carolyn Lloyd Brown and Phoebe MacLeod, fearing the worst I think when they heard of my book, came out in full support and provided material that had been lost in the mist. Their contribution along with Colin's is invaluable, for whilst it's my memoir, it is our story.

John Oxley MBE FSA, former City of York Archaeologist, who was the City Archaeologist at the time of the 1st publication., a very well qualified reader and a wonderfully approachable and scholarly man. Douglas Comer, an American intellectual of international standing, archaeologist, author, conservationist, all round great bloke, and a big fan of the Jorvik Viking Centre. And someone else who's a fan, Francis Pryor, archaeologist, author, populist, and a regular presenter on Channel Four's Time Team. Professor Pryor, who is also a sheep farmer, gave up his valuable time to write a testimonial for this book, as he said pulling off his wellies, 'as a break from being up to my neck in wet sheep'. Thanks Francis, and thank you sheep.

Patrick Argent, designer, teacher and producer and a selfless supporter of others, especially in the field of design. Caroline Watson, a dear friend possessed of a brilliant talent for words and a blessed sense of humour. Miriam Cintron, a New Yorker through and through who is an insightful and talented photojournalist of the New York City scene. Irene Lipton, one of those rare people who can turn their fine arts talents to commercial projects. Tony Patrick, a designer who used to work with me on projects who always tells it like it is. And finally, David and Jenny Hann, artists, storytellers, brilliant conversationalists, fonts of ideas with mercurial minds who have stripey little people in the form of badgers come to visit their magical cottage high on a cliff above the North Sea. They asked the badger family what they thought of my book, and they gave it a 'paws up'. However, the general consensus was, there should have been more worms in it.

Thanks also to three other singular people who live here on our Spanish mountain. Together they helped cross the last 't' and dot the final 'i'. Izzy Shaw, who saw the words through the trees and managed to dig up a few more grammatical worms. Emma White, graphic designer, whose cool-headed creative and technical expertise put this book under its covers and so to bed. And Sally Freeman, whose clear vision and love of words helped us clean up and polish the final words of the changes to the second edition. All of these smart and lovely ladies prove the point; that special talent is usually on your doorstep even if your doorstep is a mountain.

Lastly, a special and personal thanks to my dear wife and muse Kathy who, back in 2005 in New York City where we were living and working, said with typical New York directness, 'Why don't you get off your butt and write your memoir before your last brain-cells get lost on the subway?' Since then after spending countless hours, days, weeks, months and years cleaning up after my grammatical messes and transatlantic anomalies, she's still speaking to me, but only in the supermarket on Wednesdays in the cheese aisle. Don't ask why. I don't know. I'm just glad she is. I'd be lost without her.

John Sunderland

February 2014 and September 2021